LIBRARY OF SECOND TEMPLE STUDIES

82

Formerly the Journal for the Study of the Pseudepigrapha Supplement series

Editor
Lester L. Grabbe

The "Whole Truth"

Rethinking Retribution in the Book of Tobit

Micah D. Kiel

t & t clark

Published by T&T Clark International
A Continuum imprint
The Tower Building, 11 York Road, London SE1 7NX
80 Maiden Lane, Suite 704, New York, NY 10038

www.continuumbooks.com

British Library Cataloguing-in-Publication Data
A catalogue record for this book is available from the British Library

ISBN: HB: 978-0-567-45885-8

Library of Congress Cataloging-in-Publication Data
A catalog record for this book is available from the Library of Congress

Typeset by Free Range Book Design & Production
Printed and bound in Great Britain

FOR ELEANOR

"If you do not expect the unexpected, you will not find it . . ."
Heraclitus

CONTENTS

Abbreviations

AB	Anchor Bible
AB	Codices Alexandrinus and Vaticanus
ABD	David Noel Freedman (ed.), *The Anchor Bible Dictionary* (New York: Doubleday, 1992)
ANET	James B. Pritchard (ed.), *Ancient Near Eastern Texts Relating to the Old Testament* (Princeton: Princeton University Press, 1950)
AOAT	Alter Orient und Altes Testament
BETL	Bibliotheca Ephemeridum theologicarum lovaniensium
Bib	*Biblica*
BR	*Bible Review*
BSO(A)S	*Bulletin of the School of Oriental and African Studies*
BZAW	Beihefte zur Zeitschrift für die alttestamentliche Wissenschaft
CBQ	*Catholic Biblical Quarterly*
CBQMS	*Catholic Biblical Quarterly*, Monograph Series
CCSL	Corpus Christianorum: Series Latina
CEJL	Commentaries on Early Jewish Literature
ConBNT	Coniectanea biblica, New Testament
CRBS	*Currents in Research: Biblical Studies*
DJD	Discoveries in the Judaean Desert
ExpTim	*Expository Times*
FoSub	Fontes et Subsidia ad Bibliam Pertinentes
HDR	Harvard Dissertations in Religion
HTR	*Harvard Theological Review*
ICC	International Critical Commentary
IDB	George Arther Buttrick (ed.), *The Interpreter's Dictionary of the Bible* (4 vols.; Nashville: Abingdon Press, 1962)
IDBSup	*Interpreter's Dictionary of the Bible, Supplementary Volume*
JAL	Jewish Apocryphal Literature Series
JBL	*Journal of Biblical Literature*
JJS	*Journal of Jewish Studies*
JQR	*Jewish Quarterly Review*
JSHRZ	Jüdische Schriften aus hellenistisch-römischer Zeit
JSJSup	*Journal for the Study of Judaism*, Supplement Series
JSOT	*Journal for the Study of the Old Testament*

JSOTSup	*Journal for the Study of the Old Testament, Supplement Series*
JSP	*Journal for the Study of the Pseudepigrapha*
JTC	*Journal for Theology and the Church*
LSTS	Library of Second Temple Studies
MT	Masoretic Text
NAB	New American Bible
NTS	*New Testament Studies*
NRSV	New Revised Standard Version
OBO	Orbis biblicus et orientalis
OCD	*Oxford Classical Dictionary*
OL	Old Latin
OTL	Old Testament Library
OTP	James Charlesworth (ed.) *Old Testament Pseudepigrapha* (2 vols.; New York: Doubleday, 1983)
PVTG	Pseudepigrapha Veteris Testamenti Graece
RB	*Revue biblique*
RevQ	*Revue de Qumran*
S	Codex Sinaiticus
SBLDS	Society of Biblical Literature Dissertation Series
SBLEJL	Society of Biblical Literature Early Judaism and Its Literature
SBLSCS	Society of Biblical Literature Septuagint and Cognate Studies
SBLSP	Society of Biblical Literature Seminar Papers
SBLSymS	Society of Biblical Literature Symposium Series
SHR	Studies in the History of Religions (supplement to *Numen*)
STDJ	Studies on the Texts of the Desert of Judah
SVTP	Studia in Veteris Testamenti pseudepigrapha
TBT	*The Bible Today*
USQR	*Union Seminary Quarterly Review*
Vg	Vulgate
VL	Vetus Latina
VT	*Vetus Testamentum*
VTSup	*Vetus Testamentum*, Supplements
WMANT	Wissenschaftliche Monographien zum Alten und Neuen Testament
WUNT	Wissenschaftliche Untersuchungen zum Neuen Testament
ZWT	*Zeitschrift für wissenschaftliche Theologie*

PREFACE

This book is a revised version of my dissertation, completed in 2008 at Princeton Theological Seminary. I have many people to thank who have helped see this project to its completion. First, I owe much gratitude to the department of Biblical Studies at Princeton Theological Seminary for allowing me to focus my work on the book of Tobit. The interests and passion of the faculty—those still present and those who have passed on—constituted a significant part of my formation at PTS. The myriad ways I am indebted to my fine instructors will perhaps be obvious to the understanding reader. In particular, I fondly remember Don Juel, whose passion for scripture continues to inspire and inform me. His untimely passing coincided with the beginning of my doctoral studies, but his refusal to accept readings of texts that seem too comfortable and easy has impacted my reading of the book of Tobit, especially its ending.

This project would never have left the ground were it not for the support of Clifton Black. His encouragement to trust my instincts at times when all I had was a hunch have not gone unnoticed or unappreciated. His attention to matters both great and small has improved my work significantly. James Charlesworth and Dennis Olson also provided invaluable expertise and guidance in this process. More recently, Loren Stuckenbruck was kind enough to comment on my manuscript and offer his insights. Finally, Lester Grabbe generously read the manuscript and made comments, despite its many dissertation-like idiosyncrasies. Certainly no critic will ever be completely in agreement with all my arguments; any errors of omission or commission, however, are nobody's fault but mine.

I would like to thank the Theology Department and administration at St. Ambrose University for support of this project. They provided me a one-course release during the 2007–2008 academic year, without which I would not have had time to finish and graduate. The friendship and support of my colleagues at St. Ambrose are a source of joy in my life. I am lucky to have a wonderful job and wonderful colleagues with whom I work. I have been aided by the help of students as well, especially Ross Epping and Kaitlyn Koniuszy. The St. Ambrose library has also made the completion of this project possible. In particular, the interlibrary loan staff swiftly made available to me books from all over the world, titles which our library will never hold permanently.

I type this, sitting in an empty classroom while my son Harrison watches construction vehicles in the middle of campus outside the window; hopefully my other son, Brendan, is asleep. Thank you to my family for fun, support, and unending adventures. I owe thanks to my parents, who helped instill in me a desire to explore the world. They supported me—and continue to do so—unfailingly in many endeavors. My in-laws also deserve some credit, if for nothing else than for letting their daughter live in Princeton, NJ for seven years. And as for that daughter, Eleanor, no words can express my gratitude. Her constant light and grace never cease to amaze me. I dedicate this work to her, for its completion is due in no small part to her.

Micah D. Kiel
Davenport, IA
July, 2011

Chapter 1

INTRODUCTION

Humans, by nature, question life's events. Religious rhetoric often accompanies such inquiries, claiming to explain experiences suffered, their origin, and the reason for their genesis. In Puccini's opera, *Tosca*, the scheming Scarpia forces the title character to choose between her chastity and the life of her betrothed. In her second-act aria, *Vissi d'arte, Vissi d'amore*, Tosca laments over her undeserved predicament:

> I have lived for art; I have lived for love.
> I have not harmed another soul that is living.
> In secret I have aided many who are unfortunate.
> Always with a sincere faith,
> My prayer rose to the holy shrines.
> Always with a sincere faith,
> I placed flowers on the altar.
> In the hour of ache,
> Why, why, O Lord
> Why have you repayed me like this?
> I have given jewels for the Madonna's mantle . . .
> In the hour of ache,
> Why, why, O Lord
> Ah, why have you repaid me like this?[1]

Tosca's lament is reminiscent of that of Tobit (3.1–6) because the two characters share one assumption: upright behavior should elicit an appropriate divine response. They both lament because God seems to treat the formula cavalierly.

Over one hundred years ago Abrahams wrote: "There is a general consensus of opinion that the Book of Tobit was written with a tendency" (1893: 348).[2] Today there is general consensus with regard to Tobit's tendency. It has become commonplace to refer to the book's Deuteronomistic theology—the retributive perspective assumed in Tosca's lament—which

---

1   Author's translation. Throughout this work, if no indication is given, the translation is my own.
2   Abrahams' goal was to demonstrate that there was no consensus regarding Tobit's specific tendency: was it intended to advocate a certain piety marked by doing good works, or was its tendency more specifically tied to burying the dead?

claims that God rewards according to human action. This formulation of retribution holds that if you do right, God will do right by you. And it assumes that the reverse is true: do wrong and God will punish you.[3] As we will see in the following pages, there are some significant problems with finding this doctrine as Tobit's tendency. When the book is compared with contemporaneous Jewish literature, it appears to proffer a much more complex understanding of retribution.

At the core of this study lies the question of theodicy—the justice of God in the face of evil—and Tobit's particular working out of this problem.[4] Are the difficulties experienced in this life the result of God's retribution?[5] Are they connected to the deeds of humans? Or, is there another explanation for why people like Scarpia succeed, why individuals suffer calumnies, why they go blind, and why the Jewish people are under Gentile rule?

I. Introduction to this Study

a. The Problem

Scholars commonly refer to the Deuteronomistic perspective of the book of Tobit. As Carey Moore states, "the Deuteronomistic idea of 'sin or win' pervades the entire book" (1996: 263). Joseph Fitzmyer's more recent commentary has repeated this reading of the book: "Tobit's thinking sums up 'the great Deuteronomic equation,' viz. that those who love God and fear him will be rewarded, whereas those who do not will suffer" (2003: 332). Calling Tobit "Deuteronomistic" or "Deuteronomic" sometimes means that the book incorporates and emulates many of the central theological tenets of the book of Deuteronomy. The seminal effort in coordinating Tobit with Deuteronomism is Alexander Di Lella's article in the *Catholic Biblical Quarterly* (1979: 380–9), in which he posits 14 points of contact between Deuteronomy and Tobit's farewell discourse in chapter 14. Too often, however, the

---

3   Further parts of this study will demonstrate amply how this view pervades Tobit scholarship. At this point, we can simply note the perspective of Carey Moore, who claims that the "Deuteronomistic idea of 'sin or win' pervades the entire book of Tobit" (1996: 263).

4   Portier-Young offers a contrary opinion here, claiming that "no biblical theology offers a satisfactory explanation of the origin of or the reason for individual human suffering. Nor does the book of Tobit seek to answer this difficult question" (2001: 37). The futility of the endeavor, however, does not necessarily mean that the book of Tobit does not attempt an answer. Portier-Young argues instead that Tobit is meant to show how God is present in the lives of those who suffer.

5   Portier-Young (2001: 37) claims that Tobit has no interest in the origin of suffering, only in how God responds to it and how humans should respond in light of this reality. She claims that the Deuteronomic program has no place for the individual, a conclusion with which I will disagree later in this study.

word "Deuteronomistic" is used to describe Tobit's perspective on retribution. For example, after his sight returns, Tobit specifically coordinates his situation with God's retribution by claiming that it was God who had scourged him in the first place (11.15). Carey Moore calls this Tobit's "Deuteronomistic creed," an idea that he claims "pervades the entire book" (1996: 263). Attaching the word "Deuteronomistic" or "Deuteronomic" to this concept is misleading because it does not do justice to the theological complexity of the book of Deuteronomy nor to Tobit itself.[6] As we will see, a more accurate label for the type of theological idea with which the book of Tobit allegedly interacts is a "simple doctrine of retribution" or perhaps a "straightforward retributive theology." There is good reason to discuss retributive theology in Tobit (e.g., Tobit's retribution-laden prayer in ch. 3). There are two problems, however, with the way in which scholars have developed this premise.

1. Problem one: lack of precision

Scholarly attempts to pin the book of Tobit with a Deuteronomistic perspective are hindered by imprecision and a lack of contextualization of retributive theologies. These problems take shape in two specific ways:

1. First, there is a lack of titular precision. Frequent use of the adjective "Deuteronomistic" invites confusion. What is meant by this word? Does it refer specifically to the theology of the book of Deuteronomy? Does it refer to the so-called "Deuteronomistic History" in Joshua through 2 Kings? The word most often, in descriptions of Tobit, is meant to describe the book's retributive perspective. The term, however, is too imprecise and speculative to be helpful in descriptions of Tobit unless it has been defined carefully.

2. Second, scholars have not paid sufficient attention to variant forms of retributive theology contemporaneous with Tobit. Although perhaps misguided in naming Tobit's perspective "Deuteronomistic," scholars generally have not placed Tobit among wider conversations about retributive theology during the early Hellenistic period. As a result, one major component of the argument presented here will be to examine closely what exactly Deuteronomistic theology—or, in our new terminology, "straightforward retributive theology"—is. What are its biblical antecedents and what was its status during the period in

---

6   See Weeks (2011), who recently has come to a similar conclusion. He rightly notes, as do many, that Tobit is indebted to many parts of Israel's heritage and he puzzles at how Tobit has so quickly been pinned with a singular ideological point of view. He claims that to speak of only Deuteronomic influence "would be to underestimate the complexity of the picture which the author paints for us, and it seems astonishing that recent scholarship on Tobit has become dominated by a paradigm of the book as a quintessentially Deuteronomic work" (390). Weeks' essay appeared simultaneously with my article (2011), which similarly questioned the enterprise of attributing to the book of Tobit a singularly Deuteronomic point of view.

which Tobit was written? This is not to say that influence directly from Deuteronomy is impossible. Di Lella's work (1979), however, launched a scholarly trajectory that canonized Tobit's "Deuteronomistic" stance. Subsequent work has generally neglected critical analysis regarding similar and contrasting views of retribution in the Second Temple period.

2. Problem two: not attending to the whole story

A second problem is that many treatments of "Deuteronomistic" theology in Tobit do not necessarily attend to the entirety of the text and story of Tobit. It is undeniable that Tobit's prayer in chapter 3 and his singularity in keeping the law of Moses while in exile indicate that the book has employed language and ideas indicative of a straightforward doctrine of retribution, irrespective of whether or not it is named "Deuteronomistic." In many of these verses, Tobit claims he is guilty by association, lumped together with the sin of all his kin that instigated the exile. Although these ideas and themes are in the text, this does not mean that they are the overall message the author intended to convey. In a simple doctrine of retribution—what Tobit scholarship tends to call "Deuteronomistic theology"—reward and punishment are based on obedience. The present study will suggest to the contrary that this formula may not underlie all the unfortunate events in the narrative of Tobit. The suffering experienced by characters in the book does not result from an individual's ability to keep certain statutes, because it is not immediately clear why Tobit loses his sight, why a giant fish attacks Tobias, and why a demon afflicts Sarah.

The arc of the story also may not uphold a straightforward retributive theology, according to which one expects either immediate, or at least eventual, reward for good or wicked deeds.[7] The ending of Tobit's story does show some resolution and restoration: Tobit's sight is returned, Tobias marries Sarah, and Nineveh gets its recompense. One of the core problems of the story—Israel's subjection to foreign rule—is not resolved. Nineveh is destroyed but is replaced by another foreign power. For a straightforward doctrine of retribution to hold, one must find the resolution of the problems afflicting Tobit and Sarah as anticipatory of what will be the eventual end of the Diaspora. Carey Moore perceives this issue and argues that it is not a problem for the book's retributive perspective. He claims that the "Deuteronomic principle was still intact" because the help that comes to Tobit and Sarah represents "divine assurance of other more wonderful

---

7   Moshe Weinfeld finds a tendency in the wisdom literature to explain current sufferings as only a temporary delay. Many sapiential texts alleviate the problem of theodicy through the concept of אחרית, the "latter end," an idea "according to which the prosperity of the wicked and the suffering of the righteous are only transitory states. The decisive factor is the 'latter end'" (1972: 316). Weinfeld also finds this idea in Deuteronomy itself, but it is focused there on the nation instead of the individual.

things to come" (1996: 298). Such a reading is possible, but not necessary. In a novella where much of the action of God—like an iceberg—lies well beneath the surface of human intelligibility, perhaps the ending hints that the characters are never fully "in the know." Tobias rejoices over the destruction of Nineveh, but one wonders why Tobias does not realize that the core problem of subjugation to foreign rule has not been resolved. In brief, the narrative itself offers some reasons why the so-called Deuteronomistic rhetoric—especially as stated in Tobit's prayer in chapter 3—might not be the only or even primary tendency the author intended to convey.

b. A Way Forward

Many scholars encounter the problem outlined above: that, despite the book's seemingly straightforward retributive theology, parts of the narrative strain against it. For instance, William Soll claims that one has the feeling that "there should be a better fate for people like Tobit" (1989: 224). This disjunction is exhibited in Irene Nowell's reading of Tobit (1983). She claims that although the book is characterized by irony and delayed reward, the basic principle is affirmed that God rewards the righteous and punishes the wicked (229–32). Nevertheless, the story of Tobit strains against this conclusion sufficiently to force Nowell also to say that even though Tobit eventually receives his reward, "the doctrine of retribution is not a simple equation" (233). Nowell claims that the "fundamental irony" of the book is that "God blesses the righteous and punishes the wicked; yet God is free" (233). Later in her study, Nowell claims that "the foundation of the theological statements in the Book of Tobit is the belief that God is free" (270), a freedom she attributes to influence from Deuteronomy. Nowell quotes Deut. 32.39 as proof of God's freedom: "see now that I, even I, am he; there is no god besides me. I kill and I make alive; I wound and I heal; and no one can deliver from my hand" (NRSV).

Nowell's quotation here is problematic and selective. This verse does seem to assert God's freedom to treat retributive formulae cavalierly, should God so wish. The problem is that this verse comes in the context of Moses' song, in which he recounts God's deeds for Israel (32.10–15a) and Israel's spurning of God (15b–18). Because Israel was not mindful, God was jealous and resolved to hide from the people (19–20). The whole of the song seems to support the idea that God punishes the wicked: "I will take vengeance on my adversaries, and will repay those who hate me" (32.41b NRSV). Nowell's attribution of freedom to God results from her encounter with the ways in which the narrative of Tobit does not exemplify its widely purported exhibition of Deuteronomistic retribution. While Nowell is correct in pointing out the theological complexity of both Tobit and Deuteronomy, her assessment here contains a more problematic underlying assumption. It is so commonplace to assert the book of Tobit's Deuteronomic stance that any theological idea in Tobit must be squared with Deuteronomy. This constrains a free inquiry into the theological intentions of the author of Tobit, especially the book's perspective on retribution.

Nowell should be commended for her insightful assessment of the story of Tobit, but her attribution of the freedom of God to the theology of Deuteronomy as a way to explain inconsistencies in the retribution exhibited in Tobit seems problematic.[8] Whether exhibited in Deuteronomy or not, could the author of Tobit not have introduced a corrective theological viewpoint? Or, more pointedly, if Tobit is found to have a complex theological iteration, must that complexity be found in Deuteronomy itself, as if Tobit could not have other influences or an original theological expression?[9] These questions do not, however, taint the basic premise of Nowell's investigation: that there is much in Tobit that does not work out according to a straightforward retributive formula. Nowell is struggling to put her finger on an aspect of Tobit's narrative that does not cohere well with the Deuteronomistic formulation as it is so often described in Tobit scholarship. It is this problem—inaptly called "God's freedom" by Nowell—that provides the impetus for the present study. The elements of the story that could be attributed to God's freedom are actually not to be so interpreted, and instead come from a more apocalyptic understanding of the genesis of evil in the world.

In light of the foregoing summary, the argument to be presented here will proceed in two major parts. The first part of this study, comprised of chapters 3–5, will contain an analysis of conceptions of retribution—especially those named "Deuteronomistic" by some scholars—at a time roughly contemporaneous with Tobit. Sirach will provide a point of comparison from which we can ask how Tobit does or does not cohere with such a doctrine. The narrative of the book of Tobit itself will also be examined for the actual argument it presents in its entirety. The second part of this study, containing chapters 6–8, will examine some of the earliest Jewish apocalyptic traditions, those contained in portions of the collection of apocalyptic texts called *1 Enoch*. These will be investigated specifically with regard to retribution and the origin of evil in the world. As we will see, they offer a very different conclusion from that in Ben Sira. When Tobit is compared to these apocalyptic writings it will become clear that a reassessment of Tobit's purported Deuteronomistic perspective—its straightforward retributive theology—is in

---

8   As we will see later in this study, there were many emendations to the Deuteronomistic theory and, in the case of Ben Sira, much anguish resulting from the difficulty of affirming this doctrine in light of contradictory human experience. The "freedom of God," however, does not seem to be attested anywhere as one of the ways with which the difficulty of this doctrine was treated. To the contrary, the assurance of God's action and character is of utmost importance in such discussions.

9   The work of John Gammie is important here (1970: 1–12). Gammie emphasizes that there is a strong theocentric aspect to retribution in Deuteronomy, which gears well with Nowell's references to God's freedom. Such an emphasis on God's role was meant to offer "deliberate corrections" to what had become a problematically "hard and fast dogma" (11). These arguments will be dealt with more fully in chapter 3 below.

order. The book of Tobit also displays affinities with Israel's earliest apocalyptic traditions. The intention here is not to set straightforward retributive theology and apocalyptic traditions as completely contradictory. There are many ways in which much apocalyptic thinking as represented in the early apocalypses is influenced by such thinking, not the least of which is the belief that God will punish the wicked and reward those who endure in righteousness.[10] To some early Jewish apocalypticists, however, evil is not of human origin, but is imposed upon humanity as an outside force. These theological aspects of early apocalypticism in Israel illuminate elements of the book of Tobit and reorient their significance. Tobias' encounter with a meddlesome fish, Sarah's demonic menace, and Tobit's scurrilous sparrows all are manifestations of a world gone awry, corrupted by sin and evil.

The book of Tobit, ultimately, offers a theological interpretation of life's events that is complex, supple, and commensurate with human experience. The book's views are forged in consultation with traditional answers to deep human questions, while at the same time taking account of more contemporary innovations. While Tobit's folk-tale genre has generally excluded it from the pantheon of great theological thinkers in the Second Temple period, the study that follows aims to show that segregating Tobit in this way is a tragedy. The book of Tobit puts forward an erudite theological composition, told as an entertaining narrative, that grapples with suffering in a way that exudes deep thinking, complexity, and awareness of the human condition.

---

10   One major difference lies in the timing of these events. The reward and punishment, as envisioned by some apocalypticists, does not come until after death, which is a significant divergence from Deuteronomistic theology, especially as conveyed in Sirach.

Chapter 2

THE BOOK OF TOBIT: LANGUAGE, DATE, PROVENANCE, INTEGRITY

The goal of this chapter is to discuss some of the major interpretive issues one faces when studying the book of Tobit. Tobit has a complicated textual history, and offers little that allows its place of creation to be pinpointed with any precision. In what follows, the language, date, provenance, and integrity of the book will be discussed, which will help situate the book sufficiently so that we may proceed with the arguments about its theological viewpoints in what follows.

The Original Language of the Book of Tobit

As is the case with most text-based forays into antiquity, one must establish what text will be the basis for inquiry. The textual history of the book of Tobit is complicated. Manuscripts of the book exist in at least nine different languages in close to twenty variations. An exhaustive treatment of the situation will not be possible here. A few salient points, however, should establish the texts on which this study will be based and how they will be evaluated.

Two separate discoveries in the modern era have proved epoch-making in the history of scholarship on the book of Tobit, especially with regard to the understanding of Tobit's textual history. The first is the discovery of Codex Sinaiticus by Tischendorf in 1844. Prior to this date the primary recension of Tobit in use was the so-called "shorter" Greek text, represented most prominently by the Alexandrinus (A) and Vaticanus (B) codices, thus its common siglum in Tobit parlance: AB (named G^I in Hanhart's edition [1984]). A longer recension of Tobit was known, represented by an eleventh-century manuscript (MS 319) and a sixth-century papyrus (MS 910). The version of Tobit discovered in Codex Sinaiticus cohered with this longer version and was significantly different from AB. The discovery showed the importance of this longer Greek recension (with reference to Tobit, called S or G^{II}), which instigated new interest in Tobit in the latter half of the nineteenth century. The *Vetus Latina* (VL), or Old Latin (OL), also shows similarities to the longer recension.[1] With the exception of two lacunae (4.7–19b and 13.6–10b), S contains the entire text of Tobit. The first lacuna can be filled by MS 319, but the second needs to be covered by using either VL or AB.[2]

The question of which of these two Greek recensions is older was an immediate matter of contention among scholars. David Simpson's influential introduction to Tobit in Charles' *Apocrypha and Pseudepigrapha of the Old Testament* argued strongly that S was original and that it was based on a Semitic *Vorlage*, claiming it as "the nearest approach which can be made to the original text whether the latter first appeared in Greek or in a Semitic language" (1913: 1:175). Nevertheless, in 1972, Thomas stated that there still was not consensus on the matter (463–4). Thomas' analysis indicates that there is enough verbatim conformity between S and AB to conclude that one was a direct revision or expansion of the other. According to Thomas, the Greek linguistic evidence indicates that either AB is an adaptation of S intended to improve the Greek of S, or S is an emendation of AB that intended to make the Greek more Semitic and add redundant material (467–8).

Close analysis seems to indicate, however, that at the many points where AB is shorter than S, a logical reason can be surmised, usually an attempt to remove redundancy or to make the language more idiomatic. For example, in 12.14 Raphael reveals two pieces of information previously hidden from the characters in the story. He claims that he was sent to heal and to test Tobit (ἀπέσταλμαι ἐπὶ σὲ πειράσαι σε). Raphael's mission as it is actually described in the narrative, however, makes no mention of testing, whereas healing is a definitive part of his mission according to 3.17. The AB text removes the reference to testing, presumably because healing is more indicative of Raphael's mission throughout the text. This is easier to explain as AB removing the reference to testing as opposed to S adding it for some reason. Fitzmyer summarizes the differences between the two texts: "It is clear that the differences between G^{II} and G^{I} [i.e., S and AB] are most easily accounted for by a process of curtailment and the elimination of Semitisms that are found in G^{II}" (2003: 5). Thus, the most likely conclusion is that AB is a revision of S. Here, contrary to the often-quoted dictum in text-critical studies, the shorter reading is not the preferred one. In the specific case of the Greek texts of Tobit, the longer recension has a greater claim to antiquity.[3]

---

1   For a fuller discussion of Tobit's textual history, see Fitzmyer (2003: 3–15). The transmission of the Old Latin (OL) itself is difficult, and it is problematic to refer to it as a unified tradition (Gathercole 2006). More details will be provided below.

2   Auwers (2005) argues that the OL should be given more consideration in these reconstructions, claiming that "the type of text" might be more important than "the language in which it is preserved" (17, author's translation).

3   This is not to say, however, that the Greek text of S is without its own infelicities. When evaluating the textual tradition in S, reference to the OL can be helpful because it generally conforms to the long text (Skemp 2000: 3). The OL itself, however, does not have a stable textual tradition; to refer to it as a single text or textual tradition is misleading because it exists in at least 18 different recensions (Gathercole 2006: 5–11).

The second major, epoch-making discovery in Tobit studies is the collection of fragments of Tobit found at Qumran.[4] Four manuscripts have been found in Aramaic and one in Hebrew.[5] Despite the existence of some Hebrew loanwords in the Aramaic (such as אליל, "idol" and תהלין, "psalms"), Fitzmyer maintains that this is not sufficient evidence of Hebrew as the original language because Hebrew loanwords were not uncommon in Aramaic of the period (2003: 22–5).[6] Fitzmyer argues that Aramaic was the original language, based mostly on his judgment that the fragments portray "good examples of Middle Aramaic" and are related to other Qumran texts (2003: 26).[7] Jerome offers a tantalizing claim that he worked from an Aramaic version that he put into Latin with the help of a translator.[8] Modern studies show, however, that Jerome's work was based significantly on the OL and contained some original emendations as well. The similarities between the Vulgate and the OL are close enough that Vincent Skemp (2000: 455) calls Jerome's work a revision of the OL rather than a translation from another source. If Jerome's claim to have used an Aramaic version is true, his text must have differed significantly from the Aramaic preserved at Qumran; the two do not show a great deal of resemblance.[9] The majority of scholars now consider Tobit as originally written in a Semitic language, with most opting for Aramaic, although some do argue for Hebrew.[10]

Not only did the Qumran fragments provide a basis on which to argue for Aramaic as the original language, but their conformity to S established

---

4   The importance of this discovery is obvious and need not be overstated. Fitzmyer (2003), for instance, divides his discussion of Tobit's textual history into two epochs: before 1952 and after 1952. Carey Moore (1989) dedicated an entire article to discussion of the implications of the Qumran fragments for study of Tobit. See also Fröhlich (2005) and Dimant (2009a).

5   Joseph Fitzmyer (1995) was responsible for publishing the fragments of Tobit from Qumran. Fitzmyer's transcription and translation of the five fragments of Tobit, labeled 4Q196–200, are on pp. 1–76 and correspond to plates 1–10.

6   Fitzmyer here argues against Beyer (1984), who claimed Hebrew as the original language of Tobit and then classified the Aramaic copies of the book as *Targumim*. Cook (1996: 154–5) agrees with Fitzmyer's criticism of Beyer.

7   Fitzmyer provides seven examples that help prove his point about the language of the fragments. For Fitzmyer, middle Aramaic is the period from 200 BCE to 200 CE, although, because he sees Palestinian Aramaic as a direct descendant of official Aramaic, it is perhaps possible to extend the beginning of that date back somewhat (1979: 57–74).

8   This translator, according to Jerome, actually first put Tobit in Hebrew, which Jerome then translated into Latin (Skemp 2000: 1). There are also medieval Aramaic versions of Tobit, which date from no earlier than 700 CE. They seem to have been translated from Greek and do not bear enough resemblance to the Vulgate to be Jerome's *Urtext* (Skemp 2000: 4–5).

9   Fitzmyer (2003) and Skemp (2000) are in agreement here. Skemp claims that the correspondences between the two are "minor and coincidental and probably come via [Vetus Latina]" (466).

10   As noted above, the strongest proponent of Hebrew is Beyer (1984). Note also that one exception to the Aramaic consensus is Deselaers (1982), who argues for Greek as the original language. His book will be dealt with in greater detail below.

that text as the more original Greek recension. As Fitzmyer notes: that the Qumran fragments would correspond most closely with the longer recension (S) was an occurrence that "no one suspected before 1952" (2003: 9). Such was, however, the case; the Qumran fragments cohere most closely with S, and at times are even longer than S, the longer Greek recension. This affirms the "very early character" of the S tradition (Weeks, Gathercole, and Stuckenbruck 2004: 3). One can observe this conclusion visually by paging through the *Polyglotte* of Tobit compiled by Christian Wagner (2003). He arranges the most significant Greek, Latin, and Syriac texts in parallel columns. Because there was not ample space for the Qumran fragments in the parallel format, he colors the Greek, Latin, or Syriac texts in blue font any place where they overlap with the Qumran texts. By flipping through the pages one can note that the blue font is much more pervasive in S (Wagner's *Langtext*) than in any other recension.[11]

The implications for modern study of Tobit are as follows. The Qumran Aramaic and Hebrew fragments should have priority, being by far the oldest extant texts of the book and, in the case of Aramaic, the likely original language of composition. Their fragmentary nature, however, makes necessary the use of another text. Because of its general affinity to the Qumran fragments and the likelihood that it preceded AB, the Greek text of S will be the base text for this study. Whenever possible, the Qumran texts will be utilized. The Greek text should always be checked against the OL, which generally coheres with S, although the OL does not have a unified textual history, and must be used on a case-by-case basis (Skemp 2000; Gathercole 2006).

II. Date of the Book of Tobit

The book of Tobit is very difficult, if not impossible, to date with precision. It makes no clear references to contemporaneous political events and contains no traditions that might indicate precisely when and where it was written. For dating the book, however, there is enough internal and external evidence that some broad perimeters can be established.

One can initially notice that the story as reported in the book of Tobit is not historically accurate.[12] The book's narrative setting is the eighth–seventh century BCE in the Neo-Assyrian Empire. The background to the opening scenario in chapter 1 is the Assyrian deportation mentioned in 2 Kgs 15.29: "During the reign of Pekah, king of Israel, Tiglath-pileser,

---

11   Wagner (2003) does include the Qumran fragments at the end of his *Polyglotte* (pp. 181–204).

12   Although, note the objections of Dimant (2009b: 354, n. 25), who says that "scholarly assertions of the 'non-historicity' of the Book of Tobit" should be "qualified." She bases her opinion here on how the "general conditions" of the Assyrian Diaspora as represented in Tobit have been "strikingly confirmed" (354).

king of Assyria, came and took Ijon, Abel-beth-maacah, Janoah, Dedesh, Hazor, all the territory of Naphtali, Gilead, and Galilee, deporting the inhabitants to Assyria" (NAB). This event is presumed as the background in the beginning of Tobit. The first verse of the book claims that Tobit is from the tribe of Naphtali and that he was taken captive from Thisbe. In 1.2 the Greek text (both S and AB) explains that Tobit was taken captive in the days of ἐνεμέσσαρος, which is probably a corruption that should read "Shalmaneser," as represented in most Old Latin manuscripts, the Vulgate, and the Medieval Hebrew manuscripts of Tobit (Salmannasar; שׁל מנאסר). Historical analysis indicates that, although Shalmaneser started the siege of Samaria in 722, the capture and deportation were not completed until two years later by Sargon, who succeeded Shalmaneser to the throne (Moore 1996: 101–2). Tobit 1.15 claims that Sennacherib succeeded Shalmaneser to the throne, but this again is an anachronism. Sargon, not Sennacherib, followed Shalmaneser. Such historical infelicities show that it was written at a time much later than that in which the story itself takes place.

Knowing that Tobit does not accurately represent its purported era allows one to look elsewhere for clues as to the time in which it might have been written. A likely *terminus a quo* is sometime after the fourth century BCE. Tobit refers to "the prophets of Israel" (14.4) and quotes Amos directly (2.6), which indicates that the prophetic books were in some sense authoritative or canonical for the author. The author also refers to the book or law of Moses (e.g., 1.8).[13] Both of these developments indicate a date later than the fourth century BCE. The Qumran fragments provide a definite *terminus ante quem*. Based on paleography, Fitzmyer (1995) dates the earliest of these between 100 and 50 BCE.[14] The fact that the Qumran fragments offer four different texts of Tobit, one of which is in Hebrew and the others in Aramaic, means that some copying of the text had occurred by 100 BCE and its composition must have been some time earlier.

Frank Zimmerman attempted to place Tobit's composition within the Maccabean period by taking burial as a "distinctive clue" (1958: 24). He claims that Tobit reflects the situation in 2 Macc. 9.15, in which Antiochus IV considered Jews not worth burial. One must, however, take note of the differences between the situation in Tobit and those circumstances indicative of the Maccabean period. Tobit does not seem to show any significant knowledge of the Maccabean movement and does not reflect any of the upheavals associated with Antiochus IV Epiphanes and his reforms (Moore 1996: 41; Fitzmyer 2003: 51). Moore (1996: 41) disagrees with Zimmerman because Tobit does not show any of the "ethnic and religious hatred" from the Maccabean period. Tobit also does not portray any characteristics of other distinctly Jewish movements in the second century BCE. Fitzmyer, in his commentary (2003: 51–2), claims that a date before 150 BCE is likely because

13   See Gamberoni (1977: 227–42).
14   Fitzmyer dates 4Q196 and 4Q198 to between 50 and 100 BCE.

Tobit does not show any of the developments associated with or similar to Qumran sectarianism, such as apocalyptic expectation and messianism. Although a Maccabean date is possible, Zimmerman's argument about burial is not sufficient proof because other aspects of that movement are absent in Tobit, making sometime before 175 BCE a more likely *terminus ad quem*.

While a precise date remains impossible to pinpoint, the evidence mentioned above does provide some sense of when Tobit was written. A date sometime between 250 and 175 BCE seems most likely. Within that range it is difficult to speculate further, although this specific range is important for avenues of the present study. In the chapters that follow, Tobit will be compared to texts with which it is roughly contemporaneous. Situating it in the middle third to early second century BCE helps provide warrant for comparing Tobit to texts such as Sirach and the earliest traditions in the Jewish apocalyptic collection of *1 Enoch*, especially the portions known as the *Book of Watchers* (chs. 1–36) and the *Astronomical Book* (chs. 72–82), both of which are dated to a similar time.[15]

III. Provenance of the Book of Tobit

The provenance for the book of Tobit is also difficult to pinpoint. Choosing to have its main character's heritage be from Israel and not Judah is "unique" in ancient Jewish literature, and the reason for this choice for the title character and his family is not "self-evident" (Dimant 2009b: 348). In determining the location of the book's composition, three major proposals have been offered.

a. Egypt

The first proposal is that Tobit was written in Egypt, a conclusion for which David Simpson (1913) has argued strongly. He claims that a major impetus behind the writing of Tobit was to respond to the Tractate of Khons, a tale from a fourth- or third-century BCE Egyptian stele telling a story set in the reign of Ramses II (thirteenth century BCE).[16] The

---

15   Although the dating of these texts will be dealt with in much more detail in turn, at this point we may note the following observation from Grabbe: "The *Book of Watchers* was probably already taking shape in the late Persian period. Since it is not unusual to put the origins of the *Book of Watchers* fairly early in the Ptolemaic period, the tradition would have been extant in some form before the end of the Persian period" (2003a: 33). See also Charlesworth, who concludes: "the consensus is now that the Book of the Watchers was composed by the early Hellenistic period and may reflect the struggles of the Diadochi after the death of Alexander the Great in 323 BCE. Thus, the writings now called the books of Enoch originated before 200 B.C.E., and conceivably as early as the end of the fourth century B.C.E." (2005: 446).

16   "The Legend of the Possessed Princess" (*ANET*, 29–31).

tractate tells of a princess who is afflicted by a demon. Khons expels the demon, thereby providing pious propaganda asserting the power of the Egyptian god. According to Simpson, the author of Tobit intended to counter Kohns' tale and its Egyptian propaganda with a Jewish counterpart (1913, 1:185). This in turn leads him to suggest Egypt as the origin for the story of Tobit; only in Egypt would a response to the Tractate of Khons make sense. Simpson further claims that the medicinal parts of the fish in Tobit chapter 6 are related to the crocodiles in the Nile, which are often shown to have similar properties in Greek and Latin writers. The mention of Egypt as the binding place of Asmodeus indicates that the author viewed Egypt as the dumping ground of all evil (1: 186). The author of Tobit also knows the Ahiqar tale, which, according to Simpson, was known in Egypt but not in Palestine at this time.[17] The author of Tobit intentionally avoids any reference to daily Egyptian life, and instead places the story in the distant world of the northern deportation, a situation similar to that of Ahiqar. Simpson ultimately posits that the book of Tobit's beginning was connected with the garrison at Elephantine and associated with the reforms of temple-based worship there after the exile (1: 186–7).[18]

Simpson's arguments are presented with two significant problems. First, his reconstruction of the book of Tobit's origin rests upon an assumption that Diaspora life in Egypt would have been difficult for Jews in the third and fourth centuries BCE. This difficult life, he claims, explains why the author did not mention daily life and set the story in a distant land. Egypt instead was the proper burial ground for demons. Simpson, however, provides no warrant for this situation. To the contrary, in the third century BCE. Jewish life in Egypt likely was stable and not marked by persecution or hatred. The evidence, limited in this period to inscriptions and papyri, suggests that Jews were in the army, were granted land, and worked as farmers, craftspeople, and even as tax collectors and administrators (Barclay 1996: 64–77; Collins 2000: 64–78). According to Strabo, the Jews also had some political autonomy and were given the right to an *ethnarch* (Fraser 1972: 1:54–5).[19] There is no trace of anti-Semitism in the early Ptolemaic period; the Jewish acculturation exhibited in the use of Greek forms of literature, religion, and language—work of "superior quality" (Fraser 1972: 1:57)—does not

---

17   We now know considerably more about Ahiqar than did Simpson. The name Ahiqar occurs explicitly on a tablet discovered in Uruk during an excavation in 1959–1960. Ahiqar is listed along with other wise sages (*ummanu*) who occupied a high place: "in the time of King Assur-ah-iddina, Aba'Enlidari who is called by the Ahlamu [i.e. the Aramaeans] Ahuqar was the *emmanu*" (Greenfield 1981: 331).

18   More recently, Deselaers (1982) has also argued for an Egyptian provenance for Tobit. He posits a four-stage development of the text of Tobit, two of which take place in Egypt, an argument that will be dealt with in more depth below.

19   Fraser claims that, although Strabo is from a later period, the situation he describes for the Jews was one that likely originated in the Ptolemaic period.

indicate forced cultural assimilation. The Jews remained distinct, generally did not intermarry, and expressed themselves naturally in the Greek forms of religion, philosophy, and commerce in their specific locale. The book of *3 Maccabees* does show some unrest under Ptolemy IV Philopater, but because this work comes from the Roman period when Jews were being persecuted, it is hard to know how well this reflects the actual situation in the third century BCE.

Another significant problem with Simpson's argument that Tobit originated in Egypt is the book's Eastern setting. Although Simpson and others argue that the inaccurate geography in Tobit indicates that it could not have been written by somebody in the East, such a conclusion is not necessary. The geography in Tobit may simply be symbolic (Zsengellér 2005). Like its treatment of history, the book of Tobit may have goals for its geography other than the standards set by modern cartography.[20]

b. The East

Precisely because of its Eastern setting, many scholars have argued that this is indeed the place of origin for the book. In 1900 James Moulton argued that Tobit originated in an Iranian milieu. Moulton claimed that there were two aspects of Magian religion that struck outsiders: their method of disposing of the dead, which was to leave a body to be picked clean by birds, and the glorification of consanguineous marriage. He posits that in a *Vorlage* for Tobit a Magian hero was praised for doing these two things and that the author of Tobit then adapted it to fit Jewish burial practices. Other elements point toward an Eastern provenance for Tobit. The dog was a sacred animal to the Persians, which may help explain its existence—otherwise almost unintelligible— in a Jewish novella.[21] Finally, the demon's name, Asmodeus, is Persian. These details and the narrative's setting indicate that the book could have originated in the Eastern Diaspora.

c. Western Levant

Finally, some have argued for a setting closer to the western Levant, a category under which we will consider Damascus, Samaria, and Jerusalem as proposals. In the later Persian and Early Hellenistic periods it is often difficult to distinguish whether or not a book was written in a Diaspora setting or in Palestine. Tobit may also be difficult to delineate by such indicators, which often are more a scholarly construction than a

---

20   The book of Tobit would not be alone in the ancient world in its employment of symbolic geography. For instance, both the gospels of Mark and John seem more interested in the symbolism of their geographical references than their accuracy.

21   See Winston (1965: 194, n. 29) for a discussion of the sacred status of dogs in ancient Persian culture. Note also Moore (1996: 197) who calls the dog "the only gratuitous piece of description in the story." See also Miller (2008).

historical reality.[22] J. T. Milik (1966) argued that the mention of Thisbe as Tobit's original home should be associated with the city of Thebez, which is 10 miles northwest of Samaria. He connects Tobit's story with that of the Tobiads,[23] claiming that it was intended to show a positive portrayal of Jewish people working and succeeding while under the rule of a foreign government. Zimmerman (1958) places Tobit in similar environs. As noted above, he connects Tobit with 2 Macc. 9.15 and the lack of proper burial for Jews. This leads him to consider Antioch, the seat of Seleucid government, as the book's origin, a city with a Jewish population and exposed to diverse cultural resources. In his scenario, Zimmerman posits that "Nineveh" in Tobit is a cipher for Antioch (1958: 19–21).[24]

Devorah Dimant has recently shown how the situation of the Assyrian Diaspora as depicted in the book of Tobit has been "strikingly confirmed" by documents and archives from the appropriate period (2009b: 354). The fact that key members of Tobit's family or close acquaintance have been dispersed from one another (Tobit in Nineveh; Gabael in Ecbatana; Gabael in Rages) and Tobit's occasional ability to work freely within the foreign government are indications of the "authentic backdrop" that the book presents (Dimant 2009b: 355–6). While this, she suggests, should cause scholars to qualify their alacrity to declare the book of Tobit's ahistorical nature (354, n. 25), she does not press the data far enough to determine a likely setting for the book's author. The evidence that Dimant discusses—Tobit's reports of Galilee that are heavily based on "previous biblical literature" (356) and its historically plausible description of the exilic situation—could lead to the conclusion that the book itself was composed in the Eastern Diaspora. Although Tobit's description of the exilic setting has an "authentic ring," she stops short of suggesting the East as the author's setting because information about such settings could have "well reached the land of Israel" (356–7). It could have been written in the East, but also, Dimant suggests, by a Jewish author "living in the Land of Israel as a guide for Jews living outside the Land of Israel" (357).

Dimant has almost simultaneously addressed this topic in another essay that approaches the question from a different perspective (2009a). When comparing Tobit with Qumran Halakhah, she notes that the presence of Tobit among the Qumran scrolls "intimates its links with the Qumran community" (2009a: 122). The references to the law of Moses in Tobit

---

22   The specific example of Greek Esther comes to mind. A colophon indicates that it was created in Palestine and meant to be read in the Diaspora, but without this introduction to the book, most scholars might posit its origin as from the Diaspora.

23   Josephus (*Ant.* 12.154–236) recounts the story of the Tobiad family, who served as tax collectors for the Ptolemies in the third century BCE.

24   Fitzmyer (2003: 53) questions Zimmerman's claim, especially regarding Nineveh as a cipher for Antioch, because Tobit does not use other code words for Assyrian kings.

chapter 1 are not based on "disparate Torah formulations" but instead "reflect a well developed exegesis of such ordinances" (125). Some of the parallels between Tobit and the Qumran scrolls suggest that scholars should take a "fresh view" of the book of Tobit, which, for Dimant, means taking more seriously the possibility that it was composed within the "Land of Israel" (140). According to Dimant, "the author was seemingly close to, or a sympathizer of, the Qumran circles," which may account for copies of it among the Qumran scrolls (140).

In the end, there are reasons for and against each of the major suggestions regarding Tobit's provenance. If written in the East, one must explain the geographical errors.[25] If one suggests Egypt, then the Eastern setting of the story and its Jerusalem-oriented ending present difficulties. Finally, if one posits the western Levant, then the Diaspora setting and issues are difficult to explain. The original language of Tobit—most likely Aramaic—does little to indicate where it was written. If it had been written in Hebrew a Palestinian provenance would be more likely, but Aramaic means it "might have been composed anywhere in the Fertile Crescent" (Fitzmyer 2003: 53).

The suggestion that Tobit was written somewhere close to the western Levant seems to make best sense of all the evidence. The book's exilic setting is a cipher used to explain Jewish subjugation to gentile rule, but, in the third century BCE, such a situation was not confined to the Diaspora. If the book truly issued from the Diaspora, one might expect more interaction with non-Jewish characters in the story as one sees in Daniel and Esther, but such is not the case.[26] In 1.4 the text seems to describe cultic sites in various locations throughout Galilee, but, at the same time, it seems to presume a broader cultic connection for all Israel between Jerusalem and certain feast days.[27] It was not impossible for a Diaspora Jew to base his or her piety on Jerusalem and the temple, but if Tobit were written in northern Palestine, its Jerusalem orientation might be more intelligible. The piety in the book also seems to presume at least intermittent travel to Jerusalem (1.6; 5.14). The author may have been close enough that occasional travel to Jerusalem was possible, an activity in which Tobit the character is proud to have engaged. A setting in the East or in Egypt would make this scenario more difficult. The proposal by Milik that Tobit was written in Samaria might have much to commend it. Galilee is also possible, given Tobit's association with the tribe of Naphtali. Either of these can provide plausible intermittent travel to Jerusalem. The evidence, scant though it may be, seems to suggest that Tobit was written somewhere north of Jerusalem, a place for which Jerusalem was firmly on the conceptual and physical horizon, but a locale governed by gentiles and not predominantly Jewish.

25   Torrey (1922) attempted to find plausibility in Tobit's geography by looking at ancient caravan routes. He claims that Tobit's Nineveh must really have been the city of Seleucia.

26   This is a point also made by J. Collins (2005: 39).

27   Weeks (2011: 3).

IV. Has the Book of Tobit been Redacted?

Scholars discussing the book of Tobit have found several reasons to question its integrity, often positing a text that changed over time and gained accretions at different points of redaction. There are two significant and enduring reasons for these theories. First, the book begins with first-person narration, which abruptly changes to third-person narration after 3.6.[28] This has led many scholars to posit the combination of two originally separate narratives. James Miller (1991) finds evidence of redaction in Tobit by comparing it with a similar shift from first- to third-person narration in the *Genesis Apocryphon*. He claims that both texts combine a pseudepigraphic first-person narrative with one that was originally third-person. As a result, there "is a direct connection between the two works" because they similarly bridged a pseudepigraphic first-person narrative with a narrative in the third person (58). Irene Nowell's (1983) literary analysis of Tobit, however, concludes differently. One of the first to apply literary criticism to the book of Tobit, Nowell engages in a thorough investigation of the narrator's voice in Tobit. She concludes that, with only a few exceptions, the first-person and third-person narration share the same perspective and angle. Both have a similar sense of omniscience. Nowell notices that Tobit the narrator relates that Anna received a salary for her work and that she was given a goat (2.12). Tobit the character, however, wallows in his own misery and claims that the goat must have been stolen (2.13). This demonstrates a separation between Tobit the narrator and Tobit the character; the narrator has an omniscience not available to Tobit the character. The narrator in Tobit is also brief and reliable according to Nowell, characteristics portrayed consistently in both the first- and third-person narration sections. Although the person changes, the style and perspective of the narration does not. Miller's essay notwithstanding, recent consensus, informed largely by Nowell's analysis, indicates that the shift in narration between 3.6 and 3.7 is the result of a conscious literary style and not the inept editing of originally distinct sources.[29]

The second reason redactional layers are often posited in the history of Tobit arises from the apparent conceptual clash between chapters 13–14 and the rest of the story. The narrative could end nicely after chapter 12, and chapters 13–14 seem to some a burdensome, unnecessary addition. As early

---

28   The Vulgate changes the narration to third person throughout. All other Greek versions and the Qumran fragments attest the change in narration.

29   On this point, see also McCracken (1995). Although he disagrees with Nowell about the difference in narration, claiming that there is a significant difference between first person and third person, they both agree on a more central point: that the switch in narration is a result of literary design, not redactional seams. Nowell's conclusions are based mostly on formal matters while McCracken sees the literary design as one where the first-person narration allows the reader to see some folly in the title character.

as 1800 Tobit's integrity was questioned.[30] Because of the subject matter of chapters 13 and 14—the future of Jerusalem and the restoration of Israel— these two chapters were thought to have been added after 70 CE, reflecting a despondency similar to that in *4 Ezra*. The comments of Zimmerman on this point are typical. He says that in chapters 13 and 14, "we are in a different climate" and that:

> The conclusion would seem to be inescapable. It is evident that Jerusalem has been destroyed, with the Temple as well; the walls, towers, and battlements overthrown; the people scattered, captive, and in mourning. The date of this psalm [i.e., Tob. 13] suggests itself, sometime after the destruction of the Temple. (1958: 24–5)

On the particular point of chapters 13–14, however, the discovery of the Tobit fragments at Qumran provided a watershed in understanding the ending of the book. Portions of both final chapters were found among the Qumran scrolls, proving that these chapters, in some form, were part of the book long prior to 70 CE.[31]

The discovery of the Qumran fragments did not stop all attempts at redactional literary-critical work on Tobit's narrative. Paul Deselaers (1982) was one of the first scholars, after the discovery of the scrolls, to revive redactional theories in the study of Tobit. Although his book was published before the Qumran fragments were widely available, their existence was well known, and his work basically ignores them.[32] The subtitle of his book indicates clearly his purpose: *Studien zu seiner Entstehung, Komposition und Theologie.* Much of his book focuses on the "emergence" (*Entstehung*) of the book of Tobit. Deselaers employs a literary method that seeks the diachronic development of the book, basing his work on a very close reading of the text.[33] In part one of his book he engages in a literary-critical analysis of Tobit, finding ways to determine different *Erweiterungen* (expansions). These could range from an interest in wisdom learning to the preponderance of a *Stichwort*, such as Jerusalem (50–1). Part two explores the *Grunderzälung* (base story) of Tobit, which he claims was written in Alexandria in the middle of the third century BCE. Part three takes up each of the *Erweiterungen.* The first expansion includes 2.11–14, 3.6, and parts of 4.3–21, which emerged from Jerusalem c. 220 BCE. The second expansion develops the first-person perspective in chapters 1–3 and has a relationship

---

30   See Moore (1996: 21), who claims Karl Ilgen, *Die Geschichte Tobi's* (1800), as one of the earliest to question Tobit's integrity.

31   4QpapTob[a], fragment 18, covers Tob. 13.12–14.3. See Fitzmyer (1995: 29–31, plate V). He dates the paleography to 50 BCE.

32   Fitzmyer notes that Deselaers' commentary on Tobit has found little following because his work "has been spun out of whole cloth by someone who had not seen the Semitic texts of Tobit" (2003: 19).

33   See, for example, his claim that Tobit's reaction to Anna is "carefully told" (376, author's translation).

(*Verwandtschaft*) with Ahiqar (424). Deselaers' discussion of the third expansion focuses mostly on the eschatological portions, especially chapters 13–14.

Deselaers concludes his book with a small booklet attached to the back cover containing his German translation of Tobit, delineating his four redactional layers in different typefaces. His work is very detailed and finds many literary seams in the text, sometimes even dividing individual verses and sentences (e.g., the interpolation of καὶ δικαιοσύνης into Tob. 1.3). His analysis of the theology of the book is also very thorough, focusing on word studies that he finds pertinent (e.g., ἐλεημοσύνη, which occurs over 10 times in Tobit) and on broader concepts with reference to Deuteronomy and Jerusalem. One of the main problems with Deselaers' argument, however, is his starting place. Suggesting Alexandria as the original provenance for the story is a perspective not advocated since Simpson's introduction to Tobit in Charles' *APOT*.[34] Since each of his *Erweiterungen* (expansions) are closely tied to a specific *Sitz im Leben*, an erroneous starting point could lead the redactional theories astray. More problematic is Deselaers' argument that Greek is the original language of the story and that the shorter Greek recension (AB or G^{I}) is the original version. Most striking, however, is the fact that Deselaers wrote his book without apparent awareness of the evidence provided by the Dead Sea Scrolls. Such evidence may have caused him to find fewer seams or helped him find warrant for conflicting themes in the text without expansion-based hypotheses. For example, had Tobit been placed in the larger context of Qumran and some of the theological tendencies of the scrolls, a wisdom tradition similar to Ahiqar and eschato-logical speculation about the future of Jerusalem may seem less disparate. The tenuous point from which Deselaers begins makes all the more difficult his subsequent detailed redactional arguments.

A second study in German, similar in method to that of Deselaers, was published by Merten Rabenau in 1994. Rabenau disagrees with Deselaers on many points, most notably when he argues for a Semitic, probably Aramaic, original and for S as the older Greek version. Methodologically, however, Rabenau is quite similar to Deselaers, engaging in a literary-critical reading of Tobit that looks for seams and inconsistencies in the text in order to delineate different levels of redaction and expansion in the book. In chapter 4 of his study, Rabenau treats the *Grunderzälung*, a story about an individual with an angelic guide meant to exemplify how to live a faithful life in the Diaspora. Not to be outdone by Deselaers, Rabenau also ends his book with a German translation of Tobit that highlights the expansions with differing typefaces. Much like the work of Deselaers, Rabenau's study is detailed, nuanced, and helpfully contextualized with other texts from Israel's traditions. His analysis significantly improves on that of Deselaers because he starts with the assumption of Semitic texts as the original language. In

---

34   Simpson (1913: 1:185–7).

the work of both Deselaers and Rabenau, Tobit is a book that started as a small folk tale that, through multiple episodes of redaction in specific times and places, gained accretions over time. It remains to be seen, however, whether such a redaction-critical approach can best explain the theological complexities of Tobit.

A brief treatment of Tobit by Lawrence Wills (1995) argues in favor of some significant redactional activity in the history of Tobit's text. Wills provides five reasons why he thinks chapter 1 comes from a different hand. Among these reasons are the fact that chapter 1 has a more Western orientation, which contrasts with the decidedly Eastern references of chapters 2–12.[35] He also notices a difference in the use of the word "mercy" in the two sections. David McCracken (1995) has argued against this perspective, claiming that chapter 1 is meant to portray Tobit's own attitude so that it may be satirized later in the narrative. Wills rejects this position because he does not think it satisfactorily explain all the differences. Chapters 13–14 also show a "difference in tone," which indicates for Wills that "a redactor has added this testamentary ending and done it rather awkwardly" (1995: 86–7). Wills summarizes the impact of the additions and simultaneously seems to judge one portion of the narrative as better than the other: "the spirited novel of chapters 2–12 has become heavily laden with theological pretension" (91). The contrasting threads of the narrative, however, could lead to different conclusions. The various points of view may be exactly the point, meant to juxtapose them in such a way as to make a more complex theological statement. Later portions of this study will attempt to show that the whole of the story of Tobit forms a cohesive, complex theological statement.

In a recent essay, John Collins (2005) has affirmed a more moderate view of the perspective adopted by Deselaers, Rabenau, and Wills. Although he is skeptical of the minutiae in the hypothetical division of sources offered by Deselaers and Rabenau, Collins distinguishes between the frame (chs. 1, 13, 14), which concerns Jerusalem, and the core (chs. 2–12), which tells the story of a family. It is only the frame of the story that places it in the "broader context of the history of Israel," a concern that is "extraneous to the core story" (25). For Collins, the frame has been added to the core story in order "to provide a theological and historical frame, from a Judean, Jerusalemite perspective" (25).

One can see, then, that—despite the evidence from Qumran that chapters 13–14 were part of the story by the first century BCE—the differences between chapters 13–14 and the rest of the narrative still suggest editorial activity in many estimations. Many scholars still posit these chapters as a later addition, but shift the date of its addition to sometime prior to the first century BCE, rather than post-70 CE. As a result of this shift, scholars no longer have a significant event or change in *Sitz im Leben* that may have

---

35   A similar point is made by Zsengellér (2005).

spurred such an addition to Tobit. One may also question the conceptual basis on which these theories rest. To what standards of coherence do we hold an ancient author? Can one work not contain more than one set of distinct themes? If another set of themes is found, must a second *Erweiterung* (expansion) be posited? George Nickelsburg, in his review of Rabenau's book, has stated this issue pointedly:

> Does a coherent set of themes necessarily indicate a compositional stratum that is to be differentiated from other strata composed of their own sets of coherent themes? Do narrative tensions necessarily reveal the hand of an editor who is bringing together disparate material or expanding received tradition? . . . Need we reduce the heart of a book to a single theme or set of themes, or can an author's composition embrace a number of related and sometimes disparate matters? (1997: 349)

Traditions and texts may have picked up accretions, but suggesting redaction and expansion in the text's history may not be the most adequate response to literary tensions.

Many scholars have rejected redactional theories in Tobit and argue in favor of the book's literary integrity. In important commentaries, both Joseph Fitzmyer (2003) and Carey Moore (1996) show their allegiance to those arguing for the unity of the work. Fitzmyer calls the literary-critical method "strange and extreme" (2003: 43) and, in reference to Deselaers and Rabenau, asks whether either of their analyses is plausible (45). Moore allies himself strongly with the perspective of William Soll. Soll, in his folklore analysis of Tobit (1989), finds chapters 1 and 13–14 as the places where the story most deviates from the folk-tale morphology.[36] At the end of his article, Soll argues that the framing chapters are nevertheless essential components for the argument of the author. Chapters 13–14 are not "merely tacked on, but are necessary in view of the way the author has portrayed the initial situation as one of exile and has explicitly connected the villainies or lacks that befall the Tobit family to that exile" (230). Steven Weitzman (1996) makes a similar argument. The strategy of allusion he finds between Tobit 13 and Deuteronomy 32 is indicative of a larger strategy throughout the work, which therefore implies the book's unity. For Weitzman, the hymn in chapter 13 is "inextricably related to the poetics and ideology of Tobit as a whole" (51).[37]

---

36   He identifies three "moves" or tales: Tobit's poverty, Tobit's blindness, and Sarah's misfortune. The first of these is evidenced especially in the "framing" chapters. The framing chapters, however, deviate from the fairy tale in their similarity to biblical genres, especially prophetic and wisdom literature. They also place the story more firmly in a specific place and time, including a specific genealogy, which runs counter to a fairy tale (219).

37   J. Collins (2005: 25, n.11) responds directly to Weitzman's claim by saying that a later redactor could have perceived the allusive strategy and been influenced by it. Collins does not respond specifically to Soll's argument.

Francis Macatangay (2011) has offered a robust narratological assessment of the book of Tobit and comes to a similar conclusion: that there is ample internal evidence to posit the book's integrity. Based upon the allusions throughout the work and its narrative structure, Macatangay concludes that "the structure of the narrative indicates a well-conceived design, not a draft left to the hands of redactors to gather additions and insertions along its literary way" (2011: 43).

In the end, the evidence from Qumran is important but obviously has not provided enough basis for scholars to reach a consensus on the book's literary integrity. It is possible that chapters 13–14 were added to the story at a point prior to its being copied at Qumran. More important, however, is what chapters 13–14 *do* to the story, whether they were added later or are an original part of the composition. The ending jolts readers.[38] The rollicking tale becomes speckled with theological intention not with "theological pretension" (Wills 1995: 91). Rather than strip the story of a conclusion that groans under the weight of pressing theological concerns by positing it as later redaction, interpreters of Tobit should read the story as a whole, as all extant textual evidence suggests it was intended to be read. The conclusion in chapters 13–14 does cast a pall over the entire narrative. There is a "certain tension and foreboding" (Macatangay 2011: 128) that recommends that the ending be taken seriously. Could the entire narrative adopt a theological intention for whose interpretation chapters 13–14 help provide the key? One can glimpse this perspective when examining Tobit's prayer in chapter 3. All narrative indications to the contrary, Tobit asserts his own guilt, which comes from nowhere else but his association with Israel as a whole (i.e., the sins of his forebears mentioned in 3.3). While one could claim this as a later addition, it places the fate of the nation at the center of Tobit's problems. Simultaneously, this one example shows a coherence between the central portion of the story and the framing chapters, which seems particularly problematic for the redaction theories in their most basic form.[39]

This study will proceed, then, based upon the argument that the book of Tobit is from the hand of a single author who intended to imprint it with a specific, albeit complex, theological perspective.[40] In the words of Abrahams with which we began, it has a discernable and coherent "tendency" (1893:

---

38   One could point to any number of other texts with similarly jolting endings. The *Similitudes of Enoch*, for example, end with a shocking revelation that Enoch himself is the Son of Man (*1 En.* 71.14). This, along with other considerations, leads J. Collins (1998: 187–91) to suggest that this final chapter is redactional.

39   J. Collins (2005) tries to avoid this problem by claiming that the exilic interests of the framing chapters are in no way the cause of the misfortune in the central story (26–29).

40   As the above summary shows I am not alone in this decision and assessment. See also the summary by Fröhlich: "despite the heterogeneity of its literary material the Book of Tobit is a consistent narrative," and today's consensus "dismisses claims of multiple authorship and theories of various textforms. The great majority of scholars think now that the book is the product of just one author" (2005: 58).

348). From this starting point also comes a major impetus for this study: if the eschatological material in chapters 13–14 is taken seriously in interpreting the book, does it change the way one should view the overall orientation of the book's perspective and the intention the author may have had in creating it? Benedikt Otzen has assessed the situation similarly:

> If Tobit 13–14 is left out, the book of Tobit is deprived of an important theological dimension. The book is not just an innocent tale about the exciting experiences of the Tobit family, it is a book that on a high artistic and theological level takes up the existential problem of the exile, and in a most sophisticated way helps the Jews in the eastern Diaspora to survive and not give up the hope of return. (2002: 45)[41]

To Otzen's statement I would add that it not only addresses the problem of the exile and hope for return, but that it simultaneously addresses human complicity in enacting retribution in daily life.

V. Conclusion

While there are many complexities and uncertainties regarding the details of the origin of the book of Tobit, there is enough solid ground to proceed with a close analysis of the book's theology. The book of Tobit's likely date, provenance, and language of composition all provide some warrant for the comparisons in the following chapters. Sirach and *1 Enoch* both provide roughly contemporaneous and geographically compatible bodies of comparative material which will help contextualize the story in Tobit. At the same time, there seems to be enough evidence and scholarly precedent for the argument that follows to build upon the idea that the book of Tobit is the product of one author. By attending to the entire story and comparing Tobit to some contemporaneous texts, we will better be able to perceive the theological complexities of the book.

41   Benedikt Otzen (2002: 45).

Chapter 3

The Origin of "Deuteronomism" in Hebrew Bible Studies and its Purported Place in the Book of Tobit

The book of Tobit contains a strong doctrine of retribution. In chapter 3, after a series of unfortunate events, Tobit prays for death and claims that he and his kin experience problems because of retributive justice: "They refused to listen to your commandments. So you handed us over to plundering, captivity, and death" (3.4a). Because something terrible happened to him (blindness, derision from neighbors, and insults from his wife), Tobit knows that he must have done something wrong, and he piously enumerates any imaginable way he might have erred: "do not punish me for my sins, nor for my unwitting errors, nor for those of my ancestors which they sinned before you" (3.3b). Later in the story, after the restoration of his sight, Tobit reaffirms the retribution he had experienced: "for [God] afflicted me" (11.15a).[1] The book of Tobit also ends with retribution. After Tobit dies, his son hears of the destruction of Nineveh and the exile of the city's inhabitants and praises God: "He [Tobias] praised God for all he had done to the people of Nineveh and Assyria; before he died he rejoiced over Nineveh and he blessed the Lord God forever and ever" (NRSV).

Most scholars, when discussing the view of retribution operative in the book of Tobit, do so in terms of a Deuteronomic or Deuteronomistic theology—one that is in concert with the book of Deuteronomy or the ideology of the Deuteronomistic History in Israel's scriptures.[2] The following comment from the introduction to a collection of essays is typical: Tobit has a "theology based on the Deuteronomic system of rewards and punishments, whereby the devout are eventually rewarded" (Corley and Skemp 2005: xiii). Note also the following assessment of Tobit from Fizmyer's commentary: "Tobit's thinking sums up 'the great Deuteronomic equation,'

---

1   AB, VL, and Vg all add a reference to mercy following this statement that makes it into many English translations (e.g., NRSV and NAB), probably influenced by the Vulgate, even though there is no basis for it in S.

2   In the following discussion it will be helpful to distinguish between two different terms. The words "Deuteronomic" pertains specifically to the language and thought of the book of Deuteronomy, while "Deuteronomistic" refers more broadly to the thought and ideology of Deuteronomy as dispersed in those books thought to comprise the Deuteronomistic History.

viz. that those who love God and fear him will be rewarded, whereas those who do not will suffer" (2003: 332).[3] Both of these quotations assume that the Deuteronomistic formulation has, at its core, a theory of retribution, and that the book of Tobit's perspective on retribution has been specifically coordinated by the author with the book of Deuteronomy. Before positing the specifically Deuteronomistic formulation as the central perspective of the book of Tobit, however, one should be aware of two factors. First, other theories of retribution in the Hebrew Bible exist and may play some role in the shape of the narrative in the book of Tobit. Second, it is simplistic to assert and repeatedly assume that there is a single retributive perspective inherent within the so-called "Deuteronomistic" perspective. In ascribing the "Deuteronomistic" perspective to Tobit, the issue of retribution often is not sufficiently nuanced, a problem that this chapter aims to correct. In what follows in this chapter we will examine what Deuteronomistic theology is, especially its place in Hebrew Bible scholarship, and then examine how and why scholars have posited it as the core perspective of the book of Tobit.

I. Retribution and Deuteronomism in the Hebrew Bible

a. Retribution and the Fate-working Deed

Although most scholars explain Tobit's perspective on retribution in terms of its Deuteronomistic stance, this is not the only formulation of a doctrine of retribution in Israel's scriptures. Klaus Koch (1955) has demonstrated a *Tun-Ergehen Zusammenhang*—a connection between act and consequence—that is not a doctrine of *divine* retribution per se.[4] Koch begins his study by noting how commonly in studies of the Hebrew Bible the connection between actions and consequences is linked to "*die Vergeltung Jahwes*," (the retribution of Yahweh) whether it is applied to individuals or the entirety of Israel (Koch 1955: 1).

According to Koch, most scholars assume that retribution has two major components. First, retribution has a juridical nature: the reward or punishment is set according to an established norm. Second, God plays an active role as the one who metes out the retribution. In the book of Proverbs, for example, a doctrine of retribution seems prominent. In chapters 25–29 one finds strong statements of retribution:

---

3   Weeks (2011: 390, n. 4) roundly critiques Fitzmyer here, claiming that the religious impulse as described by Fitzmyer is general enough that it is difficult to see how almost any biblical author, save perhaps Job, could not agree with it. But, to label it "Deuteronomic" seems "selective." At the same time, the Deuteronomic perspective to which Fitzmyer refers is itself an abstraction and based on a particular interpretation of that book, "not something ever expressed by Deuteronomy itself."

4   For the English translation, see Koch (1983: 57–87).

The one who digs a pit falls into it; and the one who rolls as stone, upon him it will return. (26.27)

The wicked one flees when no one pursues him; but a righteous one, like a lion, feels secure. (28.1)

A ruler who lacks understanding causes great oppression. But the one who hates unjust gain will lengthen his days. (28.16)

These examples from Proverbs indicate that blessing follows an action that is faithful to the community while an action judged to be wrong brings disaster. The problem, as Koch points out, is that these proverbs do not say "that Yahweh is the one who sets this disaster in motion" (1983: 58). The consequence instead seems to come from a connection to the act itself. A second problem arises from the assumption that the judgments are made according to a previously established norm. In Proverbs there is very little reference to such a norm, which suggests that there must be a different relationship between the consequence and action (Koch 1983: 59).

Koch faces a problem in Prov. 25.21–22: "If your enemy be hungry, give him food to eat, if he be thirsty, give him to drink; for live coals you will heap on his head, and the Lord will vindicate you" (NAB). The final clause, וַיהוה יְשַׁלֶּם־לָךְ, where the word שָׁלַם is often translated "vindicate" or "reward" (NRSV), seems to indicate *divine* retribution. Such a claim challenges Koch's conclusion that the retribution enacted is not directly connected with God. According to Koch, שָׁלַם in the piel (יְשַׁלֵּם) indicates a non-juridical sense of reimbursement and should be translated as "make complete."[5] In Prov. 25.22 Yahweh is not giving a reward commensurate with a certain action, but rather "this text presumes that an action and its consequences have to have an inherent relationship to one another, linked hand in hand" (Koch 1983: 60). Yahweh is certainly a higher authority but is viewed as a midwife rather than as a judge. God facilitates "the completion of something which previous human action has already set in motion" (Koch 1983: 61).

Koch goes on to investigate the idea of retribution in the prophets (focusing on Hosea) and in the Psalms. The retribution in Hosea is best described with an agrarian analogy: one reaps what one sows. In Hos. 5.1–3 the people have the correct rhetoric for a return to God, but the transitory nature of their attitude precludes God's direct action. The actions of the nation produce unavoidable circumstances: "Their deeds do not allow them to return to God" (Hos. 5.4a). According to Koch, the people are "so weak

---

5   Koch (1983: 60). Koch here is parsing things closely. With regard to his reading, which removes God several steps from the equation, one could still ask: Is it not God who built such consequences into reality? Ultimately, it is God's disposition that is in question—here, that God functions as a facilitator rather than as a judge.

that there is no way [God] can reinforce [their good actions]" (1983: 66). When reaching out to help them, God is confronted with all their sins (7.1–2). Koch therefore claims that the author is working from an idea that "actions have built-in consequences" which result in the "onset of disasters" (1983: 66). The issue is not God's punishing sin but a *schicksalwirkender Tat*, a fate-working deed (Koch 1955: 12).

In the Psalms Koch finds a more active role for Yahweh in the midst of the fate-working deed. Many Psalms, such as 74.18–19, speak of remembering:

> Remember this, O Lord, that the enemy taunts,
>   and a foolish people despises your name.
> Do not surrender the life of the dove to the beast;
>   do not forget forever the life of your afflicted.

Here and in other similar formulations (e.g. 132.1; 137.7) the psalmist calls for the fate-working deed to take effect because "the correspondence between actions and consequences where it actually takes effect is the result of God's faithfulness at work" (Koch 1983: 73). In contrast to Proverbs, God does not simply speed up the consequence but plays an actual role in the process. Even when Yahweh functions as a judge (e.g., Ps. 58.12), the divine role only completes the consequence already begun by the action: "Rise up, judge of the earth; return recompense on the proud" (94.2). According to Koch, there is "not the slightest hint of a theory of retribution according to which Yahweh either punishes or rewards someone for their actions according to a previously established norm" (1983: 74).

Koch's argument based on the above texts concludes that consequences are the direct result of human action. Any role for Yahweh is one of either quickening or ratifying the result; in either case, a "*Wirkung göttlicher Treue*," a working out of divine justice (Koch 1955: 21). The result itself, however, comes from the original human action, whether individual or collective; there is a "*Korrespondenze von Tun und Ergehen*," a correspondence between act and consequence (Koch 1955: 21). While Koch's theory is energetic and strongly argued, there are some problems with his thesis. The material he has chosen is highly selective. It would be much more difficult for him to make his case in Deuteronomy, where God sometimes plays a more active role (e.g., Deut. 32.20) and judgments are made according to a previously established norm (Deut. 4.1–2, 23). James Crenshaw notes that Koch's theory has been met with "energetic resistance" and that Koch's metaphor for God's role—a midwife assisting at a birth—does not adequately explain the "inevitable consequences of behavior" (1988: 82, n. 2). Nevertheless, Koch's theory sufficiently establishes the complex nature of retribution in Israel's scriptures. One can best proceed from Koch's analysis by not making assumptions about God's role in the consequences of human action.

b. Deuteronomistic Retribution

In the book of Deuteronomy one finds a strong doctrine of retribution paired with a role assigned to God that differs somewhat from that described by Koch. While Ecclesiastes says, "When you make a vow to God, delay not its fulfillment. For God has no pleasure in fools" (5.3, NAB), Deuteronomy adds: "for the LORD, your God, will surely require it of you and you will be held guilty" (23.22, NAB). This one simple example demonstrates how, in Deuteronomy, "YHWH is clearly responsible for bringing about the consequences" (Seow 1997: 66). Although many of the details are debated, there is general scholarly agreement about the preponderance of a strong divine sense of retribution, labeled "Deuteronomistic," among the Israelites during and after the exile. The best way to summarize this ideology of retribution is from Deuteronomy itself: "If you do not observe to do all the words of this law that are written in this book and fear the name of this honored and fearsome Lord, your God, God will smite you and your seed with extraordinary wounds, great wounds, lasting sickness and lasting evil" (Deut. 28.58–59). In Deut. 30.15–20 a choice is presented to Israel: obey and they will grow numerous and be blessed in the land; if they turn away, they will perish.[6]

The theory of a Deuteronomistic history originates with Martin Noth, whose book, *Überlieferungsgeschichtliche Studien* (1957), pointed out similar theology, language, and ideology in Deuteronomy, Joshua, Judges, 1–2 Samuel, and 1–2 Kings. The compiler of this history had a clear purpose: to show that Israel was experiencing the exile because of its failure to follow Deuteronomic law. Israel's failure resulted in the destruction of the nation. While Noth's basic thesis was immediately influential, some scholars took issue with the completely negative intentions of this hypothetical author. Most notably, von Rad pointed out that the Deuteronomistic History has positive motifs along with the negative ones highlighted by Noth.[7]

There have been many emendations to Noth's theory, such as proposals of two themes in the Deuteronomistic History and a double redaction of the texts in question.[8] Although many of the details of Noth's account

6   Later in this study we will have opportunity to examine closely the argument of Gammie (1970: 1–12), in which he adds much nuance to the perspective on retribution in Deuteronomy. At this point, we are only concerned with the basic perspective, as represented in Deut. 28.58–9, because this formulation is the one that has had the most influence on theories of a Deuteronomistic history.

7   See Coggins (1999: 23) for further discussion.

8   For the theory including more than one theme, see Cross (1973). Cross asserts that literary tensions in the historical books indicate a pre-exilic and exilic setting for divergent texts, which gave new voice to the positive aspects of the Deuteronomistic History, whereas Noth emphasized the pessimism in these texts. Nelson (1981) builds upon the work of Cross by defining more precisely the intentions of the pre-exilic and exilic editors. The pre-exilic author intended to tout the Davidic dynasty and the policies of Josiah. On the other hand, the exilic editor wanted to justify Israel's punishment by

of the Deuteronomistic History have been questioned, his most influential legacy is the attribution of the Deuteronomistic History to a single author. Steven McKenzie calls it the aspect of his thesis that has "elicited the most discussion" (McKenzie 1992: 2:162). With Noth's theory as a foundation, scholars erected the concept of a Deuteronomistic "school," a hypothetical sphere of influence that shaped the ideology of many texts in the Hebrew Bible.[9] The existence of some type of Deuteronomistic editing and authoring in the books from Joshua through 2 Kings "has now become part of the received wisdom of Hebrew Bible scholarship" (Coggins 1999: 29). The theory of the Deuteronomistic school allowed scholars to suggest its ideological influence outside of the specific Deuteronomistic History as outlined by Noth. Scholars have discerned Deuteronomistic editing in the Pentateuch (Rendtorff 1990), the prophets (especially Jeremiah [Coggins 1999: 29–30]), and the Book of the Twelve (Nogalski, 1993).

The Deuteronomistic ideology is one that contains a number of related themes and concepts that arise in Deuteronomy and those books thought to be influenced by its tenets. Moshe Weinfeld concludes his study of the relationship between Deuteronomism and Wisdom (1972) with a list of Deuteronomistic *topoi*, including such ideas as warning against foreign worship, polemic against idolatry, centralization of worship, monotheistic creed, observance of law, inheritance of the land, and fulfillment of prophecy. For each of these, he lists occurrences of the language across the face of the various Deuteronomistic books (320–65). Based on Weinfeld's taxonomy, one can easily conclude that the Deuteronomistic perspective is one in which humans, both collectively and individually, are directly responsible for their actions. God then treats humans according to their actions.

The foundation of Noth's theory (and that which has been built upon it) is showing a few cracks. An entire volume of essays titled *Those Elusive Deuteronomists* (Schearing and McKenzie 1999) was published in order to assess the place of this theory within scholarship. The first problem seems to be a growing lack of specificity with regard to what the term actually means. Richard Coggins, here, is instructive:

> We need, it seems, to be clearer than we have often been in distinguishing between what can properly be said about a particular book and its immediately related congeners; what can be said by way of describing a literary process through which other pieces of literature reached their final form; and what can be said about an ideological movement which played a major part in shaping the self-understanding of Judaism. To use the same name for them all is to invite a breakdown in understanding. (1999: 34–5)[10]

emphasizing the disobedience and obstinacy of the people and the leadership (especially Manassah).

9   For an example, see Person (1993), who argues for the existence of a Deuteronomistic school in the post-exilic period, particularly visible in Zechariah.

10   See also Noll (2007), who argues that Deuteronomy was part of a larger debate

In a similar call for conceptual and methodological rigor, Norbert Lohfink (1999) discerns two trends in treatments of Deuteronomistic influence. The first trend is that scholars no longer proceed from the source itself (i.e., Deuteronomy) in determining what is Deuteronomistic; any of the books from Joshua through 2 Kings may now serve just as well. The problem here is that some texts can now be labeled Deuteronomistic that might not be if the comparison were limited to Deuteronomy itself. In a second misguided approach, according to Lohfink, texts are labeled Deuteronomistic simply for their association with a book that is within the Deuteronomistic canon. He therefore advocates "reserving the use of the word 'Deuteronomistic' for describing textual affiliation, thereby avoiding pan-Deuteronomistic chain reactions" (1999: 39).[11]

While the above scholarly conversation may appear to end in a stalemate, it suggests some conclusions important for the current study. First, one cannot assume what the word "Deuteronomistic" means. Does the phrase refer specifically to the book of Deuteronomy or to the alleged school associated with its name? Second, any attempt to describe a text or a theological perspective as "Deuteronomistic" must be as specific as possible. Positing Deuteronomistic influence on the basis of a general or abstract concept of Deuteronomism proceeds from a nebulous assumption if it is done without recourse to specific texts. In other words, showing an actual connection or similarity between texts will prove much more convincing than a comparison of one text with an abstracted idea. The next step of this chapter will be to examine how and why scholars posit Deuteronomistic influence on Tobit and to evaluate the success of these efforts.

II. The Deuteronomistic Ideology in Tobit

Having established some sense of where the idea of a Deuteronomistic ideology in Israel's literature and theology originated, we move now to the arguments of several scholars who find Deuteronomistic expression in the book of Tobit. The arguments are made in a variety of ways, and the Deuteronomistic theology highlighted in Tobit's narrative is elicited by various methodologies. The approaches to be outlined below can be grouped into three categories: direct textual and conceptual influence; morphological/genre adaptation; and intertextual. In each case the bottom-line assumption remains the same: the book of Tobit espouses a

---

about ideas with which scribes interacted across the face of the Deuteronomistic History, but that their analysis was not always positive. Noll continues to assume, however, that "Deuteronomism" was a real thing and that the book of Deuteronomy presented a unified ideology with which Israel's tradents could interact (317).

11   For Lohfink, "textual affiliation" refers to a discernable linkage between two texts, something more than a general theological similarity.

theology in which God punishes the wicked and rewards the righteous based upon human action.

a. Direct Textual and Conceptual Influence

Alexander Di Lella's *CBQ* article from 1979 is most often noted as the original and strongest formulation of the concept of Deuteronomism in Tobit.[12] Di Lella delineates nine "points of contact" between Deuteronomy and Tobit's farewell discourse in 14.3–11. These points of contact are not mere coincidences but are "more or less definite indications that the author not only based Tobit's address on the speeches of Moses but also shared many of the same intentions of the final redactors of Deuteronomy" (1979: 380). The points of contact that Di Lella finds are as follows: long life in the good land and prosperity that is dependent on fidelity (Deut. 4.40; Tob. 14.7); the offer of mercy after sin and judgment (Deut. 30.1–4; Tob. 14.4–6); rest and security in the land (Deut. 12.10–11; Tob. 14.7); the blessing of joy (Deut. 12.12; Tob. 14.7b); fear and love of God (Deut. 6.13; Tob. 14.6, 9); the command to bless and praise God (Deut. 8.10; Tob. 14.2, 7); theology of remembering (Deut. 5.15, 7.18; Tob. 3.7, 14.7); centralization of cult (Deut. 12.1–14; Tob. 14.7); and final exhortation (Deut. 30.15–20; Tob. 14.9).

Di Lella posits this influence on the basis of lexical similarity. Similar viewpoints on the offer of mercy after sin and judgment are indicated by use of the same word in both texts, διασκορπίζω, to describe the scattering of a people. In discussing the theology of remembering in the two books, he notes that remembering (μνήσκεσθαι/μνημονεύειν) occurs 14 times in religious contexts in Deuteronomy and 13 times in Tobit. Di Lella also founds his comparison upon a general understanding of Deuteronomic theology. Tobit shares with Deuteronomy more than detailed similarities but also "many of the same intentions of the final redactors of Deuteronomy, viz., encouragement of the depressed people and exhortation to remain true to the faith" (380–1). Thus, the book of Tobit becomes a "well constructed narrative in the service of Israelite religion" that expresses "genuine Deuteronomic doctrine and practices" (387). This Deuteronomic outlook, for Di Lella, is a "theology of history" that sought to explain the "calamities that the faithful believed to have been caused by the direct intervention of Yahweh" (388).

While a full-scale discussion of these ideas as applied to Tobit will be reserved for later in this current project, at this point a couple of observations are worth making. Based upon the above summary of critique of "pan-Deuteronomism" (Schearing and McKenzie 1999; Coggins 1999; Lohfink 1999), one can quickly question Di Lella's methodology and conclusions. His formulation of "genuine" Deuteronomic doctrine (387)

---

12   One could also point to the study of Gamberoni (1977), which is similar methodologically although not arguing for the singularity of Deuteronomy as an influence on Tobit in the way that Di Lella does.

may be based on a certain interpretation of Deuteronomy that may not completely be supported by the book's constituent parts.[13] At the same time, one wonders how a text so erudite as the book of Tobit can so quickly be subsumed under one, specific, ideological agenda. This ascription, which has become commonplace in scholarship on Tobit, is indeed "astonishing" (Weeks 2011: 390).

Di Lella is not alone in his assessment of the Deuteronomistic theology of Tobit. John Craghan's description of Tobit sounds vaguely similar to that of Di Lella: "For the author [of Tobit], Israel's past offers lessons for coping in the present. Deuteronomy's doctrine of fidelity/prosperity and infidelity/disaster is judged to be a viable theology of history for the ongoing covenant community" (1982: 133). Craghan goes so far as to call Tobit "Deuteronomy revisited" (133) because of the way the book exhorts its hearers to carry out the covenantal arguments of Deuteronomy. Benedikt Otzen, also writing an introduction to Tobit, assesses the overall point of the book similarly: "those who abide by the Law of Moses are under the protection of the God of Israel" (2002: 27).[14]

The two most influential English language commentaries read the book of Tobit in the same way. Moore, for example, claims that the "Deuteronomic idea of 'sin or win' pervades the entire book" (1996: 263). Fitzmyer also works from this perspective, citing Di Lella at length when noting "Deuteronomic retribution" as a core teaching of the book (2003: 47). Both Moore and Fitzmyer certainly coordinate Tobit with many other theological ideas and point out other aspects of the book, but they both nevertheless seem to assume a Deuteronomic perspective as the core of the book.

b. Morphology and Genre-based Analyses

William Soll (1988; 1989) also posits a Deuteronomic influence on Tobit. Soll advances the study of Tobit's folk-tale elements by using the morphology of Vladimir Propp (1968).[15] In contrast to the Finnish school of folk-tale scholarship, which sought motifs and tale-types for a

---

13   Weeks (2011) points out what he calls the "questionable assumptions" in Di Lella's work, namely that the borrowed language and phrases "must reflect a corresponding dependence on Deuteronomic ideas, especially when the concepts [i.e., those in Deuteronomy and Tobit] are, at times, clearly very different" (395).

14   One could also point to the recent essay by Hofmann (2003: 311–42). He comes to several conclusions similar to those of Di Lella, and his methodology—a conceptual/linguistic comparison—is similar. The overall goal of his article, however, is not to make a specific argument about Tobit, per se, but to create a larger taxonomy of Deuteronomic reception in the Second Temple period.

15   Tobit has long been studied as a folk tale. Popular tales, such as the story of the Grateful Dead, were thought to have influenced the earliest stages of the story. One initial problem is that there is little evidence for the existence of these folk tales in antiquity. The closest that has been found is a story in Cicero (*Div.* 1.27). For a treatment of the folk tale most commonly associated with the book of Tobit, see Gerould (1908).

means of comparison,[16] Propp instead looks for a "single compositional theme" on which all fairy tales are based (Soll 1989: 213). Propp isolates 31 different functions within a folk tale (e.g., villainy, misfortune, magical agents, journey, and return), many of which have multiple attestations in the story of Tobit. Such an analysis, according to Soll, helps one to see the folk nature of Tobit by illuminating the structure of the plot. Although Tobit is indebted to the heroic fairytale genre, it also portrays "more distinctively Jewish features" (Soll 1989: 220). The compiler of Tobit has combined the fairy tale's "eucatastrophe"[17]—the problem that is turned into good—with the central Jewish problem in the story, which is the exile. This exilic problem is expressed in Deuteronomic terminology. According to Soll, one finds "explicit and detailed affirmation of the Deuteronomic theology of God's just judgment on Israel" (1989: 224).[18] Tobit is righteous and probably deserves a better fate, but he is swimming against "a current ultimately propelled by divine judgment" (224). In other words, Tobit's life has been engulfed by the tragedy of exile and he is guilty by association; the problems that accost the main characters are shown to be "acute manifestations" of the exile itself (225).[19] The folk tale did not provide the "ultimate model for the resolution of evil"; the author of Tobit turned instead to Deuteronomic theology as his "ultimate model for interpreting the exile" (230). Thus, according to Soll, the author of Tobit has emended the morphology in favor of theology.

Soll's analysis is helpful, in so far as it coordinates the theological perspective of the book with a specific narrative strategy. It also improves the study of Tobit and folk-tale theory. Soll does not, however, take account of all of the details of the story. He claims that Deuteronomic theology explains the resolution to the problems of Tobit and Sarah, but this says nothing about the theological interpretation of their origins, which so-called Deuteronomic theology could also attempt to explain. Soll also struggles to explain the unfinished ending of the story, one that leaves the reader wanting a fuller implementation of Deuteronomic rewards.

c. Intertextual

The final scholar to be examined here who has explored Deuteronomistic

---

16   See the commentary by Frank Zimmerman (1958) for an example of one scholar who depends heavily on the folk-tale background as understood by the Finnish school.

17   Here Soll (1989: 221) is borrowing a term from J. R. R. Tolkein.

18   Soll notes that this perspective is particularly evident in Tobit's prayer in chapter 3.

19   One could inquire to the contrary about how the fish that attacks Tobias or the bird feces in Tobit's eyes are the result of the exile. It is not germane at this point to discuss the viability of Soll's claim in depth. His argument will be taken up again later in the present study.

theology in the book of Tobit is Steven Weitzman (1996), who uses inter-textuality to understand Tobit's use of biblical materials for aesthetic or rhetorical purposes.[20] As the beginning point of understanding Tobit's inter-textual intentions, Weitzman points to Raphael's farewell exhortation to Tobit and Tobias (Tob. 12.17–20) and its similarities to God's instructions to Moses and Joshua in Deut. 31.14–30. Moses is ordered to write down a song; similarly, Tobit and Tobias receive instruction to praise God and to write down all that happened to them. In comparing the song of Moses with that of Tobit, there are enough similarities to posit links between the two texts. Weitzman summarizes these similarities: "Both songs are performed by pious sages shortly before their death; both appear near the end of the books within which they appear; both are followed by an address from the dying sage to those who will survive him" (53).[21]

Weitzman also finds more detailed parallels. In 13.2 Tobit describes God as one who "leads down to Hades in the lowest regions of the earth and brings up from the great abyss, there is nothing that can escape his hand"; Deut. 32.39 states, "I kill and I make alive . . . and there is none that can deliver out of my hand." Weitzman also notes a parallel that is actually a contradiction: Tobit's statement that God "will not hide his face from you" sounds similar to Moses' remembrance of God's words: "I will hide my face from them." Although these words in Tobit are not verbatim correlations, they nevertheless "clearly echo" the contents of Deuteronomy (Weitzman 1996: 55).[22] Weitzman claims that the similarities between Tobit chapters 12–13 and Deut. 33.1–32 follow a larger pattern of alluding to Deuteronomy that pervades the whole of Tobit, citing Di Lella's work as documentation.

Weitzman bolsters his argument by showing how Tobit's strategy fits a larger pattern of biblical allusion from the Second Temple period. Deuteronomy 32 was frequently read as a literary model for the dying words of the pious.[23] Songs contemporaneous with Tobit's hymn also evoke biblical language and images, such as Judith's hymn (Jdt. 15.14–16.17) modeled on Exod. 15.1–19 and Judg. 5; and Luke 1.46–55, which emulates Hannah's prayer in 1 Sam. 2.1–10.[24] Weitzman also demonstrates how Tobit has a larger agenda of emulating the patriarchal narratives. The stories of

20   Weitzman himself tends to avoid the term intertextuality. He uses the language of echo and allusion, and notes (56, n. 18) his methodological indebtedness to Richard Hays (1989).

21   While Weitzman is correct in noting these similarities, the aspects by which he compares the two are basic *topoi* within the testamentary genre of this period.

22   Weitzman bolsters his argument here by noting the way Deuteronomy 32 was read in the Second Temple period, pointing to Philo and *Targum Onqelos*. Deuteronomy 32 was not thought to be a chastisement from God upon Israel but an act of praise from Moses to God.

23   One could obviously also mention here Genesis 49, Jacob's testament to his sons.

24   Weitzman (1996: 56–7). Wilson (2006, 436–56) has argued that the circle of intertextuality in Luke extends also to Judith.

Abraham, Joseph, and Job[25] provide a template for much of the narrative in Tobit. The allusions to the patriarchs at the beginning of Tobit's story and the evocation of Deuteronomy at the end of the narrative traces "the entirety of pentateuchal history . . . almost as if to enclose the experiences of Tobit within pentateuchal bookends" (59). This perceived emulation increases the likelihood of a single allusive strategy behind the use of scripture in Tobit. The point for the author of Tobit, according to Weitzman, is that the patriarchal stories take place outside the land of Israel—exactly where Tobit's community finds itself. Thus the emulation of the Song of Moses occurs at a turning point in Israel's history; they are on the cusp of entering the land, and the author of Tobit wants to assert that the end of the exile is near.

III. Conclusion

The idea that the book of Tobit has a Deuteronomic/istic theology has become a truism in study of the book, as the following statement from a summary of recent Tobit scholarship makes clear: "most scholars now emphasize that the basic theological perspective of Tobit is the theology of retribution derived from the book of Deuteronomy . . . [It] has become a fixture in most treatments of Tobit" (Spencer 1999: 160).[26] While the above studies of Tobit are well researched and make significant contributions for understanding and interpreting the book, they all, for the most part, share three significant problems.

First, the brief summary of Koch's work should indicate that retribution in Israel's scriptures is nuanced and multi-faceted, and a facile formulation of an understanding of retribution within a so-called Deuteronomistic theology—if such a thing can even be discussed—is not tenable.[27] While Di Lella's vanguard essay coordinated Tobit's theology specifically with the book of Deuteronomy (thereby adhering to Lohfink's call [1999] for textual linkages when arguing for Deuteronomic influence), most subsequent work assumes Tobit's Deuteronomic stance based either on Di Lella's work or on an abstract concept of Deuteronomistic theology.[28]

---

25   At the time, Job was thought to be one of the patriarchs from Genesis, associated with Jobab the descendant of Abraham.

26   Note again the statement from the foreword to Di Lella's *Festschrift*, with which we began this chapter: Tobit and Ben Sira "share a theology based on the Deuteronomic system of rewards and punishments, whereby the devout are eventually rewarded even if they have first to undergo probationary suffering" (Corley and Skemp 2005: xiii).

27   This is a conclusion to which we will return, exploring it in much greater depth in the following chapter.

28   One could note here the work of Kraft (2007), who is adamant that scholars recognize the complexity of the ancient world as it is studied. He notes that there is a "large body of material (both text and tradition, as well as artwork and stones and buildings) that was respected and taken seriously by the people and cultures we study" (27).

Second, none of the above studies contains a sustained account of what the status of a doctrine of retribution might have been at the time Tobit was written.[29] Di Lella, again, made his argument specifically regarding Deuteronomy. Intervening tradition should not be ignored, however. Noting a contemporaneous assessment of theories of retribution will provide a point of reference in discerning its role in the tale and theology of Tobit.

Third, more attention needs to be paid to the overall narrative in the book of Tobit.[30] That parts of the story and the rhetoric of certain characters espouse straightforward retributive theology is undeniable. Its existence in the story, however, does not necessarily indicate that this theological perspective is the only or even primary one the author intends to assert. The movie *Lost in Translation* (2003) serves as an instructive example. In the movie, many of the characters use modern devices and technology in an attempt to connect with other human beings. Characters use cell phones, fax machines, advertising, and press conferences in an attempt to communicate. The movie's point, however, is to show how these devices are not a substitute for intimate human interpersonal connection. To say that the movie affirms the use of cell phones because characters in the movie use them *ad nauseam* is to miss the point entirely. Such may be the same with Tobit. Noticing straightforward retributive theology on the lips of the main character does not in itself establish this as the text's overall perspective. In response to these problematic aspects of the study of Deuteronomism in Tobit, the following two chapters will examine the perspective of retribution in the book of Sirach and use it as a point of comparison to understand better its existence in the narrative of Tobit.

29   Weitzman (1996) is not as culpable in this critique as others. He does pay some attention to traditions that would have mediated the message of Deuteronomy between the time of its writing and the time of Tobit. While he does this for certain detailed aspects of his study (e.g., how the Song of Moses was being read), he does not do it with the concept of Deuteronomistic retribution per se.

30   Weeks points out how the author of the book of Tobit was more preoccupied with "characterization and plot development" than with promoting a specific ideology (2011: 398). His observation on this point is about how the book of Tobit does not promote specific legal principles, but could be taken more broadly to show how the book does not function as a mouthpiece of "Deuteronomistic Theology" as perfectly as many scholarly treatments allow.

Chapter 4

RETRIBUTION IN BEN SIRA: "DEUTERONOMISM" OR "STRAIGHTFORWARD RETRIBUTION" IN THE SECOND TEMPLE PERIOD

The foregoing review of scholarship on the book of Tobit indicates that Tobit contains some aspects of a straightforward retributive theology. As was noted above, most assessments of this theology—often called Deuteronomistic—do not refer to specific texts, especially not those contemporaneous with Tobit. A logical move in attempting better to understand the narrative of Tobit is to examine closely the parsing of retribution in such literature. In doing so, one must be judicious and selective; there is not adequate space for a review of all potentially relevant literature. The text to be examined here is Sirach, in which the author struggles with the question of God's retribution—at its core, the issue of theodicy—and how to reconcile potentially contradictory doctrines about God and humanity. What will emerge from this analysis is not an exhaustive taxonomy but rather heuristic points of reference in order to help contextualize the book of Tobit and provide contemporaneous textual arguments with which Tobit might be compared and contrasted.

I. Signs of Revolt

In the previous chapter we briefly examined the so-called Deuteronomistic History and its perspective of retribution. The view of retribution undergirding the Deuteronomistic perspective is one in which God repays according to human action—there is a connection between actions and a consequence meted out by God. One consequence of this formulation was the problem of theodicy: the question of God's justice in the face of seemingly undeserved suffering, which often led to a rejection or questioning of the formulations of a close connection between act and consequence. Certain points in Israel's scriptures, most notably Job and Ecclesiastes, show "signs of revolt" against these widely exhibited forms of religious thought and practice (Coggins 1999: 32). A simplistic, straightforward theory of retribution was one that naturally incited skepticism.[1] The rhetoric of Job's friends claims God's justice and its implications in the human sphere:

> If you make iniquity far from your hand
>> and do not let iniquity dwell in your tent,
> surely then you will lift your face without blemish;
>> you will be firmly established and will not fear.
> Then you will forget your trouble;
>> you will remember it like waters that have ebbed away.
>
> (Job 11.14–16)

The friends believe that God repays according to one's actions, judged by God's own justice: "For the work of a human he renders to him, and causes a man to find [that which] is according to his path. Surely God will not act wickedly; the Almighty will not pervert justice" (Job 34.11–12). They are not able to make sense of Job's situation without positing Job's culpability.

Job himself rejects his place in the simplistic, straightforward retributive theology suggested by his friends. Job can no longer comfort himself with the knowledge that he is experiencing only a temporary delay (Koch 1983: 80): "I am blameless! I do not know myself! I reject my life . . . both the blameless and the wicked he destroys" (9.21–22). Job was not the first to suppose that not all suffering is self-wrought, but it is true that "he protests against such a doctrine, which lies in the mouth of Job's friends" (Rowley 1970: 18). Leo Perdue (1991; 1994) places the book's opinion about the origin of evil within the larger context of creation theology. According to Perdue, part of the argument of the book of Job is that, "through continuing acts of creation, including sustaining edict and violent battle, the integrity of the structures of life is upheld" (1991: 262). Terence Fretheim (2005), also emphasizing creation theology in Job, concludes differently. He agrees with Perdue that the structures of creation are upheld, but argues that those structures are different from the world Job thinks God should have created. Job the character is essentially correct in arguing that the world does not evince a "strict retributive orthodoxy where there are, or should be, no 'loose ends' to God's creation" (234). According to Fretheim, the book of Job suggests that God intended a world that does not operate in a precisely ordered way (235). Whether attributable to Koch's formulation of a correlation between *Tun und Ergehen* (act and consequence) or more specifically to a simplistic

---

1   This is a point also made by Crenshaw (1980). He claims that the theory "encouraged the rapid growth of skepticism" (11). Crenshaw also appropriately points out that this skepticism did not begin with Job and Ecclesiastes but had its origin earlier in Israel's history (see pp. 5–9). It is tempting to go further and say that the Deuteronomistic formulation had become orthodox in Israel and that Job is rejecting it. For a discussion of this possibility, see Pope (1965: lxxviii).

retribution where God plays a role,[2] Job rejects the justice of the correlation because it no longer fits his experience. As Perdue summarizes the perspective in Job, "Reality countenances no simplistic theory of retribution which must logically gear to a static order uninterrupted by intrusions from another world of disarray" (1991: 262). Carol Newsom's work on Job (2003) heads in a slightly different direction. She argues that the author of Job provides a "contest of moral imaginations." She resurrects the perspective of Job's friends as legitimate alongside the perspective of Job. The truth in the book is found in the dialogue between differing perspectives. Thus, the emphasis is not so much on revolt, but on continuing conversation. The point still stands, however, that Job evinces differing operative perspectives on retribution.

The book of Ecclesiastes also struggles with a doctrine of retribution: "In my days of vanity I have seen it all: there is a righteous one who is destroyed in his righteousness and there is a wicked one who prospers in his evil" (7.15). C. L. Seow summarizes Qoheleth's perspective by saying: "the traditional doctrine of retribution is contradicted in reality. The righteous and the wicked do not always get what they deserve; sometimes the results are contrary to human expectations" (1997: 50). Qoheleth ultimately recommends mirth because the world is too unpredictable: "there are just people treated as if they had done the work of wicked ones and wicked people treated as if they had done the work of just ones" (8.14). Qoheleth rejects the "facile dogma of retribution" seen in parts of Deuteronomy (e.g., 30.15–20) and in the collection of wisdom in Proverbs (J. Collins 1997b: 14). Now God's actions are "incomprehensible random activity" (Koch 1983: 80).

The rhetoric and theology in Job and Qoheleth indicate that a doctrine of straightforward retribution had achieved a status significant enough that two authors could revolt against it, or at least place it in conversation with a differing perspective. James Crenshaw describes the authors of these two texts as individuals who "refused to take confessional statements concerning divine control of human events at face value" (1980: 15). Qoheleth, focused on earthly things, posits God's indifference to human beings, while Job, focusing on God's retribution for good and evil, is forced to forgo previous rational arguments. While it may go too far to say that straightforward retributive theology was orthodox, it was pervasive enough as a traditional explanation that Job and Qoheleth could strain against it. These texts will provide a backdrop for better understanding the arguments of Ben Sira, to be examined next.

---

2   The situation in Job has been discussed in terms of either of these two options. Koch (1983) argues that Job has only an act–consequence connection, while others are more eager to discuss the book with reference specifically to Deuteronomistic theology (Rowley 1970: 18).

II. Retribution in the Hellenistic Period: Ben Sira

In the Hellenistic period, Jewish texts continue to interact with formulations of straightforward retribution, but the turn to skepticism seen in Job and Qoheleth does not necessarily become the theology *du jour*. What we find in some instances instead is a "renewed confidence in divine retribution" (J. Collins 1997b: 15), exemplified in the wisdom theology of Jerusalem-based sage, Ben Sira.

a. Introduction to Sirach

Jeshua ben Eleazar ben Sira (mentioned in Sir. 50.27) was a teacher in Jerusalem in the early part of the second century BCE. His book of wisdom, originally written in Hebrew, was translated into Greek by his grandson.[3] The long hymn of praise for Simon son of Onias (50.1–21) probably refers to Simon II, who served in the high priesthood from 219 until 196 BCE (Skehan and Di Lella 1987: 550). Ben Sira's understanding of wisdom can be found in the series of poems or hymns to wisdom that pervade the work. Wisdom is from the Lord (1.1–10), engenders fear of the Lord (1.14), and offers rewards (4.11–19). In Sirach 24 Wisdom speaks in the first person: "'I came forth from the mouth of the Most High, and like a mist I covered the earth'" (24.3). This figure of wisdom, dwelling with God, was directed to abide specifically with Israel: "Then the creator of all things commanded me, and the one who created me chose the place for my tent. He said, 'Make your dwelling in Jacob, and in Israel receive your possession'" (24.8). It is this high view of wisdom and its origin with the Lord in which Ben Sira locates his ethical exhortations, which include topics such as self-control (18.30–33); interpersonal associations (13.1–13; 36.18–27); child-rearing (7.23–28; 30.1–13); and use of material possessions (3.29–30; 29.1–20; 31.1–11).

On the issues of divine retribution and theodicy Ben Sira's work is an amalgamation of Israel's traditions that, according to some, does not successfully cohere. Ben Sira holds a view of the origin of sin that is unseemly in its misogynistic formulation (25.23–4) and seems loath to implicate God in the origin of evil (15.11–12).[4] At the same time, Ben Sira's view of creation

---

3   The basis for the work here will be Hebrew whenever possible, taken from Beentjes' *The Book of Ben Sira in Hebrew* (1997). Not all portions of the book are extant in Hebrew, in which case one must have recourse to the Greek translation (LXX). For a discussion of Sirach's translation into Greek, see Wright (1989). For clarity, I will follow the versification in the LXX. If a Hebrew text is not mentioned, the translation comes from the LXX.

4   At the time of Ben Sira there were competing views on this topic. As chapter seven will explore below, the myth of the rebellion of the watchers (*1 En.* chs. 1–36) offers a different, sectarian view of the origin of evil in which it is not from humans and is not from God. Randall Argall (1995) argues that these two traditions were aware of and competed against one another.

is such that all are clay in the creator's hands and the path of an individual is determined by God (33.10–13). Ben Sira struggles with the question of theodicy; his explanation of God's justice and retribution in the face of evil is not immune from critique. His lack of a satisfactory result could be characterized negatively: Ben Sira is more concerned with passing on "the hodge-podge of tradition than with achieving consistency" (J. Collins 1997b: 95). While Ben Sira certainly is in conversation with a hodge-podge of tradition, his lack of consistency is not the result of a wishy-washy theological explanation but derives from the rigorous adherence to two contradictory theological suppositions. Ben Sira proclaims a good creation that has been marred by human culpability. At the same time, Ben Sira propounds that there is duality inherent in creation, a duality created by God that sets humans on a determined trajectory.

There are any number of ways that Ben Sira's approach to the question of theodicy and retribution could be organized, but it would be a mistake to focus only on those texts in which the question of theodicy figures prominently. At the core of Ben Sira's struggles with retribution are his beliefs about God and humanity. In what follows, we will first treat Ben Sira's understanding of God, which seems to be the starting and ending points for his grappling with the problem of evil. Second will be a discussion of Ben Sira's view of human complicity in evil. Finally, we will examine the concept of "testing" in Ben Sira's thought, which provides another angle from which one may view and understand the sage's argument.

b. God in Sirach

Ben Sira strongly affirms God's sovereignty. In 42.15–43.35 Ben Sira writes a long hymn in praise of God and the divine works. The hymn begins with a statement of God's control as creator and the stability and regularity of creation: "by the speech of God his works were made; they do his will as he has ordained for them."[5] This God whom Ben Sira describes is one who knows all (42.18), has mighty wisdom (42.21), and has created a diverse and wonderful world (42.25). Toward the end of the hymn, Ben Sira declares, "terrible is the Lord and exceedingly great, and marvelous is his power" (43.29). Within this understanding of God's power and sovereignty, Ben Sira has more detailed things to say about God's compassion and creation.

One initial aspect of God's omnipotence, according to Ben Sira, is that God judges the actions of individuals: "the one who lives forever created everything; the Lord alone is just" (18.1–2). God's judgment and wrath is based on the ability to see and know all; no sinner is able to avoid detection:

---

5   The second half of this verse follows the Syriac. It is omitted in most Greek manuscripts. Hebrew B (ופועל רצונו לקחו) and M (ופעל רצנו לקחו) have an abridged version (Beentjes 1997: 168).

The man who sins against his own bed says in his soul: "Who can see me? Darkness encircles me and the walls cover me and no one is able to see me. Why should I be cautious? The most high will not remember my sins." His fear and human eyes do now know that the eyes of the Lord are ten thousand times brighter than the sun. They are attentive to all human paths and consider the hidden portion. (23.18–19)

A sinner who tries to avoid detection will be punished in the streets and apprehended when least expected (23.20–21). Ben Sira remembers those situations in Israel's past where God has punished the wicked, including those who died in the flood, the neighbors of Lot, the Canaanites, and the 600,000 soldiers who murmured against Moses (Sir. 16.7–11). These examples provide confirmation of God's justice. Ben Sira is convinced that "as great as his mercy is also his punishment; he judges a man according to his deeds. A sinner does not escape with his spoils" (16.12–13a).

There is, then, for Ben Sira, a strong sense of God's justice that entails punishment for those who do wrong. In comparison to our earlier examination in chapter three of theories of retribution in Israel's scriptures, it seems that Ben Sira's formulation would not fit Koch's theory of a general *Tun-Ergehen Zusammenhang* (connection between act and consequence) because Ben Sira envisions a very direct role for God and a standard against which humans are judged. The concept of judgment in 16.11b leaves little ambiguity regarding God's role: "on the wicked alights his wrath" (NAB). There is more at work than a built-in consequence. Similarly, the judgment in chapter 23 is such that the punishment seems to come from God; the problem explained there is that the sinner is not mindful of the Most High (23.18b). And, more pointedly, Koch's conclusion that Proverbs lacks divine retribution because the judgment is not based on a previously established norm also does not fit with Ben Sira's thought. For Ben Sira the opposite is the case. A woman who is unfaithful to her husband will be punished because she has "disobeyed the law of the Most High" (23.23), rhetoric which is intended to engender the idea that "nothing is better than fear of the Lord, nothing is sweeter than to obey the commandments of the Lord" (23.27b).

One should not force too rigid a distinction between retribution involving God and that which does not into Koch's formulation of retribution in Israel's scriptures. In reference to the narrative of Pharaoh and the plagues in Exodus, Terence Fretheim argues that the "sin–consequence schema" should not be understood in terms that are too mechanistic; there is instead a "loose causal weave" (2005: 122). Fretheim points to H. H. Schmid (1984: 102–17), who emphasizes the important and essential role of creation in the act–consequence interaction. At some level, whether God instigates the consequence or not is of little importance, "so long as the inner force of the order of creation and the action of the creator god are not differentiated" (Schmid 1984: 111–12).[6] One does get the sense, however, from Ben Sira that retribution is more than a deed returning back on the actor by way of natural processes. The sage has a more specific formulation that includes a definitive role for God for which he argues.

Although God is a mighty judge, the verdict in Sirach can often come down in favor of humanity. Part of God's power is an ability to know and understand the plight of humans. Humanity is transient; life is fleeting. The days of a life might add up to one hundred years but they amount to little more than a drop of water or a grain of sand (18.7–8). This transience is the very reason God has mercy on humanity: "for this reason the Lord is patient with them and pours forth his mercy on them. He sees and knows their destruction and that it is evil. Because of this he multiplies his forgiveness" (18.11–12). In chapter 16, as noted above, Ben Sira alludes to episodes from Israel's past that establish God's ability to punish. In chapter 2 he invokes the past to establish God's merciful tendencies:

> Examine the old generations and see: who has hoped in the Lord and been disappointed? Or who has persevered in fearing the Lord and been forsaken? Has anyone called on him and been disregarded by him? Therefore, compassionate and merciful is the Lord; he forgives sins and saves in times of affliction. (2.10–11, NAB)

In contrast to the signs of revolt in Job and Ecclesiastes, in Sirach we find what Crenshaw describes as a situation where "theology prevailed over the experiential tradition," a stance that "sets him apart from the earlier sages" (1998: 161). This is not to suggest that alternative theological formulations were not based on experience. It might be more accurate to say that Ben Sira is interested in affirming dual experiences: that of God's judgment but also that of God's mercy. It may be the one-sided nature of the skepticism in Job and Ecclesiastes that Ben Sira finds problematic.[7] Another distinction in experience, especially as communicated in Sir. 2.10–11, is an emphasis on the collective, rather than on the fates of individuals as expressed in Job and Qoheleth.

c. Humanity in Sirach

The formulations of judgment and mercy in Ben Sira are also dependent upon human action, the above discussion of God's mercy (e.g., 2.10–11;

6   It should be noted that Schmid's words here are directly related to Near Eastern texts that shed light on Israel's thinking. The concept holds true, however, in Israel's scriptures. Creation is the proper horizon in which to understand how an orderly world can be obtained.

7   It is not necessarily the case that Job expresses a one-sided skepticism. Here, again, one should note Newsom's work (2003), in which she claims that Job is meant to express a contest of moral imaginations, not necessarily to make one subject to the other.

18.11–12) notwithstanding.[8] At the core of this human disposition in Ben Sira's vocabulary is "fear of the Lord." In chapter 2, those who fear the Lord will not be disappointed while Ben Sira pronounces woe to those "with craven hearts and drooping hands" (2.12, NAB). Humans have the ability to obey or not to obey: "those who fear the Lord do not disregard his words; those who love him keep his ways" (2.15). A more extended discussion of human disposition is in chapter 15. Crenshaw isolates the phrase, "do not say" (אל תאמר; μὴ εἴπῃς), and suggests this is Ben Sira quoting those against whom he is arguing, thus giving voice to his "antagonists" (1983: 120–2). These antagonists, it seems, were claiming that, because of the omnipotence of God and God's ability to forgive, they were not culpable for their own sins. God may even have caused them.

Ben Sira rejects the suggestion that God could in any way be at fault for the sin of individuals. God does not cause one to fall away because what God hates, God does not do (15.11). Nor does God lead astray, for God has no need of a wicked person (15.12). Evoking the language of Gen. 1.1, Ben Sira proclaims that God, from the beginning (אלהים מבראשית[9]), created humans and made them with their own "inclination." The Hebrew word for inclination here is יצר, which implies the human's ability to make a free choice. As J. Collins states, "the inclination is not an external, supernatural force" but is dependent upon human volition (1997b: 83). In the next three verses (15.15–17), the word for "choosing" is used three times: if humans choose, they are able to keep the commandments; fire and water are set before individuals, from which they must choose; and before humans are life and death, between which they must choose. The point is clear in its echo of Deut. 30.15–20: humans exercise choice in keeping the law and choosing life or death. Here we see what might be called a doctrine of free will: "Ben Sira insists on the radical freedom human beings have of choosing one extreme or the other and, by implication, anything in between" (Skehan and Di Lella 1987: 272). At the same time, as if to confirm this choice and its importance, Ben Sira repeats the refrain that God is watching these choices: the eyes of God see all that has been made; "he understands a person's every work" (15.19b). This hints at the assumption that, although the choices are left to humans, God is waiting with a response commensurate with the deed. Similar sentiment can also be seen in Ben Sira's discussion of how properly to guard one's tongue (37.17), and in a clear admonition not to sin: "my child, if you have sinned, do not add to it, and for your former [sins], pray. Flee from sin as from a snake" (21.1–2a).

Ben Sira, then, views God as a powerful judge who oversees the actions of humans. God allots to humans the ability to choose their own paths. We have

---

8   The potentially contradictory stances asserted by Ben Sira will be discussed in greater depth below.

9   This is according to Hebrew manuscript A (Beentjes 1997: 44).

already noted that, in his formulation, Ben Sira places too much emphasis on the divine role to reconcile it with Koch's deed–consequence connection. Noticing similar formulations in Deuteronomy also confirms this conclusion. Recall the choice Moses sets before the people: "I have today set before you life and good, and death and evil. I command you this day to love the Lord, your God, to walk in his ways, and to keep his commandments . . . and you will live and become many" (Deut. 30.15–16). At the same time, Moses also presents the negative: "If, however, you turn away your hearts and will not listen . . . I tell you today that you will certainly perish" (Deut. 30.17–18). An accented role for God and a clearly established norm by which to judge makes a simple *Tun-Ergehen Zusammenhang* (connection between act and consequence) unlikely. Instead scholars often refer to the formulation in Sirach as "Deuteronomic."[10] Ben Sira clearly has a carefully constructed view of retribution, but it might be misleading and problematic to call it "Deuteronomic," as many scholars have.[11] Such phraseology assumes a tidy retributive formula, contained within the book of Deuteronomy and writ large across the face of the Deuteronomistic History, with which Ben Sira wholeheartedly agrees. There are two significant problems with labeling this "Deuteronomic." First, it does not do justice to the actual theological complexity of Deuteronomy, and, second, Deuteronomy and its purported "ists" (i.e., Deuteronomy's ideology in the hands of later tradents) have not cornered the exegetical market on certain conceptions of retribution in Israel's scriptures.

1. Excursus: The Appropriateness of the Notion and Adjective "Deuteronomic"

Calling Sirach Deuteronomic does not do justice to the theological complexity of Deuteronomy itself. While one can point to texts such as Deut. 30.15–16 to claim human necessity in keeping the law as an anthropocentric "Deuteronomic" view of retribution, John Gammie (1970: 1–12) has pointed out ways in which Deuteronomy contains theocentric views as well. He delineates four aspects of retribution in Deuteronomy.

1. Retribution can function in Deuteronomy as an "impersonal principle operative in society" (Gammie 1970: 6). In this idea, retribution will come upon the actor as a result of the natural order of things in a

---

10   For example, J. Collins (1997b: 83). See also Skehan and Di Lella, who claim: "His [i.e, Ben Sira's] pervading theological outlook is Deuteronomic" (1987: 75). Elsewhere (79) they refer to Ben Sira's "Deuteronomic equation." See also Beentjes (2011), who examines Ben Sira's Deuteronomic view through the specific categories of Weinfeld.
11   See Rankin (1936: 98–123) for a description of what he calls the "Deuteronomist Theory" in later Judaism, although he does not discuss Ben Sira at any great length.

way similar to what Koch called the *Tun-Ergeben Zusammenbang* (connection between act and consequence). Injustice results in this system because innocents can be impacted by the wake of the retribution as it impinges upon the wrongdoer. Thus the repeated order in Deuteronomy to "purge the evil one from your midst" (e.g., 13.2–6; 24.7).

2. A second conception of retribution suggests that there is a principle according to which the people are assured God will "inevitably operate" (Gammie 1970: 7). While God plays a role here, the basic idea is still anthropocentric. The impetus is on humans to act in a certain way and God reacts accordingly. This is the aspect of retribution in Deuteronomy that scholars deem "Deuteronomic" in discussions in Sirach and Tobit. It is this obedience that is linked to the assurance of the other classically defined "Deuteronomic" tenets such as blessing (14.28–29), long life (6.2), and possession of the land (8.1).

3. A third conception of retribution in Deuteronomy starts with a theocentric orientation. Here, it is the character of God that has primary focus, especially in the emphasis that no action on the part of Israel instigated God's election of them in the first place. God chose them to be a peculiar people (7.6). Although God still metes out punishment on the basis of human action, there is a sense that humans do not always receive the "full measure of judgment" that their actions may have warranted (Gammie 1970: 10).[12]

4. Finally, there is a tendency in Deuteronomy toward "dissolution of the idea" of retribution altogether. In this formulation, the idea of retribution "is no longer viewed as an appropriate conceptual vehicle to describe God's relationship to [humans]" (Gammie 1970: 10). The text, instead, occasionally points out the limitations in such a doctrine. The interaction of God with humanity is alternately discussed as probationary (8.2), pedagogical (8.3–5), or willy-nilly (8.17–18). Gammie posits that these directions seem like "deliberate corrections" that point out the dangers of an anthropocentric understanding of retribution (11). He claims further that the people were evidently turning the "hortatory injunctions" into "hard and fast dogma" (11).

The point of this lengthy summary of Gammie's work is to force the idea that, if one wants to refer to a "Deuteronomic" conception of retribution, one must be aware of the theological complexity of the situation in Deuteronomy.[13] The phrase "Deuteronomic," when used as a descrip-

---

12   Here Gammie provides Deut. 9.7–8 as an example in which the people deserved more punishment than they received.

13   One could also note Braulik (1994). Braulik delineates redactional strata to show the variety of perspectives in Deuteronomy. At one level, the observance of the law is the only way those in exile can hope to recover the land (156). In a different stratum, however, possession of the land is "the fulfillment of an entirely unmerited promise, an assurance of pure grace, which YHWH gave the fathers by an oath" (158). Later in the exilic period, Deuteronomy will assert that Israel "may never ascribe what it has achieved

tion of Ben Sira's view of retribution, seems limited to Gammie's point number two, above, that God offers rewards commensurate with human deeds. More recent assessments of the theology of Deuteronomy have come to similar conclusions as to the complexity of traditions contained therein.[14]

Dennis Olson has also affirmed this point of view of the complexity inherent in Deuteronomy. When examining Deuteronomy 29–32, he notes the affirmation of both divine determination and human freedom as a central paradox or juxtaposition. He claims that the authors are "bumping up" against "truths that transcend human knowing and thus require . . . contradictory positions to articulate them" (Olson 2003: 209). In another essay, Olson claims that the death of Josiah in 2 Kings 23 did not cause the connection between act and consequence to founder: "a general order of act and consequence may be operative in a loose moral weave in reality, but it does not apply rigidly or exhaustively" (Olson 2005: 136).

A second point bears mentioning, which is the fact that Deuteronomy (and those texts claimed to be "Deuteronomistic") is not the only place in Israel's scriptures where one can find expressions of a connection between act and consequence that is enacted by God. For example, the interaction between Pharaoh and Moses in Exodus 6–14 is a complex interplay of divine determination and efficacious human action. Many of the difficulties faced by the Israelite slaves in Egypt are echoed in the impact of the plagues (e.g., the cry of the Israelites in bondage [3.7] and the cry of the Egyptians [11.6]). Fretheim points out how, in Exod. 9.19–21, God allows humans to heed the divine word in order to limit the damage of the divinely decreed hail (2005: 120–3).

to its own efforts. It was YHWH alone who gave Israel the strength to procure these riches (8:17–18)" (159). Thus, the composition history of Deuteronomy both prescribes observance of the law as a prerequisite for taking the land and also asserts that there is "no causal connection" between possessing the land by an "achievement of their own" (159).

14   Here it is worth noting a recent article by Noll (2007), whose aim is to reorient discussions of the Deuteronomistic History toward an ongoing conversation on the merits of Deuteronomy's ideology rather than a straightforward acceptance and representation of that ideology. Although intended as a corrective to Noth (1948; 1957; 1981), Noll assumes a unified ideology on the part of Deuteronomy and does not consider the possibility that such an ideology could find inspiration outside of Deuteronomy itself. Note especially the assumption in his definition of Deuteronomism: "the presence of words and phrases derived from the book of Deuteronomy that seem to affirm the ideology affirmed by Deuteronomy" (317). While Noll's concept of an ongoing conversation or debate might make better sense of the evidence, his work could perhaps be better served by abandoning the concept of Deuteronomism and expanding the reconstruction to a wider, ongoing debate of themes in the Torah.

One can also point to various Psalms that express similar anthropocentric views of retribution:

> O Lord, do not rebuke me in your anger,
>> or discipline me in your wrath.
> For your arrows have sunk into me,
>> and your hand has come down on me.
> There is no soundness in my flesh
>> because of your indignation;
> There is not health in my bones
>> because of my sin.
> For my iniquities have gone over my head;
>> they weigh like a burden too heavy for me.
>
> (Ps. 38.1–4 NRSV)

Should Ps. 38 be described as "Deuteronomic" simply because it correlates God's retribution with human action? The same sense of retribution is assumed in the story of Noah's flood, but one would not call Ps. 38 diluvian. Ben Sira could be just as influenced by Ps. 38 as by Deut. 30, in which case Ben Sira's formulation is Deuteronomic only if one can guarantee that the view of retribution in Ps. 38 is influenced by Deuteronomy and/or Deuteronomistic ideals. This then runs the risk of what Norbert Lohfink calls "pan-Deuteronomistic chain reactions" (1999: 39). To call Sirach "Deuteronomic" does not do justice to the complexity of the situation. The repeated use of "Deuteronomistic" as shorthand for its perspective on retribution says too little because Deuteronomy is actually more complicated. At the same time, use of the word "Deuteronomistic" says too much because scholars can then find it anywhere.

The point here is to describe and define Ben Sira's perspective without necessarily attaching to it a macro-label from earlier parts of Israel's scriptures. Ben Sira clearly works from an understanding of retribution that can be found in many parts of Israel's scriptures, and one of his major inspirations is undoubtedly Deuteronomy. He believes that there is a direct correlation between act and consequence, with the retribution meted out by God based on available norms. Explaining Ben Sira's perspective this way is more verbose than giving it the title "Deuteronomic," but it is more accurate and representative of the complex web of influences with which Ben Sira interacted.

d. Ben Sira's Struggle with Straightforward Retribution Based on Available Norms

The problem with Ben Sira's formulation of straightforward retribution as described above was clear to him: what happens when the formula does not work? One can claim God's sovereign justice and humanity's ability to ally itself with one side or the other by fearing God, but the vicissitudes of life often challenge such a tidy formula.[15]

The human inclination (יצר), which was noted above as the corner-stone of Ben Sira's belief in a free choice, cannot be read in isolation from his argument about the clay vessel formed in the hands of a potter (יוצר) in 33.13. The inclination described in chapter 15 should not be equated completely with free will because the inclination is coordinated with a doctrine of creation wherein God allots a person's path. Just as one day is more important than another (i.e., some are festivals, others not), so it is with all humans who are made of clay: "with fullness of knowledge the Lord distinguished them and appointed their different paths" (33.11). God blesses and sanctifies some, drawing them in; others he curses and brings low, expelling them from their place (33.12). Experience tells Ben Sira that all things are created in pairs, one thing the opposite of another (33.15).[16] As such, "like clay in the hands of the potter, to be molded according to his good pleasure, so are humans in the hands of their creator, to be given to them according to what he decides" (33.13). Although he had previously described humans as having something akin to free will, Ben Sira now has described a determined fate for humans. As J. Collins summarizes Ben Sira's attempt at theodicy: "despite his vigorous endorsement of Deuteronomic theology and human responsibility [in ch. 15], Sirach's overall position remains ambiguous" (1997b: 84).

Ben Sira struggles to maintain contradictory theological suppositions in order to explain the phenomenon of evil. On the one hand, God is omnipotent and has the right to judge according to human actions. Humans are granted a degree of ability to influence their own actions and make the choice set before them. At the same time, creation is ordered in such a way that there is an inherent duality in creation that "serves the purposes of God" (J. Collins 1997b: 95). As Crenshaw describes the situation, "it is difficult to avoid the suspicion that Sirach realized in one way or another the utter futility of his efforts at theodicy" (1983: 127). This futility, however, is not lost on Ben Sira. There are two ways in which Sirach has attempted to blunt the horns of this dilemma.[17]

---

15   Such questions are often noted as the beginning point for discussions of theo-dicy in the Hellenistic period. See Charlesworth (2003: 470–508).

16   At this point, it seems Ben Sira is somewhat dependent on Stoic thought. See Collins (1997b: 85). Although Genesis chapters 1–2, 6–9 could just as likely provide the idea of things being created in pairs.

17   There are actually more than two that have been posited by scholars. For example, Crenshaw (1983: 129) enumerates six ways, among which he emphasizes Ben Sira's call to drown out the problem with praise to God and Ben Sira's attempt to move the expected but vacant retribution from current experience into the psychological realm.

1. The latter end (אהרית)

One way in which Ben Sira tries to deal with the discomfort of his explanations of retribution is to explain that, although the retributive equation may appear temporarily to be skewed, eventually people's deeds will bear the proper fruit. Ben Sira repeatedly asserts that the true character of a person's life will be revealed at his or her death: "at the end of one's life one's actions are revealed. Call no one happy before his death; a person is known by how he ends" (11.27b–28).[18] Ben Sira also claims that one who is stubborn with respect to wisdom "will fare badly in the end" (3.26a). In other words, the appearance of good or ill fortune may only be an appearance. This concept in Ben Sira is not only negative. He can also exhort the righteous to do what is right by explaining the hope for an eventual reward. After affirming that all God's works are good, Ben Sira claims that one work should not be compared with another, "for everything shows its worth in its proper time" (39.34).[19] The final exhortation of the book provides the advice: "do your work in righteousness, and he will give to you your reward in his time" (51.30).[20] Passages such as these reveal a different direction in which Ben Sira adjusts his search for the answer to theodicy, allowing him to retain his adherence to a concept of straightforward retribution by altering the timing of the event. Herein lies an admission that "things are not what they should be at the moment, since external circumstances do not always correctly mirror the inner character of [an individual]" (Crenshaw 1983: 126). The delay of reward allows Ben Sira to retain his strict doctrine of the sovereignty of God; the doctrine of reward and punishments does not have to be removed. There is, however, a "painful delay" (Crenshaw 1983: 126).

When discussing the doctrine of rewards, Weinfeld, in his study of Deuteronomy and Israel's wisdom tradition, says that any book dealing with reward/punishment cannot pass over the problem of theodicy (1972: 307). Weinfeld claims that wisdom literature "solves" the problem by connecting the painful delay with the idea of a "latter end" (1972: 316). In this endeavor, Ben Sira does not stand alone. Weinfeld offers other texts that work from the same concept of a latter end: "Look not on the wine when it is red, when it sparkles in the glass. It goes down smoothly; but in the end it bites like a serpent, or like a poisonous adder" (Prov. 23.31–32, NAB). The success of the wicked and suffering of the righteous are only transitory states.

18   From manuscript A (Beentjes 1997: 38).

19   The Hebrew here is כי הכל בעתו ינביר, from manuscript B (Beentjes 1997: 69).

20   Most translations here seem to follow the Greek, which says, ἐργάζεσθε τὸ ἔργον ὑμῶν πρὸ καιροῦ; thus, "do your work in good time" (NRSV). Manuscript B, however, has מעשיכם עשו בצדקה, which leads to my translation "in righteousness." A portion of this verse, corresponding to the last two words, was found in 11QPs[a] (שכרכם בעתו). See Sanders (1965).

The decisive factor is the latter end (אחרית), at which point the wicked will be cut off (e.g., Prov. 24.14). In the Psalms, this idea is often conveyed with the image of fading flora: "Do not envy those who do wrong. Like grass they wither quickly; like green plants they wilt away" (37.1b–2, NAB; Weinfeld 1972: 316).

Oliver Rankin has also provided a study of how texts struggled with the disjunction between an ideology of retribution and a reality that appears to contradict this ideology. His study may be an oversimplification, but he discusses the doctrine of rewards and punishments as one that had "appendices" that helped make it "elastic and durable" as a concept (1936: 81).[21] One of the appendices Rankin discusses is the fact that God could "delay action" in bringing about the proper end (82). The explanation of reality that posits straightforward retribution, with its "adjuncts," became "an extremely serviceable and adaptable instrument" (Rankin 1936: 83).[22] Rankin sees, across a wide swath of Israel's literature (e.g., Psalms, Ezekiel, Chronicles), an ability to adapt the theory without compromising its central tenets.

Ben Sira, then, attempts to address the problem of an apparent lack of justice for righteous individuals by adhering to a concept of the latter end (אחרית). In so doing, he is giving fuller expression to a theme insipient in earlier manifestations of Israel's wisdom traditions.

2. "Testing" in Ben Sira's theodicy

Ben Sira also approaches theodicy and his perspective on retribution with a concept of testing, a factor often not coordinated with his attempts at theodicy in scholarly discussions on this subject. Ben Sira establishes the concept of testing near the beginning of his text. After an opening poem in praise of wisdom, chapter two begins with a warning to be prepared: "My child, when you come to serve the Lord, prepare yourself for a test [πειρασμόν]" (2.1). The one who is wise is to be pure of heart and undisturbed in a time of adversity by clinging to God. The exhortation concludes: "accept whatever befalls you, in times of misfortune be patient; for in fire gold is tested, and those who are acceptable in the furnace of humiliation" (2.4–5). By looking at the following verses (2.7–18) we can discern Ben Sira's intentions for this testing. The test is not meant to engender mistrust or anger toward God, because the past tells us that God is faithful and those who hoped in the Lord were not

---

21   Rankin's language here uses the problematic "Deuteronomistic" and "Deuteronomic" designations. I remove them here from explanation of his work for the reasons delineated earlier in this chapter.

22   When using Rankin's language here, one must be careful to remember that he is writing before Noth's theory of the Deuteronomistic history (1948; 1957) and before Koch's contribution (1955, ET 1983), which helps one distinguish between the natural act–consequence connection and a more specifically theological doctrine in Deuteronomy and those books potentially influenced by it.

disappointed (2.7–11). At the same time, the one who is not able to endure and whose hands droop will have no recourse at the visitation of the Lord (2.12–14). The testing, therefore, is a concept that fits well with what was previously outlined as God's sovereignty in judgment, a proving that tests one's allegiance.[23] In essence, Ben Sira asks: Will you endure or allow your hands to droop? The test is a wide-angled perspective from which to view one's allegiance, as the last verse in the pericope makes clear: "let us fall into the hands of the Lord and not into the hands of humans" (2.18a).

Testing as a mechanism to determine if an individual or group is found worthy can be found as an element of divine–human interaction in Deuteronomy. As Skehan and Di Lella point out in their comment on Sir. 2.1–6: "the idea of preparing oneself for testing even though one served the Lord is part of the Deuteronomic theory of retribution that legitimated probationary suffering for the virtuous" (Skehan and Di Lella 1987: 150). The language of testing (נסה) appears at several points in the book of Deuteronomy, perhaps most strongly in chapter 8. In an attempt to make sense of the desert experience, Moses' speech claims that for 40 years they have been directed by God "so as to test you by affliction [in order to] find out whether or not it was your intention to keep his commandments" (8.2, NAB). This discipline from God is just "as a man disciplines his son" (8.5b, NAB). In v. 16 the same sentiment is repeated. The people were in the desert and fed manna so that "he might afflict you and test you, but also make you prosperous in the end." The book of Judges continues the theme. God decides not to eliminate the surrounding nations in order "to determine whether [Israel] would obey the commandments the Lord had enjoined on their fathers through Moses" (Judg. 3.4, NAB).

Ben Sira works with the concept of testing in 4.17; 6.7; 33.1; and 44.20. In 4.17, Wisdom is described as one who instructs her children. At first, she walks with him as a stranger and puts him to the test. She tests him with her discipline "until his heart is fully with her."[24] If he fails in this test she will abandon him (4.19). In 33.1 the treatise on creation and the allotment of some to God's pleasure and others to sin—a doctrine of pairs in creation—begins with the statement: "No evil can harm the person who fears the Lord; through trials repeatedly such a one is safe."[25] This is contrasted with one who hates wisdom, who will be tossed about like a boat in a storm. A final reference to testing is in Ben Sira's paean to the patriarchs. In 44.20 Ben Sira specifically singles out Abraham as one who observed the precepts of God

---

23   There is also the connotation here more specific to metallurgy, that the fire removes impurities from the gold. This aspect of the fire, however, does not seem to be Ben Sira's main focus in the verses that follow the analogy. The focus seems to be on endurance as a test of fidelity.

24   Hebrew manuscript A: ועד עת ימלא לבו (Beentjes 1997: 25).

25   Hebrew manuscript E. The last phrase is: בנסוי ישוב תמלט (Beentjes 1997: 105).

and "when tested, was found loyal," a clear reference to the *Akedah* (the binding of Isaac) and Genesis 22.

Despite the existence of testing in Deuteronomy and its existence in key places in the text of Sirach, few scholars have made recourse to this concept in discussions of Ben Sira's ideas of retribution. Crenshaw delineates six ways in which Ben Sira approaches the problem of theodicy, none of which contains the concept or language of testing (1983: 129). J. Collins, in assessing Ben Sira's attempts at theodicy as having an "unresolved tension," does not specifically treat 2.1–5 or 33.1 in explaining difficulties in this life (1997b: 83). Di Lella does treat 2.1–5 in an article from 1966, in which he equates the concept of testing with what he calls "probationary suffering" (145). He claims that, for Ben Sira, the point of the admonition is that "the virtuous should not be dismayed by ill-fortune, for eventually they will be rewarded with the usual material blessings: long life, good health, numerous children, etc." (1966: 145). Di Lella essentially equates the concept of testing with the idea of one's "latter end" as discussed above. The evidence in Ben Sira, however, does not warrant the conclusion that a protracted reward—Di Lella's "probationary suffering"—should be equated with "testing." The test is not aimed at the rewards, although the rewards may eventually appear. The test is instead an initial test of fidelity, a conclusion supported in what follows by examining more closely how Ben Sira employs the concept of testing.

Di Lella connects the concept of testing with the so-called Deuteronomistic rewards. In Sirach chapter 2, however, there is little mention of the specific Deuteronomistic rewards that Di Lella enumerates (1966: 145). There are general references to a great future (2.3) and lasting joy and mercy (2.9), but the language of rewards remains oblique. More pertinent in the context is the repeated exhortation to keep the commandments. Ben Sira claims in 2.1 that trials will arise in the context of coming to serve the Lord. Further, the pericope ends with a call to end up in the "hands of the Lord." This is reminiscent of Deuteronomy and Judges, where the trial itself acts as a crucible through which fidelity can be determined. In other words, the trial arises to find out whether or not an individual or group is able to keep the commandments in the first place. The picture painted in Sir. 2.1–18 is not one where the *Tun-Ergehen Zusammenhang* (connection between act and consequence) is temporarily skewed, a probationary period until all things become as they ought. The testing has its own purpose, namely to test and improve an individual's worth just as gold is tested in fire in order to assess and increase its purity (2.5). It seems Di Lella has conflated the idea of a person's latter end (אחרית)—when the probationary suffering ends—with a test that purifies and tests fidelity.

The idea of testing also shows up in Sir. 6.1–17. Here, although in a more mundane setting, Ben Sira's use of the concept of testing will confirm the above contention. The sage claims that, in trying to discern true friendship, one should first test a friend and not be too hasty to trust him (6.7). Just as

God tested Israel's fidelity, so also individuals are wise to test their friends in order to confirm the level of loyalty and commitment. Ben Sira clearly understands testing as an initiatory proving through which fidelity can be assessed. Finally, the example of Abraham in chapter 44 explains testing as a check for fidelity. The test revealed that Abraham was found loyal (44.19). The text goes on here to describe Abraham's blessing of great progeny, all of which occurred "for this reason" (על כן), namely Abraham passing the test of fidelity. While rewards are in sight here, in the testing, more is at stake than a hoped-for reward. The test does something—tests initial fidelity—and should not be equated wholesale with the expected rewards at a person's latter end (אחרית). The test is not contradictory with the rewards, but one is not necessarily a direct result of the other; the test itself has an independent purpose. Thus, it seems that the concept of testing in Ben Sira is different from the idea of a protracted reward that will be commensurate with the original deed as Di Lella had suggested. There is a direct divine role played in this testing, with the goal being to discern and confirm the loyalty and fidelity of the party in question.

Finally, the concept of testing in Sirach is best understood within the larger context of the work and importance of sagacious activities. In a sapiential work such as Sirach, the concepts of admonishing, discipline, and instruction find a natural home. These concepts are often tied particularly to the vocabulary for discipline or instruction (מוסר/παιδεία), which are common in Ben Sira (e.g., 6.22; 21.19; 22.6; 23.7) and in other sapiential works (e.g., Job 5.17; 12.18; Prov. 1.2–3; 3.11; 15.32–33). In Sirach, language of admonishing and discipline is used to describe the activity of the sage himself, of personified wisdom, and of God.

Sirach chapter 6 discusses an important constellation of events: a close association of the personified figure of wisdom with a first-person statement from the sage himself. In 6.18–24 the concepts of instruction and discipline are connected with the figure of wisdom and specifically with testing. To the fool wisdom is like a burdensome stone meant to test, which the fool will cast aside (6.22). This statement is followed with the comment: "for discipline is like her name, to many she is not obvious." The word for discipline, המוסר, is identical to the hophal masculine singular participle of סור, which means to depart or withdraw.[26] Thus the sage employs a double entendre: wisdom's name is both "instruction" and "withdrawn." This suggests that part of the role of personified wisdom is to discipline so as to weed out those who are not worthy.

In the very next verse, Ben Sira makes one of his few personal statements: "Listen, my child, and receive my opinion; do not reject my counsel" (6.23). He follows this statement with a metaphor: the student is to submit to the yoke and fetters of wisdom. Here the personification of wisdom and Ben Sira's own life are both used toward the same end: "to instruct disciples in

26   For a fuller discussion, see Skehan and Di Lella (1987: 193).

a certain way of life" (Liesen 2000: 70). Ben Sira expects his admonishing activity to be mirrored by those who follow his example. In a more mundane example in chapter 19, Ben Sira encourages the admonishing of neighbors and friends towards the proper use of speech and avoidance of gossip. In this case, one fulfills the law by admonishing (19.16). In 32.14 Ben Sira confirms the importance of instruction/discipline: "the one who seeks God will receive discipline."[27]

The role of admonishing, seen in human action and in the role of personified wisdom, is also ascribed to God. Within the larger concept of God's sovereignty in Ben Sira is a repeated effort to describe God's significance in terms of a wise sage. In response to an aspect of the human condition—fleeting existence and the anxiety of death—Ben Sira describes God as one who guides and teaches: "the mercy of a human is on his or her neighbor, but the mercy of the Lord is on all flesh, teaching, instructing and turning them back, as a shepherd guides his flock" (18.11–12). Randall Argall, in a discussion of Sirach 16.24–17.14 (a hymnic piece comparing the works of heaven and humans), argues that part of the sage's agenda is to claim that the Torah can be understood by perceiving the heavens, in effect projecting "a torah unto the heavens" (Argall 1995: 137). Ben Sira may be thinking similarly in chapter 18: the role of the sage as one who admonishes and tests is projected onto God and the way the divine will is carried out in the human sphere. Ben Sira creates a "sage unto the heavens" by drawing a close parallel between the role of these two entities.

The way Ben Sira projects the image of a sage onto God provides further confirmation of the fact that the concepts of the "latter end" and "testing" should not be conflated in our understanding of his attempts at theodicy. The "latter end" is a painful delay of a deserved reward, whether good or ill. Testing is a divinely instigated, sage-like activity wherein God admonishes and tests fidelity just as a sage—and especially Ben Sira himself—would a pupil. Both are components of how Ben Sira works out his understanding of God's justice in the world, "adjuncts" (Rankin 1936: 83) that helped him cope with and explain the complexities faced in everyday life.

III. Conclusion

Scholars' struggles to explain Ben Sira's argument about retribution and its implications for theodicy are commensurate with those of Ben Sira himself. Precisely what component of Ben Sira's argument comprises an original contribution, if any, is a matter of disagreement. J. Collins claims that the "original and substantial contribution" is the idea that there is a "duality" in creation—i.e., Ben Sira's doctrine of

---

27   From Hebrew manuscript B (Beentjes 1997: 59).

opposites—that serves the purposes of God (1997b: 95).[28] For Argall, Ben Sira's "contribution" is the idea that God's justice is saved for the "opportune time, a time set by God" (1995: 142), at which point the created elements will be used for blessing or wrath (e.g., 39.16, 28–35).[29] Finally, Crenshaw argues that Ben Sira contributes by punishing sinners in the psychological realm; the claim that all are under great anxiety (40.1) is tempered by the fact that this anxiety is "seven times more" for sinners. For Crenshaw this indicates a "flight into psychology and metaphysics" wherein the retribution "manifests itself in the inner life" (1983: 130).[30]

Whether described as "utter futility" (Crenshaw 1983: 127) or as an "unresolved tension" that exhibits a "naiveté" (J. Collins 1997b: 85, 91) on the part of the sage, the explanation offered by Ben Sira remains unsatisfying and perhaps inconsistent (although, to be fair, no biblical theodicy could withstand the phalanx of biblical scholarship and its scrutiny). While Ben Sira has not solved the problem of theodicy, there are several observations that can be made about the way in which he approaches the problem. First, Ben Sira's argument is forged in conversation with previous traditions of Israel. As we have seen, his formulation of retribution corresponds to a retributive ideology—best not called "Deuteronomic"—in which God judges people according to an established norm. Second, Ben Sira seems more interested in being convinced (and convincing others) of certain theological suppositions than with having a completely coherent explanation for evil. In other words, it is more important for him to affirm his beliefs about God (sovereignty), humans (some degree of free will), and creation (its goodness and consistency as a basis for praise), than to have an airtight explanation of the mechanisms of retribution.[31] Within these core convictions we have noted the roles of a person's latter end and testing, both of which allow Ben Sira to make sense of some problematic aspects of existence (2.4; 40.1; 43.13–22) without marginalizing his strong sense of God's control (42.15; 33.12–13) and creative prowess (43.1–12).

The work of this chapter will prove important in what follows. Comparing the book of Tobit to a contemporaneous text like Sirach provides a backdrop against which Tobit's perspectives can better be perceived. Such a comparison will result in some similarities and some differences, but more

---

28   Crenshaw (1983: 129) and Rankin (1936: 35) would also agree with this assessment.

29   The problem with Argall's assessment here is that this is not really an original element on the part of Ben Sira. We noted above that the concept of probationary suffering was one that existed within the book of Deuteronomy itself.

30   This is a point agreed upon by Gammie, who finds the same phenomenon at work in Sir. 14.3–10 (1990: 359).

31   One may also point out that Ben Sira avoids the explanation offered by some of his contemporaries, many of whom were positing eventual retribution in the afterlife, especially in *1 Enoch* (e.g., 1.8; chs. 103–104) and Wisdom of Solomon (e.g., 5.15–17).

specifically will help set the terms of conversation. In particular, Ben Sira consistently discusses his view of retribution in terms of the created order. This observation provides warrant for exploring the created order in Tobit to view the book's view of retribution as well.

Chapter 5

"DEUTERONOMISTIC" OR "STRAIGHTFORWARD RETRIBUTION": INAPT LABELS FOR THE TALE OF TOBIT

Having examined the scholarly and biblical origins of varying theories of retribution in the Hebrew Bible, and having looked closely at the formulation of retribution in Sirach, we are better situated to make some evaluations about this perspective and its purported place in the book of Tobit. Do those scholars who claim Tobit's core perspective as the theory of retribution put forward in the book of Deuteronomy have ample justification for their perspective? The goals of this section are twofold. The first goal is to show that it is an oversimplification to say that the theology of retribution in Tobit is "Deuteronomistic." In some part, this work was anticipated in the previous chapter, which demonstrated how calling Ben Sira's view of retribution "Deuteronomic" is not sufficient. And, second, this chapter will show that straightforward retribution—especially as distilled in much Tobit scholarship—is not an apt label or assessment of the book's theological perspective. Addressing these issues will consist of three parts: re-examining where straightforward retributive language appears in the book of Tobit (namely, on the title character's lips); looking further in the narrative beyond the specific character of Tobit himself (specifically, by examining the language of other major characters); and comparing the theologies expressed in Sirach and Job to that in Tobit. By doing this, it will become clear that there are significant reasons to doubt that the author of Tobit intended to affirm, without qualification, a straightforward retributive ideology based on a correlation between act and consequence.

I. Retribution according to Tobit the Character

The book of Tobit contains strongly retributive theology, focused in the opening chapters on the figure of Tobit. From the outset he describes himself[1] as upright and Torah-abiding. He alone among his kin travels

---

1   From 1.1–3.6 Tobit is narrated in the first person, switching to third person at 3.6 for the remainder of the text. Nowell (1983; 1988) has shown that the perspective of the narrator changes little in the two sections. See chapter two, above, for a more complete discussion.

to Jerusalem.[2] He repeatedly gives proper burial to those of his kin who have died, an activity with a varying degree of danger depending upon who happens to sit on the Assyrian throne. After another burial, an unfortunate encounter with some sparrows, and a spat with his wife, Tobit sobs and prays:

> You are righteous, O Lord,
> and all your deeds are just;
> all your ways are mercy and truth;
> you judge the world.[3]
> And now, O Lord, be mindful of me,
> and look on with care.
> Do not punish me for my sins,
> not even those that are a result of ignorance,
> and not for those of my ancestors
> who sinned against you and refused to listen to your commandments.
> So you handed us over to plundering, exile and death,
> as an example, a byword, a reproach
> in all the nations among whom you scattered us.

(Tob. 3.2–4)

Tobit attempts to explain his situation by way of two different options: his association with the collective guilt of his people and his own unwitting sins. As we will see, neither of these options explains Tobit's situation sufficiently. Up to this point in the narrative, Tobit has been described as righteous. Tobit's prayer suggests otherwise, simultaneously asserting Tobit's guilt from his own transgression and from that of his forebears.[4] Both of these explanations are based on formulations of retribution in Israel's scriptures.

In Deuteronomy, the admonitions to obey and the consequences enacted in the Deuteronomistic History are generally focused on the nation, the people whom God chose. The choice God sets before the people in Deuteronomy is a collective one with group consequences: blessing, great progeny, and long life (Deut. 30.16) or death (30.18). Tobit's prayer asserts that he is caught up in the guilt of the people that produced the exile. Even though Tobit himself is innocent, the deeds of the nation have inadvertently

---

2   This is according to 1.6, although 5.14 indicates otherwise. Those whom Raphael names as his kin are known to Tobit because they used to make the pilgrimage with him to Jerusalem where they would worship together. McCracken essentially calls Tobit's words here a lie, claiming that the discrepancy indicates Tobit's fallibility (1995: 409).

3   The Greek here is σύ κρίνεις τὸν αἰῶνα, but translating αἰῶνα as "eternity" or "age" seems awkward. Most translate with the word "world."

4   Compare this to Sarah's prayer in 3.11–15, in which she brazenly asserts her own innocence: "You know, O Master, that I am innocent of any impure act with a man, and that I have never defiled my own name or my father's name in the land of my exile."

caused his misfortune. Here we may recall the argument of Will Soll, who claimed that the misfortunes experienced by the characters in Tobit are "acute manifestations" of the exile (1989: 225). Similar on this point is Beate Ego (2005), who argues that Tobit needs to be read in a spatial perspective. Acts of charity, adherence to endogamy, and the emphasis on dietary law mediate "God's graceful acting" while in exile (Ego 2005: 52). These pious actions, according to Ego, create stability in the midst of an always-chaotic Diaspora. Such analyses indicate that one should not be surprised that Tobit is engulfed in the collective guilt of the exile.

The problem with Ego and Soll's formulations, and more pointedly, Tobit's own explanations, is that the exilic situation, a cipher for the Diaspora[5] setting of the book, is not necessarily negative. Tobit suggests that his misfortune is the result of his association with the guilt of his people, but it is not clear that the resulting exile causes his troubles. Tobit had some difficulties while in exile, but he profited from it as well. Under Esarhaddon, Tobit worked freely (2.1), and under Shalmaneser, Tobit prospered (1.13–14). Only Sennacherib made life difficult for Tobit (1.15–20). Furthermore, Tobit's blindness comes because of his unclean status and outdoor slumber, a result not tied specifically to exile unless birds do not defecate in the Jewish homeland. Tobit's fortunes are the result of whether or not he lives under a benevolent regime; they are not produced by exile per se. Tobit's situation is similar to that of Daniel, who experienced what J. Collins calls "the changing humors of Gentile kings, who are sometimes threatening, sometimes benign" (2005: 27). Finally, later in the narrative, Raphael reveals that he had been sent to test Tobit (12.14), which does not factor into Tobit's own explanation of his situation. The retribution Tobit experiences requires a more complex explanation than Tobit's being washed in the wake of the sin that eventuated in exile.

Perhaps, then, Tobit is guilty of individual transgression (e.g., ἁμαρτίαις μου in 3.3). Individual retribution occasionally applies to certain of Israel's kings. For instance, Jeroboam is told that he is not like the faithful servant David, who kept the commandments and followed God with his whole heart. Jeroboam is worse than all before because he made idols that provoked God (1 Kgs 14.5–9). Similar words of woe are pronounced to Ahab in 1 Kings 21. Tobit prays that he might not be held responsible for his deeds (3.1), even those that are done out of ignorance (ἀγνόημα, 3.3). If Tobit has committed some unwitting sin—a fact about which the narrative itself is silent—he is far from the typically wicked person experiencing retribution, like Jeroboam or Ahab. The question remains, then: Why has Tobit, as an individual, come to experience tragedy despite his good deeds and upright character? Anathea

5   Because its story takes place outside the land of Israel, the book is most commonly thought to have an origin in the Diaspora and to deal with issues related to Diaspora life. See chapter two for a discussion of the various proposals. There are some, however, who think the book was composed within Palestinian Judaism, a view most recently supported by Fitzmyer (2003: 54) and Dimant (2009a).

Portier-Young, in an article discussing suffering and its alleviation in Tobit, claims that "Deuteronomistic" retribution does not "purport to explain the unique suffering of individuals" (2001: 37). She suggests that there is not sufficient warrant to proceed by analogy from nation to person. Whether her statement is accurate or not, it warrants asking a different question: Must the book of Tobit's perspective be constrained by a preconceived notion of "Deuteronomistic" theology?[6] Here the overly simplistic formulations of Deuteronomism, when assumed as the core perspective of the book of Tobit, begin to impinge on free inquiry into its theological complexity. Stuart Weeks has recently come to a similar conclusion, claiming that it is "astonishing that recent scholarship on Tobit has become dominated by a paradigm of the book as a quintessentially Deuteronomic work" (2011: 390).

a. Moses and Tobit

A comparison between Tobit and Ben Sira suggests the appropriateness of applying straightforward retributive justice to individuals, despite the claim of Portier-Young above that such retribution only works corporately. While Ben Sira does have the nation in mind at times (e.g., 24.8), the nature of Ben Sira's wisdom and instruction to individuals about how best to live their lives orients his work, on the whole, toward individuals. The instruction is given specifically to individuals (e.g., 15.20–27; 21.1–10), and discussion of retribution has the same focus (15.11–20; 18.1–13). The interest in individual retribution in the book of Tobit is especially evident in how its title character emulates the figure of Moses from Numbers and Deuteronomy.[7]

In Tob. 1.6–7, Tobit is the only one of his people who obeys the law of Moses[8] in bringing the first-fruits of the flock and grain to Jerusalem.[9] This action is a direct fulfillment of Moses' command to the people in Deuteronomy chapter 12:

> Then to the place which the Lord, your God, chooses as the dwelling place for his name you shall bring all the offering I command you: your holocausts and sacrifices, your tithes and personal contributions, and every special offer-

---

6   These assumptions are akin to what Robert Kraft calls the "tyranny of canonical assumptions" (2007: 10–18). His point is more specifically about references to ancient texts based on uncritical assumptions about ancient canonical attitudes (e.g., references to "the Septuagint" that are too broad). Within the narrow field of Tobit scholarship, assumptions about the book's Deuteronomistic viewpoint have become tyrannically canonical to the point that all theological assessments of the book begin and end with it.

7   Some theoretical basis on which imitation may function is offered by Duyndam (2004: 7–24).

8   See the helpful essay on this topic by Gamberoni (1977: 227–42).

9   One can perhaps see an analogous interest in *Jub.* 4.26, in which Mount Zion is described as one of God's four holy places on the earth, along with Eden, Sinai, and the "mountain of the East" (perhaps the mountain Qater mentioned in 4.25).

ing you have vowed to the Lord. Take care not to offer up your holocausts in any place you fancy, but offer them up in the place which the Lord chooses from among your tribes; there you shall make whatever offerings I enjoin upon you. (Deut. 12.11, 13–14, NAB)

Such action also relates to the commands in Exodus 12–13, with its emphasis on first-fruits (see also Exod. 23.19; Lev. 23.9–12; *Jub.* 15.1–4). Tobit, though, is depicted as more than an observant person. Tobit introduces his journey to Jerusalem in 1.6 by saying, καγὼ μονώτατος[10] ἐπορευόμην πολλάκις εἰς ἱεροσόλυμα (and I alone used to go often to Jerusalem).[11] Contrasting with Tobit are his relatives and fellow Jews as described in 1.10, who lose their distinctiveness because they fail to keep food regulations: καὶ πάντες οἱ ἀδελφοί μου καὶ οἱ ἐκ τοῦ γένους μου ἤσθιον ἐκ τῶν ἄρτων τῶν ἐθνῶν (and all my relatives and those of my descent ate the bread of the gentiles). These verses describe Tobit as one who is distinct from the rest of his people, although he mentions that his grandmother Deborah taught him how to tithe (1.8), which suggests that Tobit was not the *only* righteous person left (Weeks 2011: 392).

The description of Tobit's actions—his uniqueness among his kin— resembles the place of Moses in Numbers 11 and Deuteronomy 1. The use of μόνος evokes Num. 11.14, a verse in which Moses complains to God: οὐ δυνήσομαι ἐγὼ μόνος φέρειν τὸν λαὸν τοῦτον (I alone am not able to bear the burden of this people).[12] The beginning of Deuteronomy picks up this theme of Moses' singularity by recalling Moses' words from Numbers, "At that time I said to you, 'Alone [μόνος], I am unable to carry you'" (Deut. 1.9). The theme is repeated a few verses later, but with a more negative connotation: "But how can I alone [μόνος] bear your trouble, your resistance, and your lawsuits?" (Deut. 1.12).[13] Tobit alone bears the responsibility for journeying to Jerusalem, a singularity *vis-à-vis* the Jewish people that recalls Moses' singular burden of the people.

Although Tobit had been living an upright life, stating in 1.3 that "I, Tobit, have walked all the days of my life on the paths of truth" (ὁδοῖς ἀληθείας ἐπορευόμην), he claims the opposite in 3.5: "nor have we trodden

10   In AB μόνος is used instead of μονώτατος.

11   It would be helpful at this point if portions of Tob. 1.1–10 were available among the Qumran manuscripts in order to facilitate an analysis in the Semitic languages. Unfortunately, the earliest portion of Tobit available is 1.17.

12   Although not posited as the original language, the Greek of Tobit does echo the LXX. This could be the intention of Tobit's Greek translator. The MT at this point, however, uses the word בד (לא־אוכל אנכי לבדי לשאת את־כל־העם הזה), which indicates that the echo could have existed in the Semitic original.

13   In the MT, both Deut. 1.9 and 1.11 have the same form of בד (לבדי) as does Num. 11.14. The characterization of Moses does not seem altogether consistent between Numbers and Deuteronomy. Moses' exasperation and lack of patience seems to be softened in the account in Deuteronomy.

the paths of truth" (οὐκ ἐπορεύθημεν ἀληθινῶς). In these contrasting verses, the same verb, πορεύομαι, is used to assert and then deny Tobit's upright character. The shift from first person singular in 1.3 to first person plural in 3.5 is significant. Tobit's singularity in righteousness cannot escape the collective guilt of his people, a sentiment found in the Torah (i.e., Noah's exile-like time in the ark because of humanity's wickedness) and in post-exilic thought (see Isa. 59.12; Ezra 9.6–7).[14] Tobit has a strong "sense of his innocence," and one senses that "there should be a better fate for people like Tobit" (Soll 1989: 224). Nevertheless, his fate is the same as for all of his people: guilt and exile.

Moses shares the same fate in Deuteronomy. In chapter 1 God swears out of anger that no one will look upon the land, except for Caleb and his sons (1.34–36). The evil generation has ramifications for Moses as well: "The Lord was angry with me because of you and said, 'There is no way you will enter there'" (1.37). Later, in chapter 3, Moses pleads with God for entry into the land. Moses reports God's response: "But the Lord was angry with me on your account and would not listen to me. And the Lord said to me, 'Let this be enough! Do not speak these words any longer'" (3.26). In both instances from the beginning of Deuteronomy, Moses is denied entrance to the land because of the people.[15]

After asserting Tobit's singularity in keeping the law of Moses and his burden of collective guilt despite that obedience, the end of Tobit's prayer confirms his emulation of Moses:

> And now, do with me according to your pleasure
> and command to take my spirit from me
> so that I might depart from the face of the earth and become earth.
> For it is better for me to die than to live.
> For I heard reproaches and lies and there is much grief with me.
> Lord, command that I be released from this compulsion.[16]
> Release me to the eternal place
> and do not turn away your face, Lord, from me
> for it is better for me to die
> than to see so much necessity in my life and to hear reproaches.
>
> (Tob. 3.6)

14   Moore (1996: 139).
15   Numbers 20 depicts a different situation in that Moses and Aaron are told they will not enter the land because they did not trust God. Deut. 32.48–52 seems to indicate similarly: Moses is denied entry because he broke faith with God, referring to events in Numbers 20.
16   The Greek word here is ἀνάγκης, which the NAB and NRSV translate as "anguish" or "misery." It does, at times, seem to mean something akin to misery (see Wis. 17.16; 1 Sam. 22.2). It can also simply have the sense of destiny, as is the case in Wis. 19.4 and *4 Macc.* 8.24. The Latin here (*necessitate/necessitatem*) can carry the same connotation of difficulty or straits. I have chosen here to leave my translation rather neutral. The same word is repeated in the last line, which I translate as "necessity."

Tobit's response seems extreme. He has experienced some opposition and suffering: blindness, mockery, and subsistence from his wife.[17] Things have taken an unfortunate turn. The reference to the "eternal place" probably does not indicate a sense of life after death. In Tob. 3.10 and 13.2 this place is referred to simply as ᾅδης (Hades), but there is no indication that the author views this as a place of reward or punishment. It simply connotes the end of life, entrance to the grave, and a place from which one does not return.[18] Consistent with a simple doctrine of retribution, Tobit cannot conceive of his reward coming at any time other than during his current life, even if he experiences a "painful delay" (Crenshaw 1983: 126). At this point we can recall the retributive theology as expressed by Ben Sira. Ben Sira strongly affirms the idea that one's deeds will bear proper fruit during one's lifetime. Even when the correspondence between deed and action appears to be delayed, one will receive the proper reward at the end of life: "at the end of one's life one's actions are revealed. Call no one happy before his death; a person is known by how he ends" (11.27b–28). Tobit's expectation for treatment from God commensurate with his righteousness coordinates well with the view of retribution in the book of Sirach. What Tobit eschews, however, is the endurance that Ben Sira also recommends (e.g., 2.7, 10).

Rather than endure to the end, Tobit prays for death. Moore (1996: 140) points to a spate of characters in Israel's history who also pray for death, including Job, Elijah, and Jonah, but he does not mention Moses.[19] Tobit's call for death is reminiscent of Moses in Numbers 11. After Moses declares he can no longer carry the people alone, he says to God: "If this is the way you will deal with me, then kill me by destruction, if I find mercy with you, that I might not see my affliction" (Num. 11.15). Moses finds himself so distraught over bearing the weight of his people that he asks God to kill him. The burden results in a prayer for death. The parallel with Tobit seems substantial. In the book of Tobit, the character Tobit alone remains righteous

---

17   Exegetes have found many interesting ways to read Tobit's conversation with Sarah in 2.11–14. I agree with the assessment that a modern reader may find fault in Tobit's response and suspicion of his wife. I would not go so far as Bow and Nickelsburg, however, in saying that Tobit's response indicates "a hint of self righteousness" (1991: 135–9). Although not consistent with modern sensibilities, and although there is always a "risk of approaching the characterization from too modern a perspective" (Weeks 2011: 393), it seems possible that Tobit's having to rely on his wife for survival could have been considered another aspect of suffering. See also Levine's interpretation of the different ways the narrative treats male and female characters (1992a: 105–19).

18   So Moore (1996: 140). Beyerle (2005b: 71–88) offers a slightly different perspective, arguing that there may be a hint of an afterlife in Tobit. He claims that the whole story should be re-read in the context of the temporal and spatial eschatology of chs. 13–14 (87–8).

19   He points to Job (Job 7.15), Elijah (1 Kgs 19.4), and Jonah (Jon. 4.3). Fitzmyer (2003: 145) does mention Moses as among those figures in Israel's scriptures who pray for death.

among all the people, suffers as a result of their guilt, and subsequently prays for death.

Finally, one specific Old Latin manuscript may hint at the evocation of Moses in the early chapters of Tobit's narrative. In 2.6 Tobit remembers the words of the prophet Amos that were spoken in Bethel. The quotation, from Amos 8.10, is part of an oracle against Israel, whose merchants wanted the festivals to end soon so they could resume their business of exploiting the poor (8.4–6). God speaks, claiming, "I will turn your feasts into mourning and all your songs into a dirge" (8.10a). In the Greek recensions of Tobit the first person is changed to a passive: "Your festivals will be turned . . ." (στραφήσονται ὑμῶν αἱ ἑορταὶ), a change also exhibited in the Vulgate and Old Latin (*conuertentur*). Codex Reginensis, which is a copy of the Vulgate except for Tob. 1.1–6.12 where it is a version of the Old Latin,[20] introduces the quotation of Amos differently: *memoratus sum uerborum prophetae, quod loquutus est ad Moysen in Bethel*. The addition of *ad Moysen* ("to Moses") here is unique and seems strange, but there may be some logic behind its addition in Reginensis.

Subtle aspects of the text in Amos 8 could suggest an association with Moses' activities in the Pentateuch. Amos 8.8 talks of the land trembling (רגז), which is used in Moses' song in Exod. 15.14. Amos 8.9 says that, on that day, God will make the sun go down, darkening the earth in broad daylight, which could recall the darkness of the ninth plague in Exod. 10.21–29, during which the people of Egypt could not execute their daily activities. In a scenario where Tobit's plight is brought into close alignment with that of Moses, the words of Amos might be all the more poignant for Tobit if they were originally meant for Moses, as Reginensis suggests. There is not sufficient proof to conclude that the author of Tobit gravitated toward the quotation in Amos because its larger context has resonances with the story of Moses, but it remains an intriguing possibility. It is nevertheless helpful to notice that the convener of Reginensis might have noticed the emulation of Moses in the beginning chapters of Tobit and included the reference to Moses in 2.6 in order to make the resonances stronger.

b. Initial Conclusions

The author of Tobit clearly seems invested in expressing a straightforward retributive theology. While many scholars would call the theology put forward by Tobit the character "Deuteronomistic," we have resisted such terminology here.[21] The depiction of Tobit's predicament draws

---

20   Weeks, Gathercole, and Stuckenbruck (2004: 25–6). The relationship of Reginensis to other Old Latin texts is one that they claim is still "open," although they do call attention to its similarity at times to the so-called "Third-Greek" recension in the few places where they overlap (26). See also Gathercole (2006: 5–11) and Weeks (2006).

21   Recall the above discussion of purported Deuteronomic/istic theology in Tobit, exemplified especially by Di Lella (1979: 380–9) and Soll (1989: 209–31).

upon a wider swath of scriptural influences than just Deuteronomic/istic texts. The way Tobit's character emulates Moses is based upon texts not only from Deuteronomy, but also from Numbers, which is not a specifically Deuteronomistic text. Furthermore, the type of straightforward retribution that is often labeled "Deuteronomistic" can be found outside of Deuteronomistic texts (e.g., Gen. 6–9; Pss. 38, 79). Finally, as we explored in the previous chapter, Deuteronomy itself is too complex to equate its view of retribution solely with a sense of simple, one-to-one retribution dependent upon human action (Gammie 1970: 1–12).

Nevertheless, parts of Tobit express a straightforward retributive theology. In the words of Tobit the character, this retribution is the result of both the guilt of his ancestors and his own individual guilt. As was shown above, Tobit's attribution of his guilt to his participation in the exile is not an adequate explanation with respect to other events in the narrative. It also does not square particularly well with Deuteronomy, especially those parts to which Di Lella points (Weeks 2011: 395, n. 13). The same could be said of his attribution of his situation to his individual guilt: the narrative events—which claim Tobit's innocence—contradict Tobit's own statements about his guilt. In sum, Tobit attributes his situation to his own guilt and that of his ancestors, although the narrative events of the book of Tobit do not necessarily support his claims. We now turn to a closer examination of how this straightforward retributive theology is limited, within the book of Tobit, to the title character.

II. Looking beyond the Title Character

After Tobit's prayer in chapter 3, the story switches immediately to a grieved Sarah, distraught over a demon that afflicts her and the mocking her father must endure as a result.[22] Sarah contemplates suicide but decides that such an action would only compound her father's grief. It would be better to have God kill her. In her prayer, however, she brazenly asserts her own innocence: "you know, O Master [δέσποτα], that I am pure of any uncleanliness from a man, and I have never defiled my name or my father's name in the land of my captivity" (3.14–15).[23] Sarah does not suggest any of the reasons for her misfortune that Tobit

---

22   Levine (1992a: 105–19) points out that Sarah does not actually make reference to the demon, and may even be ignorant of it. Her lament instead focuses on the derision her situation has brought to her family, and her father in particular.

23   Levine (1992a) has shown convincingly the disparity between Tobit and Sarah. Tobit is paradigmatic for the exile and the return, while Sarah may not even have full knowledge of her own situation. Levine summarizes the patriarchal nature of the text by suggesting that men try to alleviate the loss of control in a Diaspora context by subjecting women to their control: "in captivity, he can assert his freedom and his self-identity by depicting the other as in captivity to him" (117).

enumerated. She only knows that she does not deserve what has happened to her, and she tells God as much.[24]

Chapter 4 returns to Tobit. He dispatches his son to retrieve some money he remembered having deposited in Rages. This plot development is accompanied by a long section of proverbial wisdom that Tobit imparts to his son (4.1–20). The wisdom asserts the importance of righteousness, almsgiving, and endogamy, all of which are underpinned by a straightforward sense of retribution:[25]

> Do not turn your face away from any of the poor, and from you God's face surely will not be turned. (4.7)[26]

> If you serve God, it will be paid back to you [ἀποδοθήσεταί σοι]. (4.14)

The instruction concludes with the following statement:

> Do not fear, my child, because we have become poor. You will have much good if you fear God, avoid all sin, and do good things before the Lord your God. (4.21)

As the story shifts in chapter 5 and focuses on the travails of Tobias as he thwarts a great fish, expels a demon, marries Sarah, and returns with wealth (all with the help of Raphael), the sense of straightforward retribution and rhetoric fades from the story. Characters continue to exhort God to specific action or react to situations with words of praise, but the rhetoric of these exclamations seems limited to wonder and blessing. Raguel asks that Tobias and Sarah may be granted peace and prosperity (7.12). Sarah's mother, Edna, asks that the Lord might give her daughter joy in place of grief (7.17). When Tobit and Sarah pray on their wedding night they ask for happiness and old age (8.7). At the expulsion of the demon, Raguel blesses God for this miraculous event and asks that the children might be granted mercy, deliverance, and happy lives (8.17), although one wonders if he is simply relieved to have avoided burying another potential son-in-law. The story is narrated in such a way that the simple, straightforward retribution based on human action is associated specifically with the character of Tobit.

---

24   Levine (1992a) argues that Sarah's prayer lacks the paradigmatic elements of Tobit's prayer because she is not a man. A woman was not able to represent the nation in the way that a man was. On the other hand, if Tobit's theological explanation of his plight turns out to be simplistic, Sarah's character should perhaps be commended for resisting a simple doctrine of retribution to explain her own situation.

25   Macatangay (2011) has offered a robust assessment of the role of the sapiential sections of Tobit in the overall narrative. While he notes that there are ways in which the book of Tobit admits the "weakness" of a close connection between act and consequence (246), he does, ultimately, seem to think the book intends to suggest that "God truly does protect the virtuous" (248).

26   This reading is from AB, because of the lacuna in 4.7–19 in S.

The characters within the story reinforce this conclusion: references to Tobit within the story world further index him with the straightforward retributive perspective.[27] Tobit's wife throws his own ideology back at him: "Where are your acts of mercy and where is your righteousness? Behold, these things are known about you! [ταῦτα μετὰ σοῦ γνωστά ἐστιν]" (2.14). Anna's claim that Tobit's righteousness is known to others is confirmed in Raguel's indignation over Tobit's plight: "What a wretched and bad thing that such a righteous and charitable [ποιῶν ἐλεημοσύνας] man is blinded" (7.7). The interpretation of Raguel's statement here is dependent upon tone of voice. Is he sincere, or are his eyes rolling into the back of his head in a mock because he knows Tobit's theology could never square with reality? As Weeks notes, "Tobit's self-perception sits uncomfortably beside the comments of others" (2011: 392). Weeks comes to the conclusion that the attributions of "Deuteronomism" to the book of Tobit are deficient partly because the author is "driven more by the requirements of characterization and plot development" than by the inspiration of a specific ideology (398). This certainly may be true, but Weeks extends this ultimate interest in characterization and plot to suggest that the book may not even offer a coherent depiction of God (400). This pushes the matter too far. Close attention to the details will reveal that characterization is certainly important, but that the characterization is in service of an agenda meant to show the deficiencies of the straightforward sense of retribution, and, ultimately, to offer a much more complex view of retribution.

Sincere and specific straightforward retributive rhetoric based on human action does not return to the story until Tobit himself does. After his sight is restored, Tobit blesses God and proclaims that God should be praised, "because it was he who scourged me" (11.15).[28] Most English translations of Tobit add the phrase "and he had mercy on me," following the Old Latin (*et ipse misertus est mei*), AB (καὶ ἠλέησάς με), and the Vulgate (*et tu saluasti me*) instead of S, which has no reference to God's mercy here. One scholar has gone so far as to call this Tobit's "Deuteronomistic Creed" (Moore 1996: 263). While the term "Deuteronomistic" is problematic—as previous sections of this study have shown—the important thing to note here is that this simple, straightforward sense of retribution particularly characterizes Tobit himself. Tobit the character repeatedly and consistently declares that God repays according to human action, whether on an individual or corporate level. His words in 11.15 certainly recall his initial prayer in 3.1–6 in their insistence on a one-to-one correlation between act and consequence, repaid by God based on human action.

---

27   Chatman (1978: 33) speaks of how existents are "indexed." An index is an event that either exposes character (e.g., John was angry), or mediates character (e.g., Unfortunately, John was angry). Existents are indexed by a process of attributing traits to them.

28   4Q200 fragment 5 here has only retained one word from Tobit's exclamations in 11.14–15, what is probably בני (my son) in v. 14.

The expressions of straightforward retribution, then, in the book of Tobit are associated only with the blinded title character. The narrator does nothing to ratify Tobit's rhetoric,[29] and the remaining characters do not seem to use it to explain other predicaments in the story (of which there are many). Tobit's blindness is paradigmatic for the action of God hidden in the story.[30] The reader knows more than the characters, which creates irony.[31] Scholars who notice the irony of Tobit's blindness to Raphael's (and God's) role do not extend the blindness to encompass Tobit's theological explanations. They instead take the main character's statements to be in concert with the perspective of the author. Such does not need to be the case. David McCracken argues that Tobit has misinterpreted his circumstances and engaged in incorrect self-pity as a *"flawed* paragon" (1995: 408). According to McCracken, there are "flaws in Tobit's character that he does not recognize when he narrates his story" (408). Although McCracken has made this observation, he does not extend Tobit's flaws to a lack of theological comprehension. He thinks Tobit is simply self-righteous. On the contrary, not only do Tobit's eyes not work, but the theology he espouses proves to be equally as blind. If Tobit's inability to perceive extended to his own theological explanation of what happened to him, the irony would be all the more acute. Tobit's ignorance of Raphael's mission would be compounded by his fundamentally disordered and incorrect explanation of where his misfortune came from and its eventual alleviation. In McCracken's terminology, "the ego-narrator is himself fallible, just as the character is more obviously fallible" (409). In this scenario, Tobit's expressions of straightforward retribution and his emulation of Moses are more about characterization that establishes a perspective the author intends to undermine and make more complex than about the author's ultimate theological point.

a. The "Whole Truth"

The one exception—the only expression of straightforward retribution not coming from Tobit himself—comes in Raphael's speech in 12.6–10. In this speech, Raphael claims that those who give alms will have a full life, and those who do sin and unrighteousness are warlike against

---

29   According to McCracken, the author has narrated the story in such a way as intentionally to "reveal incongruities" (1995: 410). One could perhaps say that the way the story ends, with the return of Tobit's sight, the punishment for Nineveh, etc., suggests a reinforcement of Tobit's formulations of retribution. The issue of the ending of the story and its relationship to straightforward retribution will be taken up later in this study.

30   This is an obvious point and one mentioned by most studies of Tobit as the central irony in the story. For example, Nowell (1983) states that, in Tobit, the "characters' perception of their own lives is an impenetrable mixture of knowledge and ignorance" (251). See also Portier-Young (2005), who claims that Tobit "languishes in the dark, unable to discern God's plan" (19).

31   The source of irony in the book is clear, coming from what Nowell calls a "disparity of understanding" that provides the "requisite context for irony" (1983: 251).

their own soul (πολέμιοί εἰσιν τῆς ἑαυτῶν ψυχῆς). This statement, which seems to support Tobit's theological perspective of straightforward retribution, is not the end of Raphael's announcement, however. Immediately following his recitation of simple, straightforward retributive justice, Raphael says: "I now reveal [ὑποδείξω] to you the whole truth [πᾶσαν τὴν ἀλήθειαν]." The strong implication is that even what Raphael had just said is not really the whole truth. More to the point, what Raphael reveals is that God's role in Tobit's ordeal was different from that which Tobit had perceived.

A major component of Raphael's revelation is the fact that God has been behind the action of the story the whole time. In 12.14 Raphael divulges two pieces of critical information heretofore hidden from the other characters in the story. First, Raphael reveals that it was he who presented[32] Tobit and Sarah's memorial of prayer (τὸ μνημόσυνον τῆς προσευχῆς) before God, which resulted in his being sent to heal them. This refers back to the scene described in 3.16–17. Raphael arrives in the narrative during a description of the heavenly realm, at which point he is dispatched to heal Tobit and Sarah (ἰάσασθαι τοὺς δύο). Raphael's healing activity is indicative of the role he actually plays in the story. He encourages Tobias to grab hold of the fish that provides medicinal agents that chase away the demon and remove Tobit's blindness (6.1–9). Raphael also binds Asmodeus in upper Egypt (8.3), which fits his role as healer.

Second, Raphael says that he was sent to test Tobit (ἀπέσταλμαι ἐπὶ σὲ πειράσαι σε). What Raphael means by testing, however, is not clear from previous events. When looking at the narrative as a whole, there is no indication that Raphael tests Tobit.[33] Raphael plays no role in Tobit's initial troubles and does not enter the story until 3.17, after Tobit has gone blind. Is it possible for Raphael to be sent to test and, at the same time (ἅμα), be sent to heal? Raphael's double mission as expressed in 12.14 seems to have been problematic enough that the Greek AB textual tradition removes the reference to testing altogether, but the reference's existence in S and the Old Latin indicates that it likely is the best original reading.

Sirach also provides a helpful contrast at this point. In Ben Sira's wisdom theology, the concept of testing was used on several occasions with a clear function: to test an individual's initial fidelity. Testing was important to the sage's activity in general, was prevalent in Deuteronomy, and was also projected onto God as a way of understanding divine activity. If the author of Tobit had a similar understanding of the role of testing as an auxiliary component of retributive theology, the events as narrated do not seem to demonstrate it. The concept of testing, which appeared repeatedly in Sirach,

---

32   NRSV here reads "brought and read," following the OL (*et legi*), but S has only ἐγὼ προσήγαγον (I presented).

33   The fact that testing seems to stand out here as a particularly inapt explanation for previous events in the story is also noted by Weeks (2011: 400).

makes only a strange, undeveloped cameo appearance in Tobit in 12.14. Weeks makes the interesting proposal that the reference to testing may have been intended as a way of glossing over the deep theological problems raised by God's role earlier in the story, namely that at times God is intimately involved in individuals' lives (e.g., 1.13), but later allows tragedy to happen and seems "conspicuously absent" (2011: 400). More to the immediate point, however, is that in the formulations of retribution offered by Tobit the character, the idea that God may be testing him does not enter his purview. Raphael's testing makes more complex the view of retribution previously delineated by Tobit the character, whether or not it squares well with the earlier narration.

Despite Tobit's rhetoric—the claim that he is being punished for his unwitting sins and those of his kin—it is actually not clear where the troubles in the story come from. As noted above, Tobit's trouble does not emerge directly as a result of his life in exile. His success instead depends on the disposition of specific regimes. Nor does Tobit's blindness come as a direct result of transgression, whether his or that of his kin. His propensity to bury his kin properly leads to his unclean status, which presumably is why he has to sleep outside, although no extant law specifies such an action.[34] Birds and incompetent doctors cause the blindness (2.10). Some commentators point to a story in the Babylonian Talmud (*b. Pesah* 111a) that warns against the indiscretion of sleeping outside because whoever does so will have to bear the consequences.[35] Whether such a statement helps explain Tobit's predicament is difficult to know, but it indicates that, despite what Tobit himself says, his misfortune may result from little more than what J. Collins calls a "simple indiscretion" (2005: 28). Although I will propose an alternate source for Tobit's scatological misfortune and other opposition in the narrative later in this study, at this point it will suffice to observe that if the book of Tobit's intention were to ratify and encourage a straightforward retributive theology, one would expect Tobit's blindness to have been the result of inappropriate human action, whether from Tobit himself or the nation as a whole. Tobit's emulation of Moses could perhaps indicate a straightforward explanation of his misfortune. This emulation, however, seems to be intended to reinforce

---

34   Exactly what type of activity the reference to washing in 2.9 refers to (i.e., whether it was ritualistic or hygienic) is not explained. The reason Tobit sleeps outside is left similarly ambiguous, despite many modern attempts at explanation (for a review, see Moore [1996: 130]), although it is likely that staying outside would have prevented transmitting a ritually impure status to others in the house. Moore's judgment here seems appropriate: that the author does not want the reader to get "bogged down" with questions of protocol, and instead wants to communicate "the ironic fact that Tobit's blindness occurred when he was piously celebrating Pentecost and was selflessly burying a helpless corpse" (130).

35   The saying, as quoted by F. Zimmerman (1958: 57), reads as follows: "He who sleeps in the shadow of a single palm tree in a courtyard, and who sleeps in the shadow of the moon, has his own blood on his head." This saying is also noted by Moore (1996: 130) and J. Collins (2005: 28).

his character as one whose purview is dominated by a simple formulation of retribution, rather than to supply a realistic explanation of the genesis of his misfortune in the narrative itself.

Before proceeding, it may be helpful to summarize the three major observations made above:

1. Tobit, the character, attributes his own situation to guilt within the framework of a straightforward sense of retribution.

2. Other characters in the story, however, seem to operate outside of the strict confines of a theological formulation such as Tobit's.

3. The role of Raphael in the narrative and what he reveals about God creates an epistemological gap between Tobit the character and the reader. This gap allows the narrator to critique Tobit's theological formulations by way of narrative events and statements that offer conclusions contrary to Tobit's.

III. A Comparison with Job and Sirach

The straightforward retribution based on human action in Sirach, despite all of its emendations,[36] affirms a basic doctrine that does not allow God to be culpable for misfortune and places the blame on individuals: "if you choose, you can keep his commandment; it is fidelity to do his will" (15.15). For Ben Sira, a person's deeds will show their true worth at some point in her or his lifetime. Ben Sira has a strong doctrine of God that has significant implications for the created order. God clearly judges individuals (16.11b; 18.1–2; 23.18–21), but this judgment is built into the structure of the cosmos. God has ordered creation and made it an entity that works according to God's systematic intentions (16.22–28); creation never ceases from its tasks (16.25b). One task of creation is to function in the delivery of judgment. The elements of creation are good for those who are good and bad for those who are bad (39.27). The elements of creation do not deviate from God's command. When destruction must occur, God can call upon the sea to punish and appease God's anger.

In Job, we see some differences from Ben Sira, but one significant similarity as well. Terence Fretheim coordinates the perspective of Job, his friends, and God with creation theology. Job and his friends want to assert that "the world runs like a machine, so God does not act in freedom, but only reacts within a tightly woven creational system" (2005: 228). In Job, Fretheim argues, God responds by saying that "creation is not so rigidly fixed and God's relationship to that creation is not that of a micromanager"

---

36   Recall here the previously discussed ways (chapter four above) in which Ben Sira attempted to explain his position, with theories of a "latter end" and the dichotomy between human freedom and God's determination of one's path.

(228). On this point, Job and Ben Sira may disagree, in so far as Ben Sira wants to uphold the more tightly woven mechanistic view of retribution. In Job, God asserts a scenario that challenges both Job and his friends: Job's description of the world as non-mechanistic is essentially accurate, but he errs in not realizing that this is "precisely the kind of world God intended" (235). For Fretheim, Job's travails are thus attributable to natural evil; "to have elements of such disorder and insecurity is precisely the kind of world God wanted, for God did not intend the world to be a machine" (237). Fretheim's explanation of Job, although it offers a nuanced understanding of the type of world God created (i.e., one where natural evil is a built-in possibility), nevertheless attributes misfortune to a divinely intended created state of affairs. The authors of Job and Ben Sira may disagree about the disposition of the created order and its effects, but they share a more basic agreement: the created order is responsible for the way things are and it exists this way because God intended it to be so.

If we return to Tobit, with regard to the origin of misfortune, the reader is forced to read between the lines. In Job, the reader knows immediately where the suffering comes from (Job 1.1–2.10). In Tobit, this is not the case. Although privy to Raphael's real identity, the reader is not fully informed as to the source of Tobit's misfortune, even if given enough information to know that Tobit's own explanations are not altogether accurate. Tobit is not the only character in this story to experience difficulties. In chapter 3 we learn of Sarah's affliction: a demon who kills her husbands when they enter the bridal chamber on their wedding night. There have been seven such husbands dispatched by Asmodeus by the time Tobias hears of the story. In chapter 6 Tobias, accompanied by Raphael, is accosted by a great fish that jumps out of the Tigris River and attempts to devour him for no apparent reason. Treatments of the book of Tobit that emphasize its "Deuteronomistic" theology often do not venture to explain these oppositions in the story. When discussions of these elements of the story are proffered, they are often explained as vestigial remains of Tobit's folk-tale *Vorlage*.

If the story of Tobit were intended to reinforce the idea that humans are responsible—by way of their obedience—for their wellbeing in life, why would a demon and a fish afflict the central characters? It is not immediately clear whether or not the book of Tobit intends to affirm the idea seen in Ben Sira that the natural state of the created order explains retribution. According to Ben Sira, God intended creation to act as a vehicle of judgment for the wicked, but Tobit, Tobias, and Sarah should not be counted among those ranks. The text is very clear about their righteousness and the undeserved state of their situations. The misfortune of these three characters contradicts a straightforward formulation of retribution based on human action. These characters have done nothing apparent that could have resulted in their suffering. While Ben Sira proclaims a well-ordered creation that consistently does God's bidding, the situations of Tobit, Tobias, and Sarah call forth a created order that is comparably unruly. Misfortune arises from an unruly or unstable created order that allows birds to afflict Tobit, a fish to attack Tobias, and a demon to accost Sarah.

Some would suggest that Tobit, Tobias, and Sarah simply need to await their latter end. As we saw in the previous chapter, this does play a role in Ben Sira's formulation of straightforward retributive justice. As Moore states in his commentary with regard to the ending of Tobit, the Deuteronomic principle was still "intact" because of the reversal of the characters' situations by the end of the story. The help that comes to Tobit and Sarah represents "divine assurance of other more wonderful things to come" (1996: 298). The ending, however, remains a work in progress; it is decidedly "unfinished" (Nickelsburg 1988b: 60). Tobit dies well and is able to pass on what he has learned to his son. Tobias rejoices over the destruction of Nineveh. The core problem that spurred the plot in the first place, however—an exilic setting for Tobit and his kin—has not been resolved. It is far from clear that Tobit and the other characters simply need to have the patience prescribed by Ben Sira, until the point when their fortunes in life will finally be commensurate with their righteousness.

Since the suffering of the characters in Tobit is undeserved, does Job provide a better parallel?[37] One could perhaps explain the misfortune in Tobit as akin to that of Job, especially through the lens provided by Fretheim (2005). Perhaps in Tobit, like in Job, "the world does not run like a machine, with a tight causal weave; it has elements of randomness and chaos, of strangeness and wildness" (Fretheim 2005: 244). The problem with such an explanation has to do with the resolution of the misfortune in Tobit. As noted above, both Job and Ben Sira, although differing on the disposition of the created order, both view retribution and/or the experience of misfortune as something built into the cosmos. Job's misfortune and restoration are a result of the way God intended creation to be. The resolution in the book of Tobit, however, only comes as a result of a significant divine intrusion into the workings of reality. The three problems (blindness, big fish, demon) are alleviated because of an otherworldly intrusion into the human and created realms in the form of Raphael and his divine mission. The retribution evinced is not a natural *Tun-Ergehen Zusammmenhang* (connection between act and consequence) wherein God plays a limited role, nor is it straightforward retribution based on human action, i.e., that often labeled "Deuteronomic" by most scholars. The need for Raphael's mission of healing seems to go beyond divine dealings as assumed in the formulations of both Job and Ben Sira. In Tobit the created order can no longer be counted upon to act the way God intends.

Fretheim follows his estimation of the created order preferred by the author of Job by noting some ways in which the world works: "the world has ostriches and eagles, raging seas and predictable sunrises, wild weather

---

37   See, for example, Portier-Young (2005: 16), who claims that the author of Tobit intentionally used elements of plot, structure, and imagery from Job in order to "enter into dialogue with the earlier book," which then invites the reader "to do the same." See also Moore (1996: 8).

and stars that stay their courses" (2005: 244). The last of these aspects of the created order, predictable stars, raises the possibility of another understanding of misfortune in the world that may help make sense of the evidence in Tobit. In some of Israel's earliest apocalyptic literature, the world no longer functions in the exact way God intended. This rift in the created order is often foisted into the heavenly realm and described as stars that do not obey God's orders (e.g., *1 En.* 21.1–10; 80.6; cf. 75.1). Thus, the created order has been corrupted, and injustice results from the impotence or unwillingness of created things to do what they are supposed to do.

A final point of comparison with Ben Sira and Job will also confirm the conclusion that the theological perspective in the book of Tobit is not an unqualified, straightforward connection between human action and divine retribution. As those in Israel's tradition who revolted against the formulation (e.g., Qoheleth and Job) demonstrate, it is easy to muddle the straightforward formulation of retribution with life experiences that contradict its central tenets. Although Ben Sira shows a "renewed confidence" (J. Collins 1997b: 15) in divine retribution, he is not so stupid that he cannot see the potential pitfalls in the perspective. He addresses this in many different ways, as investigated in chapter 4 above. He discusses the important role of testing, he accepts the fact that there could be a "painful delay" (Crenshaw 1983: 126) before one receives a proper reward, and he suggests that some retribution may only take place in a psychological realm; all experience some anxiety in life (40.1), but for the sinner it is seven times more (40.8).[38] The book of Job is not content with a simple explanation of retribution without significant nuance. Even the book of Deuteronomy, the basis for allegedly "Deuteronomic" theology (part of which is a straightforward retribution based on human action), has a more complex view of retribution than is often recognized (Gammie 1970). In contrast to this, the retributive theology offered by the book of Tobit's title character exhibits none of this complexity or nuance. As we already noted, its expression in the book is limited to Tobit himself. No self-respecting person with any ability to perceive the surrounding world could accept such a doctrine wholesale. As we have seen in Israel's scriptures and especially in Ben Sira, the doctrine was never expressed in such a facile way as that expressed on Tobit's lips. A straightforward retributive theology, as represented in Tobit, is so simplistic and formulaic that, when compared to Ben Sira, it seems like a caricature.

---

38   Crenshaw (1983: 128) claims that Sirach believes a "disturbed mental state" can be "punishment for sin."

IV. Conclusion

The work of Randall Argall (1995) has demonstrated some sparring among different theological perspectives during the Hellenistic period. His analysis of Ben Sira and *1 Enoch* reveals some interesting ways in which the traditions in each interact with one another. For instance, when comparing the two text's views of creation, he notes the perspective of Ben Sira outlined above: creation obeys God and enacts God's judgment. In *1 Enoch* the obedience of creation is intended only to contrast the disobedience of sinners (*1 En.* 5.2–4; 100.10).[39] A component of Ben Sira's view of creation is his doctrine of opposites, but according to Argall this is a perspective that *1 Enoch* finds unsatisfying: "*1 Enoch* 4.1 takes phenomena at home in [Ben Sira's] doctrine of opposites and shows, via paradox, that reality is more complex. Possibly the paradox is offered in response to a doctrine of opposites like ben Sira's."[40] On the other hand, Ben Sira rejects the otherworldly source of esoteric wisdom so strongly represented in *1 Enoch*. Such differences, which are consciously contradicted in each text, "are indications that each tradition views the other among the disobedient" (Argall 1995: 164). The tension that Argall perceives between *1 Enoch* and Ben Sira helps provide warrant for the tension evident in Tobit's narrative; the author of Tobit may not have intended a straightforward retributive theology to have the last word in the narrative's theological import. In the author's view, reality is much more complex than that which the straightforward formulation can offer.

As Irene Nowell once noted, the doctrine of retribution in Tobit "is not a simple equation" (1983: 233). Even if one accepts Tobit's rhetoric at the beginning of the story as programmatic for the narrative as a whole, as discussed above, the story as it unfolds seems to offer a different, or at least more complicated, explanation of reality. While this current chapter has intended to problematize the position that Tobit exhibits a Deuteronomistic or straightforward retributive theology, there remains a positive aspect to this project. If Tobit is not unwaveringly intending to support a straightforward theology of retribution that ensures a divine response commensurate with human deeds, what alternative does it intend? By comparing Tobit to parts of

---

39   See Argall (1995: 159).
40   Argall (1995: 160). The respective dates of these two texts perhaps pose a problem for Argall's argument here. The origins of the *Book of Watchers* may pre-date Ben Sira by 100–150 years. Later authors and/or compilers of *1 Enoch*, however, were contemporaneous with Ben Sira and interacted directly with him, which is a major component of Argall's argument (see pp. 13, 249–55). If these later handlers of the Enoch tradition accepted and advocated some form of chs. 1–36, then it may not be entirely anachronistic to speak of its tenets in conversation with those of Ben Sira.

1 Enoch, it should become clear that this book's theology also contains ideas that align with the perspective on evil in some of Israel's earliest apocalyptic literature.

Chapter 6

THE ORIGINS OF JEWISH APOCALYPTICISM AND SCHOLARLY DISCUSSIONS OF ITS INFLUENCE ON THE BOOK OF TOBIT

The preceding section ended by asking whether or not simple, straight-forward retribution was the sole theological perspective for which the author of the book of Tobit intended to advocate. In showing how such theological language is treated—how it is limited to the char-acter of Tobit himself—another possibility was raised for the origin of misfortune in the story. A perspective in certain segments of early Jewish apocalypticism may supply a conceptual framework in which the misfortune suffered by righteous characters in the tale of Tobit can be explained and understood. Thus, the work of chapters 6–8 in what follows will take up a different comparison. Chapter 6 will offer a brief review of theories of the origin of apocalypticism in the history of Israel and the extent, albeit limited, to which scholars have coordinated this thought world with that in the book of Tobit. Chapter 7 will provide a detailed analysis of some of Israel's earliest apocalyptic literature, in this case three portions of the apocalyptic collection known as *1 Enoch*, in order better to understand how they give expression to the theological issues insipient in that literature. Chapter 8 will analyze Tobit in light of this apocalyptic literature. Like chapters 4 and 5 above, the current goal is not to try to prove specific textual linkages between Tobit and other literature but to use *1 Enoch* as a contemporaneous point of refer-ence and a heuristic body of comparative material, which will help to illuminate the theological contours of the story of Tobit and his family.

I. What is Apocalypticism? Origins, Catalysts and Scholarly Discussions

While there is literature among the prophets in the Hebrew Bible that may be labeled proto-apocalyptic (e.g., Ezek. 38–39; Joel 1–2; Zech. 14; Isa. 65), the efforts to label it as fully apocalyptic have not been wholly convincing and will be discussed further below.[1] The one example in the Hebrew Bible of an apocalypse, the book of Daniel, is not the earliest

---

1   See especially Hanson (1975).

extant Jewish apocalyptic literature (its latter chapters, 7–12, date from the Maccabean period). The earliest apocalyptic literature arises in portions of the collection of writings known as *1 Enoch*. Two portions of the Enochic corpus, the *Book of Watchers* (chs. 1–36) and the *Astronomical Book* (chs. 72–82), have origins in the third century BCE, if not earlier.[2] As J. Collins summarizes, in the last two centuries before the Common Era, "apocalypticism constituted a distinctive worldview within Judaism," even if there was diversity within that worldview (1997a: 7).

When discussing apocalyptic literature, terminological definition is necessary for clarity of expression. Within scholarly discussion of apocalypticism, lack of consensus begins when trying simply to determine which words to use. While most scholars in North America today generally avoid using the word "apocalyptic" as a noun, there is far from consensus on this matter. Lester Grabbe notes that its usage as a noun has a "long and venerable history" and that there is plenty of precedent in the English language for using an adjective as both an adjective and a noun (Grabbe 2003a: 3). He rightly notes that, in most contexts, there is "little likelihood of confusion" (3). John Collins has repeatedly argued for an end to the use of "apocalyptic" as a noun. He argues most recently that the word is "burdened by a history of usage as an all-embracing term that includes literary form, worldview, eschatology, and anything else that one might associate with this literature" (2003c: 46). Grabbe's arguments notwithstanding, the discussion that follows will use the term "apocalyptic" only as an adjective, unless it is used otherwise within quoted material. The word "apocalypse" refers most specifically to a literary genre[3] (e.g., the apocalypse known as *4 Ezra*) and "apocalypticism" refers to a specific social movement or to the thought world associated with the literature.

---

2   The details of these texts and their respective dates of composition will be dealt with in turn. At this point we may note the following observation from J. Charlesworth: "the consensus is now that the Book of the Watchers was composed by the early Hellenistic period and may reflect the struggles of the Diadochi after the death of Alexander the Great in 323 B.C.E. Thus, the writings now called the books of Enoch originated before 200 B.C.E., and conceivably as early as the end of the fourth century B.C.E." (2005: 446). To this one may also add the observation of Grabbe: "the *Book of Watchers* was probably already taking shape in the late Persian period. Since it is not unusual to put the origins of the *Book of Watchers* fairly early in the Ptolemaic period, the tradition would have been extant in some form before the end of the Persian period" (2003a: 33). *1 Enoch* has a very complicated textual history, which will be dealt with more fully in chapter 6 below. The phrase "Enochic corpus" is appropriate to the composite nature of the text. It contains several distinct sections that seem to have been collected over a period of time. See Black and Denis (1970) and Milik and Black (1976).

3   See J. Collins (1979) for the definition put forward by the SBL working group, which runs as follows: "'Apocalypse' is a genre of revelatory literature with a narrative framework, in which a revelation is mediated by an otherworldly being to a human recipient, disclosing a transcendent reality which is both temporal, insofar as it envisages eschatological salvation, and spatial insofar as it involves another, supernatural world" (9).

a. The Origins of Jewish Apocalypticism

Before proceeding with an argument about how Tobit may share affinities with Jewish apocalypticism, it will be helpful to have a sense of how scholars have discussed apocalypticism and its origins within (or from outside) Israel.

1. Persian origin?

In many of the earliest studies of apocalypticism, there was a subtle devaluation of the phenomenon. Such attitudes resulted from the obscure nature of apocalyptic texts, their lack of rationality, and their perceived incongruity with the remainder of the Hebrew Bible and early Christianity. J. Collins, for instance, describes the study of apocalypticism in the history of theological and biblical scholarship as a situation where "theologians of a more rational bent are often reluctant to admit that such material played a formative role in early Christianity" (1997a: 1). Because scholars were unsympathetic with apocalypticism and its central texts, they often looked to sources outside of Israel from which it could have arisen. As a result, many scholars argued that the catalyst for apocalypticism in Israel's traditions is provided by Persian influence. Sigmund Mowinckel, for instance, argued in 1951 that Israel's "dualistic view of life and of the world was worked out in the course of the earlier Hellenistic period, no doubt under the influence of Persian religion, which was consistently dualistic from the beginning" (2005: 264).[4]

Some of the central tenets of Jewish apocalypticism, such as dualism and the division of time into distinct ages, seem to be foreign to Israel's traditions prior to the exilic period but can be found in Persian writings. Persian texts such as the *Bundahisn* and the *Bahman Yast* reflect the Persian conceptual ideas of history, creation, and eschatology.[5] The *Bundahisn* narrates primal creation. The benevolent deity, Ormazd (Ahura Mazda), is omniscient, good, and unrivaled in splendor. An evil opponent, Ahriman, coexisted with Ormazd, and after glimpsing the light in which Ormazd existed, tried to destroy it. The subsequent conflict between Ormazd and Ahriman lasts for 12,000 years, divided into 3,000-year epochs. There is thus a stark dualism and division of the ages that could have influenced Jewish thought. The *Bahman Yast* is an example of the "apocalypse" genre.[6] In this text, Ahura Mazda gives special revelation

---

4   Originally published as *Han som kommer* (1951). One could also note here Winston (1965: 183–216), who argues for Persian influence on different segments of Judaism in antiquity. Stephen Cook (1995: 4) notes Rowley (1944) and Russell (1964) as two others who attribute many of the *topoi* in Jewish apocalypticism to Persian influence.

5   The best resource for an English translation of these texts is Edward West (1880, vol. 5). See also Boyce (1975).

6   This classification is based on the analysis of J. Collins in *Semeia* 14, whose argument will be discussed in greater depth below. See also Hultgard (1991: 114–34).

to a human recipient, Zarathushtra (i.e., Zoroaster). This text presumes much of the cosmogony as described in the *Bundahisn*.

Parts of Daniel may portray Persian influence, from which one could conclude that Persian ideas influenced Judaism, especially in its apocalyptic iterations. In Dan. 2.29–36, Daniel recounts King Nebuchadnezzar's dream, in which he saw a statue with a head of gold, chest of silver, hips of bronze, legs of iron, and feet of iron mixed with clay. A potential parallel to this occurs in the beginning of the *Bahman Yast*: "Auharmazd [Ahura Mazda] displayed the omniscient wisdom to Zaratust [i.e., Zoroaster], and through it he beheld the root of a tree, on which were four branches, one golden, one of silver, one of steel, and one was mixed up with iron" (West 1880: 5:192).[7] Such a close parallel could suggest influence of a Persian text or concept on a Jewish tradition. R. N. Frye argues against such possible connections. Even at the place of most likely borrowing, Nebuchadnezzar's dream (Dan. 2.31–49), Frye attributes any similarities to ancient myths the two cultures would have held in common rather than direct dependence in Israel upon Iranian sources (1962: 261–9). An emphasis on the succession of kingdoms, similar to that found in Persian texts, can be found early in Herodotus (1.30; 1.95), in which the kingdoms are Assyria, Media, and Persia (J. Collins 2002: 30). Noticing this fact could indicate Persian influence on Greek tradition long before the advent of Jewish apocalypticism, or more likely suggests that the succession of kingdoms was common and not a specific millenarian belief in the ancient world.

While Persian thought could supply a possible source for such concepts as dualism and division of ages in Judaism, it is difficult to prove the antiquity of the Persian sources. The Pahlavi texts—the general name for Zoroastrian religious literature, of which the *Bundahisn* and *Bahman Yast* are a part—date from the sixth–eleventh century CE. To claim influence on Judaism, one must argue that the origin of such ideas lies in the Achaemenid period of Persian history (550–247 BCE). A. Hultgard (1991: 114–34) has tried to argue that the *Bahman Yast* has its origins in the fall of the Achaemenian Empire. The text refers to a group with disheveled hair,[8] which is how Persian artists usually depicted Greeks at that time, leading him to conclude that "there is clear evidence of an ancient mythical and apocalyptic core" in the *Bahman Yast* (1991: 133).[9] Plutarch (50–120 CE) does

---

7   See also Montgomery (1927: 188).

8   See the *Bahman Yast*, where the age that is mixed with iron is the evil sovereignty of the "demons with disheveled hair" (West 1880: 5:193).

9   Persian ideas of apocalyptic woes and successive eschatological ages are also possibly exhibited in antiquity in the Oracle of Hystaspes. This oracle is quoted or referred to by a number of early Christian authors, such as Justin, Clement of Alexandria, and Lactantius. See Hinnells (1973: 125–48).

briefly mention Zoroaster, whom he calls a sage (ὁ μάγος; *Is. Os.* 46). Plutarch knows the names of the two Persian deities who are constantly at war with one another and says that even though Ahriman is now causing pestilence, he eventually will be annihilated. Plutarch bases his knowledge on Theopompus of Chios, a Greek historian of the fourth century BCE,[10] which situates this information chronologically such that it could have influenced the development of Jewish apocalypticism. Even so, the third-hand nature of this information is hardly proof that it was prevalent enough to have influenced Judaism in any significant way.

The relationship between the origins of Jewish apocalypticism and Persian influences is likely too complicated to support any definite conclusions. While many scholars have taken up this challenge (e.g., Boyce 1975: 1984) the temporal problems constitute significant difficulty. Although there are some striking parallels between Persian religious texts and Jewish apocalypticism, proving influence is a difficult undertaking. And, as we will see, not all scholars have needed recourse to Persian texts to explain the origins of apocalypticism within Israel.

2. Apocalypticism explained as an intra-Jewish phenomenon

The other most common account of the origin of Jewish apocalypticism is to find its roots within Judaism itself, whether from prophecy, wisdom, or early mytho-poetic views of creation. The most common argument is that apocalyptic literature grows out of Israel's prophets. For instance, Friedrich Lücke (1848) held the view that apocalypticism emerged from prophecy in response to disappointment in the post-exilic restoration. Lücke organized his study according to concepts. The first book of his study is called *Der Begriff und die Geschichte der apokalyptischen Litteratur* (The Concept and the History of Apocalyptic Literature), but the history (*Geschichte*) to which he refers does not offer a development or origin of the material. Instead, he engaged in what he calls "a discussion of concepts" (*Erörterung des Begriffs* [17]). Although he eventually moved to a discussion of particular texts, such as the *Sybilline Oracles*, *Enoch* and *4 Ezra*, his organization of the material is conceptual. Adolf Hilgenfeld (1857) attempted to correct Lücke by showing that all apocalyptic literature should be investigated with a view toward its development.[11] He sought to replace Lücke's dogmatic organization of the material with a more historical paradigm, although his analysis is infused with Hegelian conceptuality. According to P. Hanson, however, Hilgenfeld's reconstruction "lifted apocalyptic to an honorable position in the area of biblical studies" (1976b: 390), as opposed to its previous status as a bizarre child of prophecy best left ignored.

---

10   "Theopompus" OCD: 1505–6.
11   For a further assessment, see Hanson (1976b: 390).

Julius Wellhausen (1883) argued differently. He claimed that there was a break between post-exilic prophecy and apocalypticism, based mostly on his idea that Jesus was the true inheritor of the prophetic tradition and all intervening material was illegitimate, in so far as it was not the stump from which earliest Christianity grew. Note the subtle devaluation of the apocalyptic perspective in Wellhausen's words:

> We have already spoken of the transition from the old prophecy to apocalypse. With the destruction of the nation and the cessation of historical life, hope was released from all obligation to conform to historical conditions; it no longer set up an aim to which even the present might aspire, but ran riot after an ideal, at the advent of which the historical development would be suddenly broken off. (1957: 507)

For Wellhausen, discontinuity between prophecy and apocalypticism helped him to devalue the latter and simultaneously depict Jesus as a truly prophetic figure.

Herman Gunkel's form-critical approach (1895) stands in contrast with Wellhausen's literary one. Gunkel did not think that apocalypticism relied on or built on prophecy, but argued that apocalypticists rummaged through earlier stages of Israel's traditions, "summoning a prestigious authority comparable to, and in fact more ancient than, that of the classical prophets" (Hanson 1976b: 393). This thinking drew upon ancient myths, especially the *Chaoskampf*, a myth that includes a battle against a primordial foe represented as the sea (Isa. 17.12–14; Hab. 3.8–10, 15), Leviathan (Ps. 74.13–14), or Rahab (Isa. 51.9–11; Job 26.10–13).

The study of certain myths figures prominently in explanations of apocalyptic literature. The *Book of Watchers* (*1 Enoch*, chs. 1–36), for example, relies heavily on mythic traditions in its explanation of the origin of evil.[12] Many recent studies have shown how Mesopotamian (e.g., *Lugal-e*, *Anzu*, and *Enuma Elish*) and Caananite (e.g., *Baal*) myths contribute to Israelite cosmogony and, by extension, to the mythology latent in Jewish apocalypticism.[13] Much of the imagery that is drawn from mytho-poetic sources finds itself expressed in Israel's prophets. This, in turn, provides imagery from which later apocalypticists drew inspiration. Israel's prophets historicized the ancient myths, especially in applying the *Chaoskampf* to the exile (Day 1985: 88–139). The image of the overthrow of the primordial foe is conflated with drowning Pharaoh's soldiers in the sea (e.g., Isa. 51.9–11). Later apocalyptic authors historicized these myths as well. For example, the beast imagery in Daniel chapter 7 is interlaced with expressing the horror of Antiochus IV and

---

12   The myths focus on the enemies Shemihazah and Asael, their corruption of humanity, and their downfall at the hands of God's agents. See Nickelsburg (1977a). These myths will be discussed in much more depth in chapter 7 below.

13   See Clifford (1998: 3–38). See also the detailed studies of Day (1985) and Wakeman (1973).

his eventual downfall. Such reflection of myth, whether for Israel's prophets or later apocalyptic literature, reflects a situation where "the old myth is applied to historical events" (Levenson 1994: 23).

Gerhard von Rad offered a different opinion by arguing that apocalypticism is a direct outgrowth of Israel's sapiential traditions.[14] He dismissed the possibility of apocalypticism's prophetic roots as "completely out of the question" because the two have incompatible views of history (1965: 2:303). Von Rad described the prophetic message as one rooted in a saving history that is clearly based on election. Apocalyptic history, on the other hand, deals only with empires and, as represented in Daniel, makes no mention of Israel's history. Even the Son of Man in Daniel is not from Israel but one who comes with the clouds of heaven.[15] The "nerve-centre" of apocalypticism is knowledge, which leads von Rad to explain apocalypticism's interest in time and a secret future with recourse to Israel's wisdom tradition (1965: 2:306). The most striking contrast between wisdom and apocalypticism—wisdom's lack of eschatological interest and fervor—was not a problem for von Rad. He claimed that the sapiential focus on the "proper time" eventually developed into a concern with last things (1965: 2:307–8).[16] While von Rad's argument was not radically new at the time, he did break new ground in the singular, non-prophetic origin of the phenomenon; he posited a "one-way street from Wisdom to apocalyptic and the denial of all inner contact with prophecy" (Koch 1972: 45).

Despite von Rad's argument, many studies of apocalypticism in Israel continued to assert that its origins lie within prophecy. H. H. Rowley, for instance, claimed that, despite "obvious differences" between prophecy and apocalypticism, "that apocalyptic is the child of prophecy, yet diverse from prophecy, can hardly be disputed . . . The relation between prophecy and apocalyptic, in which the predictive element is particularly prominent, appeared beyond question" (1944: 13). In Rowley's opinion, the prophetic view of history was one where history was "swiftly moving towards a great climax" (1944: 24). From this, it was only a short leap for the apocalypticists to appropriate such views. Although Rowley makes some strong arguments for the parallels between prophecy and apocalypticism, his analysis of the latter phenomenon takes an incorrect position on the emergence of apocalypticism by claiming a late date for *1 Enoch*. For Rowley, Daniel is the earliest apocalyptic literature, which makes it easier for him to see

---

14   He first discussed this possibility briefly in his *Old Testament Theology* (1965: 2:301–8). He also works from this idea in *Wisdom in Israel* (1972: 263–83).

15   Von Rad (1965: 2:303). He also points to Syriac Baruch 85.3, which mentions the prophets as having fallen asleep, to support his view that apocalypticism did not grow naturally out of Israel's prophetic tradition.

16   In *Wisdom in Israel* (1972: 267–8) he traced the ancient concept of the appropriate times into Ecclesiastes and Sirach. Sirach applies the idea of divine determination of the proper time to a wide variety of events, especially life and death, in which the apocalyptic literature is most interested.

intra-biblical parallels between apocalypticism and prophecy.[17] D. S. Russell affirms Rowley's basic positions that apocalypticism grew out of prophecy and that Daniel is the first apocalyptic literature. Although he does not posit a specific date for *1 Enoch*, he notes Rowley's date, shortly after Daniel, and does not quibble with it while affirming Daniel's priority. He calls Daniel "the first, and greatest, of all the Jewish apocalyptic writings."[18] Recent, detailed studies of parts of *1 Enoch*, however, have concluded it to be the earliest "full blown" apocalyptic literature within Judaism.[19]

3. A social or textual phenomenon?

In *The Dawn of Apocalyptic*, originally published in 1975, Paul Hanson builds upon the work of predecessors such as O. Plöger (1959) in arguing that the origin of apocalypticism lies in post-exilic prophecy. Hanson traces a group of visionaries in post-exilic Israel that finds itself ostracized from the official reconstruction of the nation and cult. Isaiah 65 depicts a widening schism between the visionaries and those in charge of the official hierocratic reforms, and lays the groundwork for dualism and the division of ages into epochs (1975: 160). In Zechariah chapters 9–14 Hanson finds the gulf between these two groups widened. In Zechariah 9, the visionaries are not hoping to be saved *through* history but *from* history. Zechariah 14 provides what Hanson calls a full apocalypse because there is a new dimension here that carries "apocalyptic eschatology beyond its prophetic roots" (1975: 388).

Hanson advanced understanding of the situation behind Jewish apocalyptic literature by employing social-scientific models of millenarian[20] groups. His method gives prominence to the *situation* and *intent* of the literature. Hanson uses the sociological models of Ernst Troeltsch (1931), Karl Mannheim (1936), and Max Weber (1963), sociologists who discuss the conceptual and social underpinnings of religious movements. For example, Hanson discerns the struggle for power in the post-exilic situation directly

---

17   Rowley (1944: 75–80). See, for instance, the evocation of Psalm 82, Ezekiel 1, and Isaiah 6 in Dan. 7.9–14. Compare also Dan. 9.6, which clearly locates his message as one in line with what the prophets have previously spoken.

18   Russell (1964: 16). See also p. 48, where he claims Daniel is the "first of the apocalyptic writings." The perspectives of Rowley and Russell, that Daniel is the oldest apocalypse, may seem to show a canonical bias for Daniel. Charlesworth points to some scholars who were "overshadowed by forces that celebrated the dominance of the canon" (2005: 247, n. 2). In their defenses, both Russell and Rowley wrote without the detailed knowledge about *1 Enoch* provided by the Qumran scrolls of that text.

19   Much of this dating is based on evidence from the Dead Sea Scrolls, some of which are dated to the third century BCE (e.g., 4Q208, i.e. *4QEnastr^a*). G. Nickelsburg (2001a: 170) argues that the origin of parts of the *Book of Watchers* has the *Diadochoi* as its historical referent, which would push its date into the third century BCE. See also Grabbe (2003a: 33) and J. Charlesworth (2005: 446), both of whom claim that there is a general consensus on this matter.

20   "Millenarian" is the sociological term often used to refer to apocalyptic groups.

through the lenses provided by Mannheim and Weber (1975: 211–28). Hanson summarizes the post-exilic situation as follows:

> When prophets come proclaiming the advent of the longed-for transformation, they readily find a following among these alienated elements, and when that transformation is delayed and the oppressing classes remain in power, "it was inevitable that consolation should be sought in genuine otherworldly hopes." (1975: 214).[21]

The quotation within Hanson's words here is from Weber (1963), on whom he clearly relies for help in interpreting the social situation.

Stephen Cook (1995) affirms a sociological approach to understanding Jewish apocalypticism, but suggests that Hanson's picture is not adequately nuanced. Hanson's work combined two elements that should more appropriately have been kept separate. A theory of deprivation claims that apocalypticism arises in groups that are powerless and deprived: an idea from Weber (1963), who was influenced by Marxists ideals (Cook 1995: 13). Hanson, however, conflates deprivation with cognitive dissonance.[22] Cognitive dissonance results from a group with a newly ambiguous relationship with the power structures of the day but does not necessarily entail deprivation. This distinction is important because a group can experience dissonance without deprivation (Cook 1995: 14–15).[23]

Hanson has also been criticized on a completely different front. J. J. M. Roberts (1976) offered a critique of some of Hanson's early work (e.g., 1971) on which his later book, *The Dawn of Apocalyptic*, is based. According to Roberts, Hanson (1971) sets up too strong a dichotomy between myth and history in his discussion of apocalypticism in light of its Near Eastern background. Roberts claims that Hanson has confused "a *literary* category (historiography), which could include more than one genre, with a particular, though not self-evident, *philosophical* concept of history" (Roberts 1976: 3; italics original).[24]

---

21   Hanson here is quoting from Weber (1963: 140).

22   On cognitive dissonance, see also Festinger (1956).

23   One could also note here the work of Aberle (1962: 209–12), who introduces a modified version of the deprivation theory. Aberle adds a new component of relativity to the sociological understanding of millennialism. As a result, a group does not have to be deprived objectively in order to be beset with the conditions that produce millennial thinking. Instead, the deprivation is "not a particular objective state of affairs, but a difference between an anticipated state of affairs and a less agreeable actuality" (209). The important new element here is that deprivation is relative, not absolute. This still, according to Cook, links deprivation theory too closely to millennial outcomes and does not take adequate account of cognitive dissonance.

24   In his conclusion, Roberts suggests that a better way to proceed would be to base interpretations on specific texts, "through its expression in the respective literature" (1976: 13). Some of Hanson's later publications (e.g., *The Dawn of Apocalyptic* in particular) may inoculate him from this particular criticism.

Lester Grabbe builds upon Roberts' critique of Hanson by paying more vigorous attention to Hanson's approach to the study of apocalypticism. As Hanson builds his distinction between prophecy and apocalypticism, he does so partly on the basis of the difference between actions that "unfold within the realities of this world" versus a dualistic worldview in which the faithful are resurrected to a "blessed heavenly existence" (Hanson 1992: 280–1).[25] Grabbe criticizes Hanson's rigid distinction between "this-worldly" and "otherworldly," because it is a false dichotomy; "the worldview of the prophets is as mythical as the worldview of the apocalypticists" (Grabbe 2003b: 112). Robert Carroll (1979) makes a similar point, but in the context of Hanson's tendency to explain things in terms of polarization. Carroll points out Hanson's tendency to pair things as complete opposites, such as visionary and hierocrat; prophecy and cult. Carroll's critique claims that such polarization makes complex realities too simple, and "leads to false antitheses" among which he specifically mentions "myth and history" (1979: 19). Much like Grabbe, Carroll's main critique of Hanson is his "unsatisfactory" treatment of myth (20). Carroll calls it unsatisfactory because of "the way the false antithesis between myth and history operates so that prophecy is seen in relation to history and the cult in relation to myth. Yet both exist in history and operate with mythical concepts and motifs" (20). Grabbe demonstrates how the categories Hanson supplies here, and some others, are overly simplistic by viewing the similarities and differences between prophetic, apocalyptic, and mantic writings (2003b: 119–23). His examples show the significant overlap, similarities, and congruencies between these different types of literature, which recommends avoiding the overly simplistic categories offered by Hanson.

John Collins (1979: 1–59) responds to Hanson by claiming that situation and intent should not be primary considerations in classifying apocalyptic literature. Literature should be deemed apocalyptic based upon its literary *form* and *content* so that analysis of the phenomenon is limited to that which truly belongs to it, not that which is simply derivative of it. In other words, he is concerned with setting proper limits on what is "apocalyptic," which can only be done through analysis of the literature. Collins arrives at a definition of the apocalypse genre, noting that it is held together by phenomenological similarity:

> Apocalypse is a genre of revelatory literature with a narrative framework, in which a revelation is mediated by an otherworldly being to a human recipient, disclosing a transcendent reality which is both temporal, insofar as it envisages eschatological salvation, and spatial insofar as it involves another, supernatural world. (1979: 9)

25   As quoted by Grabbe (2003b: 112).

In a later essay, Collins adds to his phenomenological morphology; he updates the definition to include the qualification that the literature intends to interpret present circumstances in light of the supernatural world (1991: 19). While this added a diachronic element, it is far from taking account of the sociological models utilized by Hanson.

The admittedly cursory summary of scholarly opinions outlined above indicate the level of disagreement among scholars with regard to any diachronic development of apocalypticism in Israel. Not only are the origins of apocalypticism in Israel vague and enigmatic, but also there exists little methodological agreement among scholars as to how the phenomenon should best be studied and discussed. Hanson's use of sociological models allows him to find apocalyptic eschatology very early (between 520 and 475 BCE), while Collins' model limits investigation to those texts with generic compatibility, making apocalypticism a relatively late, Hellenistic phenomenon.

c. Implications for the Study of Tobit

The preceding summary and background of how and why scholars have studied apocalypticism, albeit brief, yields some important conclusions for this study as it moves forward. Leander Keck, writing about the apostle Paul, famously said in that context that "in antiquity ideas did not flow in pipes" (1988: 14). This simple observation could profitably be applied to the history of scholarship on apocalypticism. Clearly the phenomenon is too erudite to be traced back to a single catalyst. Interestingly, one could say the same thing about the book of Tobit. The various traditions with which it interacts—the many inkpots in which it dips its pen (Nickelsburg 1996: 340)—recommend a more vigorous investigation of the situation and thinking that lie behind the story.

At the same time, the above summary of the scholarship on apocalypticism also shows how variegated the phenomenon was. It was not necessarily isolated, especially in some of its later iterations. Authors such as Ben Sira find ways to criticize and reject it. Apocalypticism may have had a beginning in some very specific circumstances, but its crystallization into various text forms allowed its tentacles to reach into any number of corners in various ancient Jewish contexts. The author of the book of Tobit, therefore, need not have fully been an apocalypticist in order to have been influenced by theological and/or eschatological points of view related to such movements.

II. Apocalypticism and the Book of Tobit?

The foregoing summary of scholarship provides a backdrop for the following discussion of Tobit and apocalypticism. One immediate observation that can be offered is that apocalypticism is too varied and complex to be explained as a single tradition or with recourse to a single origin. A session of the Society of Biblical Literature on "Wisdom and Apocalypticism in Early Judaism and Christianity," founded in 1994, has sought to eradicate the "gulf" that so often stands specifically between wisdom and apocalypticism in scholarly conversations (Wills and Wright 2005: 2). In such work, the origins of apocalypticism are best sought not with a dualistic, "either/or" mentality (i.e., that its origins lie with either wisdom or prophecy). This new "both–and" approach has helped the book of Tobit to be recognized in scholarship on Jewish apocalypticism, because of the myriad traditions and *topoi* it employs.

There has not been extensive scholarship in which Tobit is compared to apocalyptic literature. David Simpson in his introduction to Tobit in Charles' *Apocrypha and Pseudepigrapha of the Old Testament* was one of the first to emphasize the eschatology in Tobit's final chapters. He claimed that the author, with relation to the nation of Israel,

> stands possibly almost on a threshold of the Apocalyptic tendency. He has worked out for himself a crude and simple, but yet unmistakable, philosophy of the future. Jerusalem at the end of a given period will be rebuilt and the Temple sumptuously restored, the scattered tribes reunited, and—to his credit—the heathen will worship the God of Israel. (1913: 1:197)

Simpson's reference here is to Tobit chapters 13–14, which contain an eschatological look at the future destiny of Jerusalem. Because these two chapters stand out in comparison with the rest of the story, many scholars view them as a later addition and do not consider their ramifications for the theology of the book. Even now, after the discovery of chapters 13–14 among Tobit fragments in the Dead Sea Scrolls, this view still persists.[26] It is interesting to note, however, the extent to which Simpson's assessment of Tobit stands out from the interpretations of the book put forward in the 100 years since. L. Grabbe refers to Charles as the "father of the modern study of apocalyptic" (2003a: 3). One wonders whether, by including Tobit in his collecting and editing duties, R. H. Charles inadvertently contextualized it in such a way as to make its affinities with some aspects of apocalyptic texts stand out more prominently to Simpson. Charles may also have been the father of placing the book of Tobit within that broad conceptual framework.

a. The Arguments of George W. E. Nickelsburg about Tobit and 1 Enoch

The first and only extended argument about Tobit's relationship to apocalypticism comes from George Nickelsburg. Nickelsburg argues, in a SBL Seminar Paper from 1988, that both *1 Enoch* and Tobit reflect "an older common stock of ideas, traditions, and terminology" and

---

26   For example, Deselaers (1982) and Rabenau (1994: 183–5). For a more complete discussion, see chapter 2 above.

calls the two texts "distant cousins" (1988b, 55). He readily admits the differences between the two works: one is a collection of revelatory texts transmitting secret information while the other is a narrative tale about the trials of a family in exile. Nevertheless, Nickelsburg compares the two texts in four broad categories: (1) cosmology, angelology, and demonology; (2) eschatology; (3) ethical teaching; and (4) liturgical vocabulary.

In comparing cosmology, angelology, and demonology, Nickelsburg notes the emphasis in *1 Enoch* on the description of "hidden cosmic realia" (55). In *1 Enoch* these descriptions are clustered in chapters 17–19, 20–36, and 72–82. Enoch's journeys into these realms are meant to reinforce the coming judgment on the wicked. The holy ones (or angels) are extremely numerous and fulfill a variety of functions, operating the heavenly bodies in the *Astronomical Book* (chs. 72–82) and organized like a divine army in the introduction to the *Book of Watchers* (chs. 1–5). In the *Book of Watchers*, some angels leave their appointed stations and descend to earth with various corrupting activities. In chapters 6–11 the four angels, Sariel, Raphael, Gabriel, and Michael, function as intermediaries, pleading on behalf of humanity, instigating judgment at the flood, and eventually are dispatched to destroy the evil watchers (9–10). These myths have a specific function: they explain the origin of evil and at the same time explain how that evil will be vanquished (Nickelsburg 1988b: 57).

Tobit, at first, seems to portray a very different world than that of *1 Enoch*. Tobit does not narrate vast tours of the heavens and does not look forward to the end of evil that ushers in a renewed creation. The author of Tobit does not claim to have seen the heavenly realm, although he does allude to it (Nickelsburg 1988b: 58). God dwells there in glory, surrounded by many "holy angels" (8.15; 11.14). Tobit specifically mentions seven angels, and, as Raphael demonstrates, they bring human prayers before God and are dispatched to aid humans. The author of Tobit also ascribes some level of evil to demons: Sarah's affliction comes from the demon Asmodeus. Despite these similarities there is a temporal difference between the two works. For *1 Enoch*, God's mercy and ultimate restoration lies at some point in the future, while, in Tobit, Raphael's mission is placed in historical time, indicating that God is currently present with the people in a way that *1 Enoch* does not envision.[27] According to Nickelsburg, Tobit's focus on God's presence now in people's lives distinguishes it from *1 Enoch*, in which God's will is accomplished on earth in an "eschatological denouement" (1988b: 59).

Nickelsburg next compares *1 Enoch* and Tobit on the topic of eschatology. The eschatological perspective operative in *1 Enoch* is evident from the opening line: a final judgment is coming, at which point the righteous

---

27   Compare the similar argument of Portier-Young about God's role in the lives of the characters in Tobit (2001).

will be blessed and the wicked will be punished. Nickelsburg claims that this eschatological judgment is proclaimed and emphasized "in almost all strata of the collection" (1988b: 59). God pronounces the judgment in chapters 12–16, the cosmological journey in chapters 17–19 reinforces that it is coming, and the words in chapters 92–105 assure that human deeds are subject to God's judgment. Both the *Apocalypse of Weeks* and the *Animal Apocalypse* similarly trace history from its inception to the eschaton. In comparing this to Tobit, Nickelsburg is aware of Tobit's ostensibly historical setting, but adds that it nevertheless has "a significant orientation toward the future" (1988b: 60). The plight of Tobit and Sarah is paralleled throughout the story by the misfortune of Israel.[28] The fact that Tobit and Sarah have their situations reversed only highlights the fact that, in the end, Israel's situation has not changed. Israel's suffering "remains unfinished," and the happy ending for the characters is a "paradigm for Israel's story, which remains to be concluded" (1988b: 60).

Nickelsburg sees an even closer connection between Tobit 14 and Enoch's sixth week in the *Apocalypse of Weeks*. Tobit speaks of his kin being scattered, the house of God burning (14.4), the exiles returning, and a new building in Jerusalem. On these topics, Tobit parallels the *Apocalypse of Weeks* rather closely, sometimes expressed in almost exactly the same words. These two texts are so similar in content, sequence, and wording that Nickelsburg claims they could "reflect common tradition" (1988b: 61).[29] Despite these similarities, Nickelsburg admits differences, the most striking of which is *1 Enoch*'s description of a remnant chosen from a perverse generation, which contrasts Tobit's affirmation of the post-exilic community's continued status as the nation of Israel. While both texts are in a testamentary context (Tob. 14, *1 En.* 91.1–19), Tobit does not claim to reveal specially transmitted wisdom brought from heaven as does *1 Enoch* (Nickelsburg 1988b: 62). The authority for Tobit's declaration lies instead upon the words of Israel's prophets, in this case, Nahum (Tob. 14.4).

Finally, Nickelsburg sees similarities between Tobit and *1 Enoch* in the wisdom and ethical teaching of the two works. Tobit reinforces, through direct ethical exhortation and the narrated events, the importance of sexual morality, endogamy, and proper use of one's wealth. These are central points of Tobit's testament (chapters 4, 14) and Raphael's instruction (12.6–10), elements emphasized in the narrative events as well. Nickelsburg claims that the "plot line demonstrates that God rewards the righteous, even if they suffer for a time" (1988b: 63). This wisdom in Tobit is associated, albeit

---

28   Levine has a slightly different interpretation of this, suggesting to the contrary that Tobit is given the opportunity to be more paradigmatic of the community because he is male (1992a).

29   While Nickelsburg's conclusions here are helpful, there are other ways the relationship between the two can be framed. It will be argued below that both of these texts share certain attitudes as they attempt to answer similar questions. This is not to remove the possibility of shared traditions, but to formulate a different inquiry of how they may be similar.

rather vaguely (Weeks 2011: 398–9), with the Mosaic Torah, the standard by which one will be judged. *1 Enoch* also has strong ethical exhortation, often similar in content to that in Tobit. The most significant "common assertion" between the two texts is that the "rich have an obligation to the poor and lowly" (Nickelsburg 1988b: 64). At the same time, they both posit different ends for the rich: Tobit's generosity is eventually rewarded before the end of his life, but the rich in *1 Enoch* will receive punishment because of their sin. While there is a central agreement on the importance of how one should treat the poor and lowly, the central disagreement involves the timing of the reward. For Tobit, one's reward is received during this lifetime, which proves to be the case when Tobit's fortune is reversed toward the end of the story. In *1 Enoch*, the problem of theodicy is solved with a post-mortem resurrection. Both texts posit a system of ethics that works from the idea of "two ways," but the reward for one's path has different timing, although both admit of considerable delay in divine retribution.

After summarizing his findings, Nickelsburg claims that, despite certain differences, the similarities between Tobit and *1 Enoch* are significant. The details suggest that these two texts did not arrive at similar formulations as a result of independent reading and understanding of the Hebrew Scriptures. More probably, there is some type of literary dependence between the two, knowledge of similar tradition, or common dependence on specific developments of the biblical materials (or some combination of these three). While Tobit should not be called an "apocalypse," the text does claim to know about the heavenly world, and its "impingement on human life" is "ascribed to an angelic revelation" (1988b: 67).[30]

In a later reflection on his comparison between the book of Tobit and *1 Enoch*, Nickelsburg notes the resistance to his comparison. The critique usually focused on the fact that many of the elements for comparison were "simply common coinage in Second Temple Judaism" (Nickelsburg 1996: 339). More recently, J. Collins has also questioned Nickelsburg's comparison. He claims that the most distinctive themes of Tobit—almsgiving and endogamy—are not found in *1 Enoch*; that the belief in demons and angels was too widespread in Judaism for it to be a significant parallel; and that Tobit "shows no awareness of the kind of apocalyptic revelations that came into vogue in the early second century" (2005: 37–9). In Nickelsburg's defense, Collins does not fully engage with Nickelsburg's argument about Raphael's role as helper, mediator, and one who commissioned the work in the first place. It should also be noted that Collins does not view Tobit chapters 1, 13–14 as an original part of the story; they are "extraneous" and belong to "an editorial frame" (2005: 37).[31] Collins thereby avoids making

---

30   Nickelsburg notes Raphael again here. His most prominent role is as a helper and healer, but he also reveals his and God's role in the story.

31   Some of the disagreements between Collins and Nickelsburg here could result from the fact that they are not reading the same text. Collins prefers to treat chapters 1, 13 and 14 as a later addition in Tobit's textual history.

a conclusion similar to that of Zimmermann, who claims that Tob. 14.5–7 is "apocalyptic in mode and tenor" in its discussion of the appointed season being fulfilled (1958: 25).

Despite the hesitancy of some scholars, the parallels between Tobit and parts of *1 Enoch* seem worthy of further investigation. Heretofore, no scholar has fully hoisted Nickelsburg's gauntlet and attempted to draw more significant conclusions.

b. Hints from the Big Fish

There is one specific episode in Tobit that generally garners some mention of apocalyptic tendencies: Tobias' encounter with a "great fish" in 6.2–6. While many attempts have been made to determine what type of fish Tobias encountered, the point, as Moore points out, is "*what it symbolizes in the tale*" (1996: 199).[32] An answer to what the fish symbolized—a dangerous foe—is offered in the symbolic analysis of the Venerable Bede (d. 735 CE), who claims "the huge fish, which, since he wanted to devour him, was killed by Tobias on the angel's instructions, represents the ancient devourer of the human race, i.e. the devil."[33] Irene Nowell places the importance of the fish into the larger perspective of Israel's creation theology: "the fish recalls the traditional symbolism of water and water monsters which signify chaos, but once conquered become the means of creation" (1983: 219). In a similar way, A. Portier-Young, in an intertextual study between Tobit and Job, distinguishes Tobit from Job by noting Tobit's Diaspora mentality and its "apocalyptic worldview." Portier-Young describes the encounter of the fish, which takes place at night, as one intended to "symbolize their encounter with the chaotic and unknown" (2005: 23). The great fish that threatens Tobias may not equal the terror of Leviathan, but it nevertheless "partakes of the traditional symbolism of the chaos monster" (Portier-Young 2005: 24).

The arguments of Nickelsburg and others indicate that Tobit does, at certain points, share some affinity with portions of Israel's apocalyptic literature and tradition. These similarities and comparisons, however, have yet to be taken up in Tobit in any sustained way. Nickelsburg's assessment consistently remains on the level of *topoi* and thematic comparisons with the hope of proving some type of "genetic connection" (1993: 1:264). It is striking that Nickelsburg establishes the myth of the watchers as indicating an argument about the origin of evil and sin in the world but, when

---

32   Italics original. For a discussion of the possible types of fish, which include a crocodile, hippopotamus, or a Nile perch, see pp. 198–9.

33   *In Tobiam*, CCSL 119b, PL 928.12–14 (p. 8). *Piscis enim immanis qui a Tobia cum eum deuorare appeteret angelo docente occisus est antiquum generis humani deuoratorem, hoc est diabolum.* Translation taken from S. Connolly (1997: 46).

discussing the same in Tobit, he draws no theological conclusion. Thus, while Nickelsburg's work in bringing *1 Enoch* and Tobit into conversation is helpful, his desired goal (seeking genetic connection) leaves his conclusions wanting. There are other, yet unexplored ways these texts can be compared. If one asks slightly different questions and seeks different answers, the conversation between the two texts will prove more fruitful. Comparing the theological perspective latent in each text will better clarify the complex view of retribution in Tobit. For example, the discussion of Tobias' encounter with the great fish introduces creation theology into the discussion, but with what implication? Are the struggles in the book of Tobit the result of Tobit's guilt, as Tobit himself claims, or do they come from a force invading creation that is inherently opposed to God and the righteous? These are questions that a comparison with *1 Enoch* can help answer. If one were instead looking for a common generative tradition behind such mytho-poetic vestiges, only unconvincing, hypothetical answers would result.

III. Conclusion

Apocalypticism, although its origins are obscure, becomes an identifiable reality within Judaism during the Hellenistic period. We are now set with the task of establishing a way in which the question of Tobit and its views of evil and retribution will be discussed in the following two chapters of the present study.

The attempts to explain Jewish apocalypticism with recourse to a single origin, whether from within Israel or from outside, inevitably end in failure.[34] Apocalyptic literature is built on extensive exegesis and finds inspiration from many parts of Israel's scriptures, and, at the same time, arises in varied and complex social situations. For example, the *Book of Watchers* employs language similar to parts of those of Israel's prophets, but the entire scenario is an exegetical extrapolation from the situation that precipitated the flood in Genesis, all with the likely goal of helping to exonerate a certain segment of humanity from guilt in the origin of evil. This one example illustrates that to explain apocalypticism as the end of a one-way street will produce some frustration. The literature is too complex and erudite for such a simple explanation. Partly because of this, the current project makes no claims about origins of apocalypticism. Although the comparisons to be offered—between Tobit and *1 Enoch*—are from some of the earliest extant apocalyptic literature in Judaism, the present goal is not to determine the exact catalyst for the origin of apocalypticism as manifest in any extant literature, Tobit

---

34   This is not to disparage attempts at showing diachronic development. To eschew this work would be foolhardy, and the work of this present study is built upon many scholars who engage in this type of analysis, but, in the end, I proceed on different methodological grounds.

included. Many studies of apocalyptic texts ask *what* and *whence*, but the present study instead asks *why* and *how* in order better to understand the specific theological perspective in Tobit.

When beginning to chart a course for how Jewish apocalypticism should be investigated, Hanson's summary, although 30 years old, remains instructive: the conversation is "still clouded by disagreements on matters as basic as definitions and as comprehensive as the origins and significance of this literature" (1976b: 401). One of the avenues of investigation advocated by Hanson is "typology." Much of the apocalyptic literature does not address historical situations clearly enough for scholars to determine its date and setting. According to Hanson, typology should be investigated with reference to prosody, literary types, concepts, and sociological setting. If we investigate into each of these, each one acts as a "check on the results of the other" (Hanson 1976b: 405). He continues by saying that a conceptual analysis can be very helpful: "much of their [i.e., the apocalypticists] interpretation was guided by [concepts]" (1976b: 405). One must not overlook the complexity of the phenomenon. Such an investigation must be "rigorously historical," for which Hanson advocates in hopes of avoiding ideological diachronic scenarios, whether the ultimate goal is Hegelian idealism (Lücke 1848), normative rabbinic Judaism (Moore 1927), or orthodox Christianity (Wellhausen 1883).

In light of Hanson's argument, I propose a similar method, but with slightly different terminology. Rather than speaking of a conceptual approach based on typology, this study will use a theological approach, one that analyzes and compares the understanding of God and God's implications for humanity as expressed in certain texts. Such an approach, as all the others, is precarious; without care, it could quickly become ahistorical or fall back on *dicta probantia* (proof texts) in order to support specific conclusions. It offers, however, certain advantages, one of which is that it allows a concrete comparison between texts. If searching only for an account of the origin of apocalypticism, texts such as *1 Enoch* and Tobit offer only individual voices in what quickly becomes a cacophony. Texts, as a result, are treated as repositories of data useful for historical reconstruction, rather than as theological documents purporting a specific opinion. One of the ways this present project could have been developed procedurally would have been to isolate certain apocalyptic literary forms or *topoi* and try to trace their trajectory into the text and tale of Tobit. The above summary, however, has demonstrated that the isolation of anything genuinely "apocalyptic" is fraught with difficulty and rarely rests in consensus, which makes any argument about its trajectory into a subsequent text even more hypothetical. Since the argument to be made here is not specifically about apocalyptic origins, then *1 Enoch*, as a representative apocalyptic work, can be analyzed and offer a body of comparative material against which Tobit's true colors might better be perceived. The argument here is not to say that Tobit is or is not an apocalyptic text, but rather to suggest that it has theological affinities to certain segments of *1 Enoch*, which has significant implications for understanding the theology espoused by the author of Tobit, specifically the book's view of retribution.

A second advantage of this theological approach to the literature is that it can encompass a variety of soundings into a given text. Exploring the theological perspective in a text does not mean reading the literal words directly off the page. Good theology attends to historical, literary, and social aspects of a text. It thus, in a way, sidesteps one of the major problems seen in the above summary of scholarship on apocalypticism: the tendency to attribute apocalyptic origins to a single phenomenon or catalyst. An assessment of a text's theological perspective will, by necessity, take note of exegesis (from all relevant segments of Israel's scriptures, not just one), historical situation, mytho-poetic vestiges, and literary form. Using the word "theology" to explain the perspective latent in a text will require an approach as eclectic as the final apocalyptic texts themselves.

The guild of scholars who study apocalypticism seem reticent to use "theology" to describe a method of exploration. George Nickelsburg, near the beginning of his prolific commentary on *1 Enoch*, claims: "for analytical purposes, however, it is useful to focus on these authors' [i.e., those of *1 Enoch*] beliefs about God and the interactions between God and human beings. In so doing, I avoid the term *theology* with its modern systematic connotations" (2001b, 42; italics original). One could respond to Nickelsburg's notion by saying that to avoid the word theology is to miss something that is inherent in the nature of the text itself, much less the fact that "modern" theology in its systematic iterations does not resemble the theologizing of ancients. In *1 Enoch*, for example, the *Book of Watchers* records the beginning of Enoch's words with a warning to the watchers and a message of hope for those who have experienced their corruption: "The God of the universe, the Holy Great One, will come forth from his dwelling. And from there he will march upon Mount Sinai and appear in his camp emerging from heaven with a mighty power. And everyone shall be afraid, and the Watchers will quiver" (*1 En.* 1.4; *OTP* 1:13). The apocalypse thus starts with a decidedly theological statement, a coherent affirmation of faith about who God is and what God will do. The sociological models discussed above, whether expressed as theories of deprivation or dissonance, determine that apocalyptic texts undertake theological reasoning in order to understand present circumstances. Apocalyptic texts are religious and they make specific claims about God and humanity. To avoid the term "theology" risks not being true to the original intent of the authors and their communities.

John Collins has a similar wariness for the word theology. When repudiating the use of the word "apocalyptic" as a noun, he states: "the word has habitually been used to suggest a worldview or a theology which is only vaguely defined but which has often been treated as an entity independent of specific texts" (1998: 2).[35] The term "theology" obviously raises the danger of imposing an abstract concept on a text or situation. Collins' accusation here is one that could be leveled against Paolo Sacchi (1990), who suggested one specific theological idea as generative for all Jewish apocalyptic texts and imposed an understanding of theodicy on all subsequent texts. Such an approach will be avoided here by studying specific texts and formulating the theological perspective(s) therein.[36] Using the word "theology" does not mean positing a preconceived concept or dogma that is applied anachronistically to a text. For instance, in the following section it will be argued that the *Book of Watchers* (*1 Enoch* 1–36) and the *Epistle of Enoch* (*1 Enoch* 91–108) offer slightly different resolutions to the problem of theodicy, offered here briefly as evidence that an abstract concept of theodicy is not being applied to both texts. Although the analysis of *1 Enoch* and Tobit that follows will look specifically at the issue of theodicy, this theological issue suggests itself from the texts themselves, which will be proven along the way.

Specifically with regard to Tobit, Nickelsburg (1988b) noticed similarities between *1 Enoch* and Tobit and attributed them to dependency on the same traditions or similar development of biblical reflection. As already noted, one problem with his argument was that many of the parallels were too general and common in the Judaism of the day to prove a connection. Devorah Dimant has recently argued for a "fresh view" of the book of Tobit, based primarily on its inclusion among the Qumran scrolls (2009a: 140). She notes how the scroll fragments of Tobit have been very important in philological matters, but that "less attention" has been paid to "literary and exegetical aspects of the book in relation to the Qumran literature" (122, n. 16). Her argument, based upon Tobit's Halakhic similarities to some of the Qumran scrolls, leads her to conclude that the author of Tobit "was seemingly close to, or a sympathizer of, the Qumran circles" (140). She certainly is right that Tobit's affinities with the scrolls have been an under-explored avenue in assessing the literary and exegetical aspects of Tobit. To this list, one could also add theological aspects. Scholars have not yet asked questions about what Tobit's presence among the Qumran scrolls might have to say about the book's theology. This is the same lacuna in Nickelsburg's comparison between Tobit and parts of *1 Enoch* (1988b; 1996). The similarities may not end at mere motifs and *topoi*, but could extend to the very theological center of the book of Tobit as well.

---

35   Collins' caveat is not without warrant here. He is pointing out the dangers of a macro-understanding of the core of apocalypticism that becomes the typological touchstone for finding apocalypticism in varying places in Israel's history. This does not necessarily mean, however, that apocalyptic literature is devoid of theology or theological concepts.

36   See the work of Beyerle (2005a), which concludes that there is not a single theological depiction of God in apocalyptic texts, but a variety of depictions.

In the chapters that follow, by focusing specifically on parts of *1 Enoch*, I will offer a different assessment of the relationship than that offered by Nickelsburg between the book of Tobit and some of Israel's earliest apocalyptic literature. Both texts share certain "attitudes" toward earlier, traditional ways of thinking that intersect theologically. This intersection is both negative (in rejecting a simple retributive ideology) and positive (in favoring a dualistic theory of the origin of evil that is manifest as unruly creation). In Nickelsburg's comparison between *1 Enoch* and Tobit he made theological observations about the origin of sin and evil in *1 Enoch* but made no comparative claim about Tobit's narrative. Such a comparison and claim are necessary. If *1 Enoch* has a clear theological perspective, comparing and contrasting that found in Tobit would be a helpful way forward in assessing the theological perspective latent in the text and tale of Tobit. In what follows I will use the word "theology" in its narrowest and for our purposes most exegetically pertinent sense—explicit language about God—in analyzing the perspectives on God and humanity in *1 Enoch* and Tobit.

Chapter 7

RETRIBUTION IN *1 ENOCH*: EXONERATING HUMANITY IN FORMULATING THE ORIGIN OF EVIL IN THE *BOOK OF WATCHERS* AND THE *ASTRONOMICAL BOOK*

Heretofore, we have observed some aspects of the tale of Tobit that suggest the story may not cohere with a simple, straightforward doctrine of retribution—the perspective often labeled "Deuteronomistic" in studies of Tobit. As noted in chapter 1 above, Irene Nowell (1983) once observed the ways in which Tobit strains against the formulaic expressions of straightforward retribution assumed to be the core perspective of Deuteronomy. Nowell attributed these theological flecks on Tobit's surface to God's freedom, which she also tried to find expressed in Deuteronomy. We have already seen, however, that Tobit is more than a mouthpiece for "Deuteronomistic" retribution. While the book of Tobit does express a straightforward formula for retribution, this expression is limited to Tobit the character himself. The theological perspective of the book as a whole is much more complex. It has already been suggested that certain portions of *1 Enoch* may provide a body of conceptual material to which Tobit might profitably be compared. The previous chapter indicated how George Nickelsburg (1988b; 1996; 2001b) emphasized many points of comparison between Tobit and certain parts of *1 Enoch*. His brief analysis, however, was limited to motifs and *topoi*, and did not proffer any sort of theological comparison. The next step in comparing Tobit to such literature is to examine portions of *1 Enoch* itself in order to understand Tobit's theological contours. Once this has been established, one can attempt a more direct comparison with some of the perspectives in Tobit.

I. Introduction to *1 Enoch*

1 Enoch has a very complicated compositional and textual history. J. T. Milik has argued that, by the beginning of the first century BCE, *1 Enoch* resembled an Enochic Pentateuch containing the *Book of Watchers*, the *Book of Giants*, the *Astronomical Book*, the *Book of Dreams*, and the

Epistle of Enoch.[1] More recent analysis of the Aramaic Qumran fragments, however, suggests that the picture is significantly more complicated than Milik's initial judgment.[2] For instance, the evidence indicates that 4Q203 may not belong to the same manuscript as 4Q204, which leads to the conclusion that the *Astronomical Book* was an independent text at this point (Knibb 2007: 26–7). If this is indeed the case, there is evidence of at least a loose collection of Enochic writings at Qumran containing the *Book of Watchers*, the *Dream Visions*, and the *Epistle* (Knibb 2007: 26). The *Parables of Enoch*, which were not found at Qumran, seem to have replaced the *Book of Giants* in a five-section organization of *1 Enoch* at some point after the first century CE.

The Qumran fragments virtually assure that Aramaic was the original language of these texts. However, the full corpus of *1 Enoch* has survived only in Ethiopic versions that date from the fourteenth and fifteenth centuries CE. Bridging the gap between the Aramaic fragments and the Ethiopic texts are several Greek manuscripts: Codex Panopolitanus (sixth century CE), covering chapters 1–32, and the Chester Beatty Papyrus (fourth century CE), covering chapters 97–104. In addition to short quotations or allusions in early church writers—(*inter alia*, Clement of Alexandria and Origin)—are lengthy excerpts in the chronicle of Georgius Syncellus (d. 810 CE), who often is thought to preserve a fairly reliable representation of the original text (Black and Denis 1970: 8; Nickelsburg 2001a: 12–13). To date, no critical edition of *1 Enoch* is able to deal fully with the textual complexities.[3] Commentaries by Nickelsburg (2001a) and Stuckenbruck (2007a) tend to be based upon their own eclectic texts depending on the evidence available in a given verse or section.[4] In what follows, in places where significant textual issues arise, every attempt will be made to determine the best and most likely original text, from which translations will be taken. If no indication is given, the translation quoted here is taken from *The Old Testament Pseudepigrapha* (Charlesworth 1983).

1   For a more complete discussion, see Milik and Black (1976) and Black and Denis (1970).

2   On this topic, Stuckenbruck (2007a: 15) makes two related points. First, that the materials do not seem to have been collected into this five-book format at an early stage, and second, that when they are collected together, the pentateuchal format does not seem to be the prevailing justification for doing so.

3   A helpful volume is provided by Knibb (1978). See also Uhlig (1984).

4   Nickelsburg (2001a) tries to reconstruct an earliest recoverable text, while Stuckenbruck instead offers a full translation of all the relevant versions separately, and then negotiates the differences among them (for a summary of the different approaches, see Stuckenbruck 2007a: 18–19).

II. *The* Book of Watchers

a. *Introduction to the* Book of Watchers

The *Book of Watchers* comprises the first 36 chapters of *1 Enoch*. The pervasive themes of judgment and special revelation are apparent from the opening verses, which predict the removal of the ungodly (1.2) and in which Enoch, with open eyes, sees a vision of the Holy One and heaven (1.2–3). Portions of the *Book of Watchers* have been found in Aramaic among the Dead Sea Scrolls, and Aramaic seems likely to be the original language. The manuscript 4Q201 contains fragments from chapters 1–10 and possibly chapter 12, which date from the early second or perhaps the late third century BCE (Nickelsburg 2001a: 9–10; Milik and Black 1976: 4–41). This discovery, combined with the fact that several different traditions and layers of redaction exist within the text itself, indicates that the *Book of Watchers* originated by the middle of the third century BCE (Nickelsburg 2001a: 7; Grabbe 2003a: 33; Charlesworth 2005: 446; Milik and Black 1976: 31).

The *Book of Watchers* tells a story about the period immediately before Noah's flood. According to Gen. 6.1–4, certain sons of heaven fell in love with the daughters of men and took them as wives. As a result, the *Nephilim* (Giants) appeared on the earth and became the mighty men of renown (6.4). By the time of the *Book of Watchers*, this story had gained many accretions. In the Genesis account, God does not seem pleased with the action of the angels, but the offspring they bear are good: the mighty ones of old. Genesis 6.5 then begins the flood account with the wickedness of humanity, making no apparent connection to the story of the *Nephilim*. The juxtaposition of the two episodes, however, was generative in producing the myths of rebellious angels as they exist in *1 Enoch* (Stuckenbruck 2004: 87–118).

The *Book of Watchers* tells a story that provides an etiology for sin and disaster in the world by drawing on two different traditions. In one tradition, Shemihazah is a rebellious angel who curries obedience from a small group of angels. These angels descend and impregnate women, who give birth to giants, who end up turning against humans. A second myth has Asael as the central figure, who teaches humanity different types of metallurgy and the making of swords and shields. In one myth, Shemihazah breeds destruction and sin; in the other, Asael teaches the same to human recipients (Nickelsburg 2001a: 171).[5] In both cases, the origin of sin is ascribed to the rebellion in heaven and its terrestrial fallout; the women give birth to "giants to the degree that the whole earth was filled with blood and oppression" and Asael teaches every form of oppression on the earth (*1 En.* 9.7–8). The *Book of Watchers* is thus a composite text, although one written "in a remarkably skillful and dramatic way by an accomplished writer" (Milik and Black 1976: 34). Attention will be paid here to some redactional issues, but

---

5   These two myths will be investigated in greater depth in the following section.

ultimately it is the argument of this skillful author, responsible for the final form of the text, which we seek here.

b. *God in the* Book of Watchers

An obviously significant figure, God in the *Book of Watchers* is nevertheless distant and transcendent. God's transcendence is seen in the epithets used to describe God. In 1 En. 10.1 the text offers a string of amplified language, where God is called "Most High," and "The Great and Holy One" (see also 1 En. 1.3). In 36.4, God is called the "Lord of Glory." As Nickelsburg summarizes this view of God, especially with regard to chapters 12–16:

> God is the transcendent, wholly other, heavenly king. He does not appear on earth, as he did to Abraham or Moses or Isaiah. His chariot throne does not descend to earth as it did for Ezekiel. It is fixed in heaven, the realm of spirit and holiness, totally different from the earthly sphere of flesh and blood. (2001a: 260)

In the *Book of Watchers*, God is transcendent and totally "other," which highlights the spectacular nature of Enoch's eventual approach to God's throne.

1 Enoch 14 narrates Enoch's vision of God's throne. A long buildup describes the approach to heaven with images of marble, fire, crystal, and lightning. Physical elements that normally cannot coexist emphasize the strangeness and foreignness of the experience; a house inexplicably is hot like fire and as cold as ice. When Enoch finally sees the throne, he sees the "great glory" (14.20) sitting upon it. The author applies no anthropomorphic language to God[6] and moves immediately to God's clothing (14.20b), an instance of "deanthropomorphizing" (Hanson 1977: 200).[7] The glory is such that only the angels, and certainly no one of the flesh, can face the "Excellent and the Glorious One" (14.21). The inaccessibility of the throne radicalizes Enoch's experience. The image of Enoch before the throne, juxtaposed with prohibitions to approach, augments the uniqueness and authority of the revelation he receives. The context of imagery that contradicts physical reality, injunctions against any approach, and language indicating God's transcendence, make Enoch's experience all the more remarkable (15.1).[8] God in the *Book of Watchers* is distant and transcendent but calls Enoch forward and provides the legitimization for his journey and revelation.

The depiction of God in chapters 17–19 also serves an immediate purpose within the context of the *Book of Watchers*. Scholars have suggested that

6　　Compare this vision with that in Daniel, which makes mention of hair (7.9).

7　　This was a "tendency of the Second Temple Period" according to Hanson (1977: 200).

8　　Enoch's claim to revelation, of course, is not one limited only to this portion of *1 Enoch*. Later in the corpus the *Epistle of Enoch* presumes the revelation, and the revelation is cited as an authority in later Christian literature (Jude 14–15).

chapters 17–19 are a later redactional addition to the text of the *Book of Watchers*. Carol Newsom provides some warrant for their addition. Chapters 12–16, in their focus on the sin of the watchers, calls God's omnipotence into question. The addition of chapters 17–19, however, "serves to shift this balance through its graphic depiction of God's power" (Newsom 1980: 323). Thus, the depiction of God in the *Book of Watchers* is not always simply the result of speculative formulations, but sometimes grows out of specific needs that arise while attempting to answer pressing theological questions.[9]

Finally, the work of the angels in the *Book of Watchers* also indicates God's transcendence and otherness. At the beginning of chapter 10, after the destruction wrought by Asael and Shemihazah, the groaning of the people ascends to heaven (9.10). The angels Michael, Surafel, and Gabriel ask what they should do in response (9.11). In chapter 10, the "Most High" gives specific instructions to the angels. Sariel announces the judgment of the coming flood (10.2), Raphael binds Asael and casts him into the desert (10.4–5), Gabriel is to destroy the sons of the watchers (10.9–10), and Michael destroys the giants and binds Shemihazah (10.11–15). In the end, Michael is told to destroy all injustice on the earth. The activity of God, carried out through the angels, is consistent with the characterization of God as transcendent. This general inaccessibility of God and the divine throne contrasts God's activity in the original Genesis story, in which the Lord communicates the divine plan directly to Noah (Gen. 6.13).

c. Humanity in the Book of Watchers

Similar to the characterization of God, the role of humanity in the *Book of Watchers* also changes significantly from the parent text in Genesis. Genesis separates the story of the *gibborim* (the great ones) from the flood, thereby making humanity culpable for the sinful situation in the world (Gen. 6.5). In the *Book of Watchers* the situation is reversed; sin and evil result from a rebellion in heaven and its penetration into the human realm. As Hanson describes the situation, the text "goes far beyond [Genesis] in developing a sectarian explanation of the origin of evil in the world and its ultimate eradication" (1977: 232).

1. The Shemihazah and Asael myths

The *Book of Watchers* weaves together two originally independent myths that are central in how the text expresses its view of humanity. In the Shemihazah myth, angelic beings sin in their descent to earth and union with human women (7.1). The union results in giants who turn against creation, consume all human produce, and sin against birds,

---

9   See also Beyerle (2005a: 51–186), whose study of the theophanies in the *Book of Watchers* and the *Astronomical Book* concludes that one of its main goals is to bridge the gap between the realm of God and that of humans.

beasts, reptiles, and fish (7.5). In this scenario, humans bear no culpability; the evil wrought comes from an outside force impressed upon them.

At several points the flow of the Shemihazah myth is interrupted by another that focuses on Asael. This myth is one that, if not originally based on the Azazel scapegoat tradition in Leviticus 23, eventually came to be associated with it.[10] In this myth, Asael teaches forbidden knowledge to humans (Newsom 1980). The second half of 7.1 seems to be the initial incursion of the Asael myth, although the first mention of Asael as the chief rebel comes in 8.1. The Asael myth offers a revised role for humanity by having Asael be the instigator of what humans will guiltily promulgate. Asael dazzles humans, teaching them metallurgy for making weaponry and jewelry. Humans not only absorb the knowledge, but ἐποίησαν ἑαυτοῖς οἱ υἱοί τῶν ἀνθρώπων καὶ ταῖς θυγατράσιν αὐτῶν καὶ παρέβησαν καὶ ἐπλάνησαν τοὺς ἁγίους (And the sons of men make [them] for themselves and for their daughters and they transgressed and led astray the holy ones).[11] The Asael myth finds a segment of humanity partially culpable in the entrance of evil into the world because they enticed the holy ones into rebellion. In the Shemihazah story, humans are "merely victims," whereas they are "collaborators in sin" in the Asael myth (Newsom 1980: 313). There is thus a difference of opinion between the Asael and Shemihazah strata with regard to human complicity in the origin of evil.

There has been a limited but focused scholarly discussion of these two myths with regard to their background and use in *1 Enoch*.[12] The debated issues involve the origin of the myths: are they from Ancient Near East or Greek sources and to what extent were the myths forged in exegetical consultation with Israel's scripture and ritual practice? Paul Hanson argues for a three-part growth of the tradition. The Asael myth initially was added to the Shemihazah myth in an attempt to connect the latter to *Yom Kippur*, which Hanson believes was associated with Asael (Hanson 1977: 220–32).[13] The teaching of forbidden knowledge is a third addition that becomes a "parallel motif" alongside the heavenly rebellion and cohabitation of the watchers with humans (Hanson 1977: 226). Lester Grabbe critiques Hanson's position, especially his use of פטר, which Hanson traces through *Targum Pseudo-Jonathan* back to *1 Enoch*. Grabbe offers seven points of refutation based on historical,

---

10   See Grabbe (1987: 153–4), who observes that the parallels between the Asael and Azazel stories were similar enough that ancient interpreters eventually brought the two together, even if they were not originally connected.

11   The Greek here is from the Syncellus text. There is ample support for this as an original reading of the text. For external evidence, Nickelsburg points to *1 En.* 86.1–4; *Jub.* 4.1–5; and *Targum Psuedo-Jonathan*, all of which hint at the fact that the sin of the watchers was instigated by the beauty of the women (2001a: 195).

12   In addition to the proposals to be discussed here, one should also note the work of Dimant (1974), whose work is summarized succinctly by Wright (2005: 35–7).

13   Hanson bases his argument partially on *Targum Pseudo-Jonathan* (Lev. 16.9–10, 21).

lexical, and exegetical grounds suggesting that Hanson's proposal seems not to "stand up" (1987: 154–5).

Nickelsburg argues for a separate genesis of the Asael myth based upon the Greek legend of Prometheus, which he claims was then combined with the Shemihazah story of heavenly rebellion (Nickelsburg 1977a: 383–405). In this scenario, the wrong teaching from Asael becomes the original source of evil: 8.1 states that women, adorned with beautiful metallurgy learned from Asael, lead the holy ones astray, thus superseding the Shemihazah myth's claim to explaining the ultimate origin of evil (Nickelsburg 1977a: 401–3).[14]

2. The combination of Asael and Shemihazah myths

Both Hanson and Nickelsburg point out the way in which each individual myth contributes to a discussion of the origin of evil, but neither scholar significantly addresses the resulting combination of the two myths. Although there is consensus that, in the *Book of Watchers*, two myths have been joined, there is "no consensus as to how or why [the Asael] motif came to be incorporated into the narrative" (Nickelsburg 2001a: 190); the result of the admixture of the two is "not entirely clear" (Newsom 1980: 321). At times the interpolations seem to indicate a desire simply to make Asael the main antagonist, while at others it seems that the "principal concern" was to emphasize that the result of sin is corruption of the earth as opposed to incorrect teaching (Molenberg 1984: 136). In light of the fact that one of the major contrasts in the two myths is the degree of human culpability in the origin of evil, one might expect the combination of the two to emphasize a specific role for humanity *vis-à-vis* evil over another.[15] Two main points, to be outlined in what follows, indicate that the author of this composite text intends to subdue the Asael myth and its emphasis on the culpability of humanity in the origin of evil.

i. Removing Asael's Distinctiveness

First, in 7.1–6 and 9.6–7 the motifs of the two myths are mixed together in such a way that the Asael myth loses some of its distinctiveness. In 7.1–6 the Asael myth loses its chieftain. Instead, the forbidden teaching

14   Nickelsburg reaffirms this argument in his commentary (2001a: 195). There are also some textual issues with 8.1, which will be dealt with below.

15   See the suggestion of Wright (2005), who says that the author's purpose "in including two traditions concerning the corruption of humanity could be due in part to the changing notions of the origin of sin within Judaism" (104). Although Wright's work parses the different traditions in great detail, he never offers a sustained interpretation of the results of the combined myths, later calling the Asael addition "an even greater mystery" (136). It is also worth noting that, in a different context, these "euhemeristic traditions" were employed simply to argue for the supremacy of Jewish culture (Stuckenbruck 2004: 98).

is interpolated into the procreation of the giants, mentioning medicine, incantations, roots, plants, and, according to 4Q201, sorcery (4Q201 3.15: ולאלפה אנין חרשה; καὶ ἐδίδαξαν αὐταῖς φαρμακείας καὶ ἐπαοιδὰς καὶ ῥιζοτομίας καὶ τὰς βοτάνας ἐδήλωσαν αὐταῖς). The Asael and Shemihazah traditions also are brought close together in 9.6–7, which comes in the midst of a prayer of petition, described by Nickelsburg as a "clear and pointed statement of the problem of evil" (1977a: 387).[16] In 9.6 Asael is referred to as having taught "oppression." This is immediately followed by a reference to Shemihazah and the relations with women. The two figures are combined grammatically in 9.8, with use of the third person plural, such that they are both responsible for all evil, whether by way of illicit teaching or fornication that produces defilement: "*They* have gone [ἐπορεύθησαν] to the daughters of the men of the earth, and *they* have lain with them, and have defiled themselves and they revealed to them all sins"[17] (*1 En.* 9.8). The author who combined the two myths seems interested, at this point, in bringing together the deeds of the two chief rivals, showing that they are both responsible for evil on the earth. The Shemihazah paradigm of the origin of evil has primacy here. Humans are passive, the actions of the two opponents forced upon them. As Nickelsburg states (2001a: 213), although the two chief villains are combined, "Shemihazah's primacy in the original form of the story is still evident" to the extent that the "whole earth is filled with blood and iniquity" (*1 En.* 9.9).[18] Nickelsburg's assessment suggests that Shemihazah's primacy is simply a vestigial remnant, as if its contours still shine through the heavily edited final form of the text with no help from the final author. One could read the evidence differently and suggest that the final compiler of the *Book of Watchers* intended to combine the myths so as to emphasize Shemihazah's role and its explanation of the origin of evil, specifically one that exonerates humanity.

ii. Modifying Asael's Sinful Activity
Second, Asael's activity is described in chapter 10 as corruption, not incorrect teaching. The narration of Raphael's victory over Asael (10.4–8) describes Asael's binding and eternal confinement in darkness. In the midst of ordering these punishments, the Most High makes Asael and his cohorts solely responsible; the motif of teaching remains, but in 10.7a it is described as something that has corrupted the earth and made it desolate: καὶ ἴασαι τὴν γῆν ἥν ἠφάνισαν οἱ ἐγρήγοροι (heal the earth

---

16   For some context to the issue of theodicy during this time period, see Charlesworth (2003: 470–508).

17   The Syncellus text here adds: καὶ ἐδίδαξαν αὐτας μίσητρα ποιεῖν (and they taught them to do hate-based charms).

18   Nickelsburg (2001a: 204) follows the Syncellus text in removing the reference to blood because it does not seem a good parallel to the reference to blood in 9.1.

which the watchers have made desolate).[19] The whole earth has been corrupted (ἠρημώθη) by Asael's teaching, and upon him should be written *all sin*[20] (10.8). This language of corruption and the ascription to a chief rival are more indicative of the activity of Shemihazah's watchers (as described in 7.3–6) than of the activity of Asael, whose wrong teaching would more naturally be described as impiety or ungodliness, as is the case in 8.2a (καὶ ἐγένετο ἀσέβεια πολλὴ ἐπὶ τῆς γῆς; and there was much ungodliness on the earth). The language of corruption in 10.7–8 (ἀφανίζω, ἐρημόω) is reminiscent of the language in 8.2b (καὶ ἠφάνισαν τὰ ὁδοὺς αὐτῶν; and they made desolate their paths).[21] Although the reference to corruption in 8.2 is surrounded by a depiction of Asael that is in line with its foundation myth (i.e., that Asael taught improper activity which humans then promulgated), it sits more broadly in a context in which the Shemihazah myth "dominates" and in which only "fragments" of the Asael myth remain (Nickelsburg 2001a: 196).

The ascription of "all sin" to Asael is what led Hanson (1977: 220–6) to find the origin of the Asael myth in Israel's scapegoat tradition. These words, however, have a more specific goal in their immediate context. The author portrays the Asael myth in such a way that Asael himself is responsible for sin and humans have been corrupted by his activity. The end of 8.1, where humans are made partly responsible for the promulgation of the evils taught to them, seems only the vestigial remains of a perspective the final author of the *Book of Watchers* intended to mute.

3. Conclusions regarding humanity in the Book of Watchers
In the original Shemihazah myth, humanity bears no guilt in the entrance of sin into the world. The original Asael myth, however, laid some blame on humanity; in order for Asael's teaching to be successful it needed to be promulgated by humans (as is indicated in 8.1d). As the above analysis indicates, these two myths were brought together in order to change the implications for humanity. The author has brought the Asael myth into close alignment with that of Shemihazah in order to hold both figures responsible for evil, which simultaneously mutes any human culpability.

19   This is following Syncellus text. There is not complete consistency of the terminology used for heavenly beings in the *Book of Watchers* (as the textual variations at the very beginning at 1.2 indicate). However, as Nickelsburg has summarized (2001a: 140–1), there does seem to be enough of a pattern to discern what is being discussed. It seems that the Greek translators adopted the word watchers (οἱ ἐγρήγοροι) and used it always to refer to the rebel heavenly beings, which distinguished them from other heavenly beings, which are referred to as angels (ἄγγελοι).

20   4Q202 4.5 here preserves two letters, a yod and a taw, which could be part of the construction: כול עויתא (all sin).

21   This is following the Syncellus text. Panopolitanus has this statement formulated in the passive (ἠφανίσθησαν) as does the Ethiopic (Nickelsburg 2001a: 189). Note also that the language is reminiscent of Gen. 6.11–12, in which violence filled the earth and all flesh corrupted its way on the earth: (Hebrew: שחת; LXX: ἀφανίζω).

In two separate moves, the *Book of Watchers* limits the role of humanity in the genesis of evil. First, the original situation from Genesis itself has been adapted. Humanity is no longer responsible for corruption on the earth (cf. Gen. 6.12); with the Shemihazah story, blame has been shifted to the rebellious watchers and the offspring that result from the rebellion (*1 En.* 7.1–6).[22] The Asael myth offered a different understanding of the origin of evil, but by associating Asael with Shemihazah, describing Asael's activity as the corruption of the earth, and ascribing evil to both Asael and Shemihazah, there is a segment of humanity no longer guilty. The author responsible for the final form of the *Book of Watchers*, and those who created the now-conflated myths themselves, were interested in the problem of evil, its origin, and the role of humanity (or lack thereof) in its genesis and promulgation.

d. Creation in the Book of Watchers

1. The regularity of creation and derivations therefrom

The discussion of humanity and evil in the *Book of Watchers* leads naturally to a discussion of the role of creation. Before narrating the story of the watchers, the text of *1 Enoch* 1–36 begins with a general announcement of the coming judgment followed by an exhortation to observe natural phenomena (chs. 2–5). These chapters foreshadow Enoch's travels to the heavenly realm and establish the importance of creation in the thought of the author and in the argument of this particular text. Chapter two switches to second-person address, speaking to those upon whom the judgment described in 1.9 will come. Humans are exhorted to examine God's works because they do not alter their courses (2.1). Following this exhortation are admonitions to observe the regularity of seasons, precipitation, and agrarian activities. The statement in 5.1 explains the reason for the contemplation: "understand that the living God made them thusly, and he lives for ever and ever."[23] The text contrasts this image of God as the guarantor of natural regularity in 5.1—"year after year his works do not change"[24]—with the actions of the unrighteous in 5.4: "but you have changed your works" (וְאַנְתֻּן שְׁנֵיתֻן עֹבְדְכֵן; 4Q201 2.12) . . . "there will be no peace for you" (לֵת שְׁלָם לְכֵן; 4Q201 2.14). The seas and rivers obey, but the wicked have not obeyed and as a result they will not find peace (5.4) even while the elect

---

22   It is not my intent here to imply a direct movement from Genesis to the story of the watchers as we have it in *1 Enoch*. There certainly would have been much intervening tradition, but we do not have access to it.

23   Translation here is according to the Greek Panopolitanus Codex. Nickelsburg (2001a: 150), based on evidence from 4Qen^a (הוּא לְעֹלַם דְעָלְמִין), adds the substantive phrase, "who lives for all the ages," to the beginning of the clause as part of the subject. This does not change the meaning significantly, however.

24   This is a possible reconstruction of 4Q201 2.11b–12a. The end of l.11 has "year" (שְׁנַה). This reconstruction is supported by Panopolitanus (Nickelsburg 2001a: 151).

ones will (5.7). It seems that such texts "regard observable reality as a kind of cosmic parable and exhort their readers to draw the appropriate lesson" (Argall 1995: 101). The constituent parts of the order of nature in *1 Enoch* 1–5 function as an "exemplar of regularity and faithfulness" that allows them to act as "independent personalities" (Stone 1987: 300–301).[25]

The *Book of Watchers* also evokes creation in its very specific narration of what the watchers themselves do. In *1 Enoch* 6–11, which tells the combined stories of Shemihazah and Asael, the havoc that both wreak on earth penetrates and corrupts creation. In the story of the birth of the giants, Shemihazah and those who have rallied around him impregnate human women, who give birth to generations of giant creatures.[26] The Aramaic in 7.2, with a *pe'al* participle, indicates passivity on the part of the women: והויה בטנן מנהן (and they [the women] became pregnant by them [the watchers]). The humans grow weary of feeding these giants, who consume humans as substitute nourishment (7.3). The giants then consume animals, which is directly forbidden in Gen. 1.29–30, although the prohibition changes after the flood (Gen. 9.1–3). The giants have turned their destruction against the entire created order by eating what should not be eaten. Then they begin to devour one another. Finally, summarizing the previous activity and mentioning one act more abhorrent than all the others, the text adds a final, stark statement: "and they drank the blood" (7.3). This defies the qualification of Noah's ability to eat animals: "flesh with its lifeblood still in it you shall not eat" (Gen. 9.4). *Jubilees* 7.26–33 expands and makes more extreme this injunction, claiming that anyone who drinks the blood will be blotted out from the face of the earth and suffer judgment in *Sheol*. Thus we see, in the Shemihazah myth, humans invaded by the rebellion in heaven, which results in sin of every kind against God's intended order.

The *Book of Watchers* proceeds to offer two different remedies for this corruption.

i. Healing the Earth
The first way that the *Book of Watchers* resolves the watchers' menace is by narrating how the earth itself needs to be healed. The offspring of the watchers need to be defeated themselves, dirty work that is reserved for Gabriel (10.9–10). But at the same time, the earth itself is healed of the plague that came as a result of the evil teaching and procreative activities. Asael's teaching results in the corruption of creation, which

---

25   Stone claims that *1 Enoch* has moved beyond the common expression in the Hebrew Bible, in which nature is personified only as a "literary device" (e.g., Ps. 19.1; Pss. 104 and 148).

26   The ambiguity for the name of these creatures here is intentional. While both the Ethiopic and Codex Panopolitanus attest only "giants," the Syncellus text has οἱ δὲ γίγαντες ἐτέκωσαν ναφηλείμ καὶ τοῖς ναφηλείμ ἐγεννήθησαν ἐλιουδ, which perhaps is a conflation with *Jubilees* 7.22, which mentions the *Elioud*. The Qumran Aramaic is too fragmentary at this point to provide any help in resolving this interpretive problem.

necessitates that the earth itself be healed. One best sees this perspective when observing how Raphael dispenses with Asael. The Most High tells Raphael to bind Asael in the desert and cover him with rocks (10.4–5). Raphael, whose name means "God heals," is dispatched on healing missions elsewhere in Jewish literature (e.g., Tob. 3.16–17; 12.11–21). There is not an exception here; Raphael must do more than bind Asael. He is directed to heal the earth (ἴασαι τὴν γῆν²⁷), which has been made desolate by the watchers (10.7) and by the deeds of the teaching of Asael (ἐν τοῖς ἔργοις τῆς διδασκαλίας ἀζαήλ [10.8]). There is no culpability on the part of humanity mentioned, and the text emphatically exhorts Raphael to write "all sin" upon Asael. By noting how Raphael's instructions are extended beyond binding to healing a plagued earth, one can see how the sin attributed to Asael has resulted in the corruption of creation. It seems clear that creation in the *Book of Watchers* is something corrupted and penetrated by evil that eventually will be cleansed and healed.

ii. Enoch's Otherworldly Journey
Enoch's otherworldly journey in chapters 12–36 of the *Book of Watchers* also offers a remedy, of sorts, to the scourge of the watchers and continues to express this remedy in terms of the created order.²⁸ The first manifestation of Enoch's otherworldly journey is in chapters 17–19.²⁹ Enoch sees many hidden phenomena of creation: a river of fire (17.5), a great darkness, and the storehouses of all the winds (18.1); God ordered all things that have been created (18.1).³⁰ Enoch's tour of the heavens emphasizes the inner workings of the judgment predicted in earlier sections of the book. He sees the storehouse for the angels who mingled with the women and whose offspring continue to lead humanity astray (19.1), kept until the final judgment. Just beyond these captives lies a chasm with no earthly features, a "desolate and terrible place" (18.12). Finally, in 18.14–16 there is a description of stars that have not obeyed the proper order. They anger God because they did not appear at the proper time of their rising. As a result, God has bound them until the time of the completion of their sin. Just as all the ordered things

---

27   The Ethiopic and Syncellus here have the imperative, ἴασαι. Other manuscripts, including the Panopolitanus Codex, have the future passive, ἰαθήσεται.

28   There is continuity between the two sections, even though Noah figured more prominently in chapters 6–11 and Enoch becomes the central recipient of revelation in chapters 12–36.

29   Enoch's ascent to and vision of the heavenly throne introduces his more extensive visits to the outer reaches of creation in chapters 17–36 and establishes his "credentials" for that journey (Nickelsburg 2001a: 229).

30   For a fuller discussion of lists of things revealed in apocalyptic literature, see M. Stone (1976: 414–53). Stone claims that there is a common function for the lists: "they all occur at the high point of a revelation, where a brief statement of its contents is desired, or else as a summary of what is revealed to the seer" (418).

obey (18.1), so the predicted punishment will come to pass according to God's word.

In the midst of this description of the farthest reaches of creation, the significance of the rebellion of the watchers is couched in terms of the created heavenly phenomena. The note in 18.15 regarding stars that have decided not to obey their appointed movements does more than assure the coming judgment. The description of these stars alludes to the sin of the watchers.[31] A "linkage has been made" between the rebel watchers and the stars who do not do what they are supposed to do (Argall 1995: 122). Argall argues that the reason behind this linkage comes from a desire to find "an explanation for the astronomical miscalculations of the dominant society by relating them to the hidden phenomena of transgressing stars" (1995: 122). Positing a sociological situation behind this literature is helpful, but there may be a theological impetus as well. The language used to describe the transgression of the stars echoes the language of creation in Genesis 1: καὶ οἱ ἀστέρες . . . οὗτοί εἰσιν οἱ παραβάντες πρόστιγμα κυρίου ἐν ἀρχῇ τῆς ἀνατολῆς αὐτῶν.[32] The stars who rebelled against God are described as doing so <u>in the beginning</u> of their rising. The text may be condemning contemporaneous heretical calendrical systems, but it also claims that the experience of evil in the world comes from a supra-human rebellion against the created order.

Thus, the otherworldly journeys in *1 Enoch* 17–19 make two related points. On one hand, they assert the regularity of creation, which is in harmony with *1 En.* 2.1–3. At the same time, part of the problem experienced in the current time is described as a rebellion against this very predictable order. Some of the heavenly bodies are not obeying God's command, and the rebellion of the watchers is thus described as eventuating in instability and unpredictability in creation. The ultimate point, of course, is that order will be restored: "order exists in heaven in spite of the fact that some stars and angels have rebelled and will be punished" (Argall 1995: 118). The restoration envisioned, however, should not distract from the way this text expresses the problem of evil, something experienced as a rupture in the very order of creation.[33]

---

31   This is an observation made also by Nickelsburg (2001a: 288) and Argall (1995), who says that the language here "recalls" that used in 2.1 (121).

32   Greek from Codex Panopolitanus. Only one small Aramaic fragment of 18.15 has been preserved and its identification as such is doubtful (Milik and Black 1976: 22, 228).

33   It is possible that one could see a contradiction here: How is it possible simultaneously to assert the regularity of the heavenly phenomena and discuss the rebellion of certain stars? Jackson calls attention to this potential problem but says that, even if such a tension can be perceived, it does not seem to have been a problem for the authors of *1 Enoch*. Instead, "the original regularity of the cosmos as described in *1 Enoch* 2–5 forms the basis for condemning all subsequent deviations" (2004: 140). And, at the same time, Enoch's visits to the otherworldly realms are from a time before the rebellion; it is as if he is given access to the "blueprints of this cosmic order" (140).

The purpose of the otherworldly journeys in the *Book of Watchers* is to show concretely the judgment announced against the wicked. The reliability of the judgment is augmented by the revelatory nature of the entire episode: traveling with authoritative guides and seeing visions of places to which no one else has access. In chapter 21 Enoch sees a vision of a terrible place reserved for the transgressing stars, which is followed directly by a visit to a place of fire where the evil angels are reserved forever, assuring that the judgment coming to the wicked is built into the structure of the cosmos. The text emphasizes the importance of creation in understanding both the phenomenon of evil and its rectification. The motif of the punishment of the stars, which parallels the evil work of the watchers, indicates that their misdeeds are a breaking from the order of creation. The evil wrought by the watchers is a malfunction of nature and creation itself: created entities are not doing what they are supposed to do.

2. *Conclusion to creation in the* Book of Watchers

The created order in the *Book of Watchers* contains mountains, trees, rocks, plants, bodies of water, rivers, wind, and more. But, as Nickelsburg states, "this author does not separate science from theology or history from creation" (2001a: 293). While a work that contains such cosmological speculation certainly reflects interest in the "science" of the day, references to the working of the heavenly phenomena, astronomy, and botany are all in service to the theological interests in the text. Included with the phenomena Enoch observes are "the historical evidence and enactment of human sin and divine justice" (Nickelsburg 2001a: 293). In other words, the author is expressing his or her belief about the nature of evil in terms of creation. Evil is nothing less than a rebellion against the order of creation and, as such, is manifest in creation as unpredictability (i.e., not following God's appointed regularity) and as the crossing of boundaries (especially those between heavenly beings and humans). The historical experience of the author, quite possibly one of oppression,[34] is described metaphorically as rape, ravenous devouring, and imbalance in creation. Creation is the stage on which the "cosmic parable" of the drama of the origin of evil and its rectification are played out (Argall 1995: 101).

---

34   Recall the arguments of Nickelsburg (2001a: 7); Grabbe (2003a: 33); Charlesworth (2005: 446); and Milik and Black (1976: 31) that the *Book of Watchers* most likely reflects turmoil under the *Diadochoi*.

III. *The* Astronomical Book

a. Introduction to the Astronomical Book

The *Book of Watchers* expresses its understanding of evil in the world with specific roles for God, humanity, and creation. As we move to another portion of *1 Enoch* with roots in the third century BCE, we will see some similar arguments being made. It may not have as much to say about the role of humanity, but it works from many of the same perspectives on the role of creation in explaining the phenomenon of evil.

Chapters 72–82 of *1 Enoch*, known as the *Astronomical Book* or the *Book of Heavenly Luminaries*, is, along with the *Book of Watchers*, the oldest portion of the apocalyptic collection of *1 Enoch*.[35] The Dead Sea Scrolls contain fragments that, according to Milik and Black, correspond to parts of 73.1–74.9, the script of which dates to the late third or early second century BCE.[36] The manuscript evidence from Qumran indicates that the *Astronomical Book* circulated in a longer form than that which is found in the Ethiopic version.[37] It is a tractate intended to affirm the regularity of a solar calendrical system (72.2). The angel Uriel communicates to Enoch revelation about the luminaries according to their origin and movement (72.1). The movement of these luminaries is fixed (75.1) and provides the basis for a 364-day calendar, on which festivals and agricultural work would be based. The text also polemicizes against a 360-day lunar/solar calendar, which omits four days (75.2–3; 82.4), even though there is no evidence that such a calendar was in use within Judaism (Collins 1998: 61). While this section of *1 Enoch* seems to show less familiarity with other parts of the corpus, it nevertheless seems to "reflect faithfully" many of the concepts and ideas prevalent in other parts of the work (Neugebauer 1985: 386).

b. God and Humanity in the Astronomical Book

God in the *Astronomical Book* is described with the same type of transcendent and majestic language as was used in the *Book of Watchers*.[38] The text usually uses modifying epithets with the divine name.[39] God

---

35   Milik and Black speculate that the *Astronomical Book* may even have origins in the Persian period (1976: 8).

36   Milik and Black (1976: 7). See also Nickelsburg (2001a: 10). The fragment in question is 4Q208. Stuckenbruck points out that there is nothing overtly Enochic in this fragment, but it does warrant inclusion based on its similarity to 4Q209 (2007b: 58).

37   It seems that it was copied on its own scroll because of its length. See Milik and Black (1976: 8) and Nickelsburg (2001a: 8). See also Stuckenbruck (2007b: 57–9).

38   At this point, I am using the *Book of Watchers* as a point of reference and comparison only. I am not positing the growth of the *Astronomical Book* in consultation with or directly from the *Book of Watchers*.

39   For example, one of the most direct references to God is in 81.3, where the name "King of Glory" is used.

is the one who "created all the phenomena in the world" (81.3). Enoch is shown the position of each of the luminaries according to their rank and origin (72.1), all of which is a part of what God has created. While Enoch is taken on a journey, of sorts,[40] to visit the openings for the heavenly bodies, the winds, precipitation, and the seven mountains and seven rivers, there is no approach to the throne as in the *Book of Watchers*. Nor is God mentioned as the executor of judgment on sinners. It is simply mentioned that evil things shall be multiplied on them (80.8).[41] Divine agency certainly lies behind creation and the regular workings of heavenly phenomena, the computations of which are "true" (82.7). There is, however, no theophany and no vision of the heavenly throne; God remains a distant figure.

Humanity in the various redactional layers of the *Astronomical Book* also does not differ much from the perspective thereof in the *Book of Watchers*. One of the book's major goals and emphases is to exhort humans to follow the proper calendar.[42] Although more limited in scope than the *Book of Watchers*, the *Astronomical Book* also has a revelatory perspective. Uriel acts as Enoch's guide (72.1; 80.1). Within humanity, there is a stark division between the righteous and sinners. The author draws an analogy between the shortness of the days during winter and how the days of the sinners will be cut short (80.2), which recalls the analogy contrasting the obedience of natural phenomena with the disobedience of wicked humanity in chapters 2–5.[43] At the same time, those who do what is right will not be affected by the sin of the sinners; the consequences of the evil deeds will come only to those who act wrongly (81.9). The righteous are blessed, but there is no sin like the sin of computing the days incorrectly and according to the wrong indicators (82.4) because, if they are computed incorrectly, Sabbaths, festivals, and harvests will not fall at the appropriate time.

c. Creation in the Astronomical Book

When one begins to examine the role of creation in the *Astronomical Book* an internal contradiction quickly becomes apparent. The text's initial statements indicate a regularity and orderliness to the heavenly phenomena that Uriel showed to Enoch:[44]

---

40   The journey is not as pronounced as in other parts of the Enochic corpus, especially compared to the *Book of Watchers*. A journey may be presupposed but, according to VanderKam, it is "hardly a noticeable theme in the book" (1984: 108).

41   As in the *Book of Watchers*, there are significant redactional issues in the *Astronomical Book*, which will be dealt with below.

42   For an analysis of the book's goals *vis-à-vis* calendrical systems, see Koch (2007: 119–37).

43   This is an observation also made by J. Collins (1998: 61–2).

44   The *Astronomical Book* only hints at Enoch as the recipient of the revelation, although the text itself is narrated in the first person.

The Book of the Itinerary of the Luminaries of Heaven: the position of each and every one, in respect to their ranks, in respect to their authorities, and in respect to their seasons; each one according to their names and their places of origin and according to their months, which Uriel, the holy angel who was with me, and who also is their guide, showed me. (*1 En.* 72.1; *OTP* 1:50)

Uriel shows the movement of heavenly bodies, the twelve winds, and seven mountains and rivers (77.1–9), and Enoch writes down what he sees (74.2). Chapter 75 avers that the luminaries and their leaders do not tarry in their duties: "The leaders of the chiefs of the thousands, which are appointed over the whole creation and upon all the stars . . . they do not leave from the fixed stations according to the reckoning of the year" (*1 En.* 75.1; *OTP* 1:54). All of the calculations are precise, and in 82.7 Enoch states unequivocally that the calculations about the luminaries and months are "true" because they have been revealed as such.

In chapters 80–81, however, one finds an "astrological twist" (VanderKam 1984: 106). *1 Enoch* 80.2–8 describes a disobedient heavenly realm, which contradicts the earlier assertions of creation's regularity:

In the days of the sinners the years will grow shorter, their seed will be late on their land and in their fields. Everything on the earth will change and will not appear at their times, the rain will be withheld, and the sky will stand still . . . the moon will change its order and will not appear at its normal time . . . many heads of the stars will stray from the command and will change their ways and actions and will not appear at the times prescribed for them.[45] (*1 En.* 80.2, 4, 6)

Scholars have described this section (chs. 80–81) as one that "stands out" from the rest of the *Astronomical Book* and is "in tension with the rest of the book which presupposed unchanging patterns for the luminaries" (Nickelsburg and VanderKam 2004: 7).

One indeed sees a glaring difference in chapters 80–81.[46] In 80.2–8 the regularity of creation has changed; plants now will not bear fruit and rain is unpredictable. The moon alters its order and the amount of light it gives forth. These chapters shift the scientific interest evident in the majority of the *Astronomical Book* and unexpectedly introduce a stark contrast between sinners and the righteous. Perhaps most strikingly, the chiefs of the stars make errors, change their courses, and do not appear at the times prescribed for them (80.6). VanderKam summarizes the situation in chapter 80 as follows: "prior to the end, natural laws, which are considered unchanging elsewhere in the Astronomical Book and in *1 Enoch* as a whole

---

45   Translation taken from Nickelsburg and VanderKam (2004: 110–11).
46   The glaring shift in perspective in chapters 80–81 has caused many scholars to posit it as a later addition to the text. Despite the fact that the eschatological perspective in chapters 80–81 is in "starkest contrast" (VanderKam 1984: 106) to the remainder of the *Astronomical Book*, it is nevertheless these very chapters that give the *Astronomical Book* its apocalyptic perspective.

(e.g. 2.1), will no longer apply, just as humanity will violate moral and religious laws" (1984: 106).

Scholars have not easily understood the reasons for this theological shift. For instance, VanderKam asks: "one wonders why someone chose to add a poem that conflicts so strongly with the remainder of the book" (1984: 106). In the end VanderKam offers only the explanation that it "remains an enigma" (1984: 107). Recourse back to the *Book of Watchers*, however, may help explain the intentions behind the addition.[47]

The addition of chapters 80–81 changes the overall message of the *Astronomical Book* by adding what Milik and Black call "moral considerations" (1976: 8). In the *Book of Watchers*, the regularity of the created phenomena is employed in two ways, both of which also function in the *Astronomical Book* once it has been retrofitted with chapters 80–81. First, the regularity of the heavens is used as an analogy to highlight the abnormality and unpredictability of the sinners. J. Collins also notes this parallel between the two books, claiming that, when examining chapter 80, "we are reminded of the contrast between orderly nature and sinful humanity in 1 Enoch 1–5 [i.e., the beginning of the *Book of Watchers*]" (1998: 61). Second, the deviations from regularity in chapter 80 highlight the significance of the experience of evil in the world: it hails from a disruption in the order of creation itself. The watchers, depicted as rebellious stars, are entities not obeying the rules of creation (18.14–16), which recalls the rebellious chiefs of the stars (80.6) in the *Astronomical Book*. In both scenarios the heavenly bodies are not performing their appointed tasks. The assertion of David Jackson, although made specifically regarding the *Book of Watchers*, also holds true for the *Astronomical Book*: the "regularity of the cosmos . . . forms the basis for condemning all subsequent deviations" (2004: 140).

Chapters 80–81 of 1 *Enoch*, then, reflect an individual or group less interested in the specific regulations of the calendar and more interested in the moral implications of irregularity. For the *Astronomical Book*, evil has a similar significance to that in the *Book of Watchers*; in both "right observance is determined by an understanding of the heavenly world" (Collins 1998: 62). One should do more than contemplate the created order, however. Creation also provides the arena in which evil had its beginning; evil is explained in terms of a cosmological origin and significance.[48] Emphasis on adherence to a certain calendrical system

---

47   Nickelsburg has an even more radical perspective on chapters 81–82, claiming that this text was originally a testamentary end to the *Book of Watchers* that served as a "narrative bridge" to chapters 91–105 (2001a: 335–7). For a good discussion of some problems with this theory, see the reviews of Nickelsburg's commentary by Collins (2003a: 2:373–8) and VanderKam (2003: 2:379–86) in Neusner and Avery-Peck (2003: vol. 2).

48   Collins agrees with this assessment, stating that, in the *Astronomical Book*, "earthly sinfulness has a supernatural cause" (1998: 61).

is augmented with the idea that the phenomenon of evil in the world is nothing less than a rupture in the regularity of creation itself.

In summary, in the *Astronomical Book*, the author attempts to make a pointed statement about the problem of evil and the significance of sin. While the text may have originally focused on following the correct calendar, chapters 80–81 change the function of the scientific interest considerably. In its final, quasi-apocalyptic form, the text expresses two different situations. The text first describes an orderly cosmos where everything is as it should be. With this as the backdrop, the cosmic significance of sin is explained as a rebellion from the created order. The scenario in the *Astronomical Book* is not so different from that in the *Book of Watchers*, where sin and evil are described as a fissure in the ability of creation to do its job and follow its orders. VanderKam, summarizing the perspective of both the *Book of Watchers* and the *Astronomical Book*, claims that both books "demonstrate that through inspired guidance into the mysteries of the cosmos one can arrive at theological truth" (1984: 141). In an apocalyptic community the experience of evil and the lack of ability to explain hardship in terms of doing right or wrong lead to a new explanation. The origin of evil is explained in terms of a rebellion from creation that divides humanity into two groups. A community's lack of ability to exert historical influence in the world is now attributable to a rupture in the created order itself.

IV. The Epistle of Enoch

a. Introduction to the Epistle of Enoch

The *Epistle of Enoch*,[49] comprising chapters 92–105 in *1 Enoch*, is from a later date than the *Book of Watchers* and the *Astronomical Book* and presupposes earlier portions of the corpus.[50] The section begins (92.1–5) with a narrator who claims Enoch as the author of what is to follow. Enoch then alludes to his previous revelatory adventures, saying that he is recounting what was revealed to him from his heavenly vision (93.2). There are several texts (e.g., 100.1–4; 102.1) that speak of a coming judgment in a way reminiscent of chapter 1. The righteous need not fear this judgment (102.4), which recalls assuaged fears in the *Astronomical Book* (81.9). The text itself is made up of many smaller, originally distinct, forms, including woes, exhortations, two-ways instruction, and revelatory formulae (Nickelsburg 2001a: 416–20). There is, however, enough consistency of theme and subject

---

49   The work is named as an epistle because of its self-reference as such (τῆς ἐπιστολῆς ταύτης) in 100.6, even though it evinces only a loose resemblance to a letter.

50   Stuckenbruck delineates the *Epistle* as 92.1–5 and 93.11–105.2 because it is interrupted by the *Apocalypse of Weeks*, which is usually treated as a distinct unit. He also points out that these compositions in the *Epistle* "received and interpreted the earliest strands of the Enochic tradition" (2007a: 1).

that most scholars are comfortable talking about the text as the product of a single author, in so far as it was assembled toward a specific end.[51] The *Epistle* contains apocalyptic sections, most notably the *Apocalypse of Weeks* (ch. 93), and discourses that alternately address sinners and the righteous. For all the exhortation to righteousness that the *Epistle* entails, there is remarkably little specificity. Readers are repeatedly told not to sin, to remain righteous, and to persevere, but the specifics of what to do and what to avoid are not discussed in detail. (One notable exception here pertains to wealth: the dominant ethical theme of the text is the relationship between rich and poor.) The text presumes knowledge of the *Book of Watchers* and, at the same time, is known by the writer of *Jubilees*, which sets its date somewhere between 200 and 150 BCE (Nickelsburg 2001a: 427). The *Epistle* focuses a great deal on retribution and, as has been the case above, God, humanity, and creation all have significant roles to play in this retribution, even if the *Epistle* does not always offer the same answers as did the *Book of Watchers* and the *Astronomical Book*.

b. God in the Epistle of Enoch

In the *Epistle of Enoch*, God is described with much of the same terminology as was seen in the earlier sections of *1 Enoch*. God is named with similarly transcendent language, called the "Great One" (103.1), "Most High" (101.9; 100.4), and the "Holy Great One" (98.6). Also, as was seen in earlier portions of the corpus, God is the creator (e.g., 94.11). More prominently, however, God is the arbiter of judgment. In earlier sections of *1 Enoch*, God was behind the judgment and its primary source, but the angels were quickly dispatched to execute its workings (e.g., 10.1–22). In the *Epistle*, God acts in the judgment itself. For example, chapter 100 claims that angels will gather sinners together and that the Most High will rise up in order to execute judgment on a day when horses and chariots will sink in the blood of the sinners (100.3–4). In 101.2–3 the sinners are warned about God's wrath and ability to hinder the rain and dew as means of punishment. Even more explicitly, in the days of judgment, God will hurl fire on sinners and cause them to tremble (102.1). Such language offers a fairly common description for a theophany, but is more anthropomorphized than Enoch's throne vision in 14.8–25, in which the description of God is limited. So, while God is still described as using angelic messengers and as completely in control of creation, at the same time, there is a more anthropomorphic depiction of God in the *Epistle*, especially with regard to judgment.

---

51   Nickelsburg (2001a: 426). Stuckenbruck (2007a) does not go quite so far as Nickelsburg in making this point. He does, however, note the way the originally disparate parts of what comprises the *Epistle* are combined so successfully that it is hard to distinguish their relative dates (11). This observation about their cohesive combination would seem to support Nickelsburg's observation as well.

c. *Humanity in the* Epistle of Enoch

The depiction of humanity in the *Epistle of Enoch* differs from that in earlier portions of the corpus. In the *Apocalypse of Weeks* there is a long list of rhetorical questions that ask who is able to understand all the activities of heaven (93.11–14).[52] The repeated question, "Who is able?" has only one possible answer: Enoch is able to know the workings of the heavenly phenomena. As Stuckenbruck states, "the rhetorical questions, placed within the Enochic tradition, make Enoch stand out sharply as the unique revealer of wisdom" (2007a: 237).[53] The text is alluding to Enoch's journeys as written down in chapters 18 and 72–82 and indicates that one can understand only through the special revelation that Enoch received. Although promulgating the Enoch tradition, the *Epistle* is somewhat at odds with chapters 2–5, in which sinners have sufficient understanding to examine all the activities that take place in the sky and how these do not alter their ways. The sinners can contrast their own deviant activities with creation, which acts with nothing but fidelity and orderliness.

There is another aspect of humanity in the *Epistle* that contradicts earlier portions of the corpus: in the *Epistle*, humans are directly responsible for their own righteousness; there is an "emphasis on human beings as the origin of sin on the earth" (Stuckenbruck 2007a: 249). This idea is first introduced in chapter 94, following directly after the *Apocalypse of Weeks*. The path for the righteous is described with basic two-ways instruction; there is a path for the wicked and one for the righteous. Incumbent upon the righteous is the need to do the correct things: "seek and choose for yourselves and choose righteousness and the elect life. Walk in the way of peace so that you shall have life" (94.4). This directive is followed by a series of woes to sinners, those who "build oppression and violence" (94.6). Two-ways ethical instruction was a "common metaphor" for presenting ethical exhortation throughout Israel's history (Nickelsburg 2001a: 454). This idea is joined in the *Epistle* with strong words about how an individual's deeds will be examined. In another woe oracle, the text claims that the unrighteous will be "recompensed according to their deeds" (100.7), and that sinners should fear because angels will make inquiry into their deeds (100.10). On the other hand, good things are prepared and written down for those who are able to endure to their end in righteousness (103.3).

---

52   There is a potential textual problem here that arises when one notices that these rhetorical questions follow immediately upon 93.10, which states the sevenfold instruction to be given to the righteous. Nevertheless, the Aramaic Qumran fragments indicate that 93.11–14 follows directly after the *Apocalypse of Weeks* (with the misplaced section of 91.11–17 returned to its rightful place after 93.10). At Qumran there seem to have been about 13 lines, now lost, that came between the end of the *Apocalypse of Weeks* and 93.11–14 as we now have it (Nickelsburg 2001a: 451–2).

53   Stuckenbruck further points out that these verses' placement and subject matter, immediately following the *Apocalypse of Weeks* and discussing the chosen ones to whom revelation will be given, help to highlight further Enoch's unique role (2007a: 238).

The implication of such exhortation concerns human culpability *vis-à-vis* evil. In chapter 98, in the midst of a section of oaths to those who are wise and those who sin, v. 4 claims that the origin of sin lies with humans themselves. This verse has a difficult textual history, and Nickelsburg (2001a: 468), quoted here, bases his text on two reconstructed Greek readings:[54] "I swear to you sinners, that it was not ordained for a man to be a slave, nor was a decree given for a woman to be a handmaid, but it happened because of oppression. Thus lawlessness was not sent upon the earth; but men created it by themselves" (98.4). Stuckenbruck (2007a: 336–45) emphasizes the "parallel absurdities" and gives more credence to the Ethiopic tradition and reconstructs as follows: "I have sworn to you, O sinners, that (as) a mountain has neither become nor will become a slave, nor a hill (become) a woman's handmaid, so sin was not sent to the earth, but the people have created it by themselves." In either reading of the text, the author claims, by way of "parallel absurdities" not divinely intended, that sin was not sent to the earth by outside influence. Humans are culpable for their own sin, a "hard to miss" contradiction with the *Book of Watchers* and the myth of the rebellion in chapters 6–11 (Stuckenbruck 2007a: 346). Aiding this change in the tradition is *1 En.* 100.4, which includes the watchers with all who give aid to iniquity (ἐβοήθουν τῇ ἀδικία[55]) and does not single them out as instigators, thereby treating them "discreetly" (Milik and Black 1976: 52). J. Collins notes that the *Epistle* seems to "contradict" the origin of evil in the *Book of Watchers*, and calls it a "discrepancy" that could be attributed to the updating of a growing tradition or to different provenances for the two texts (1998: 67). Nickelsburg claims that, although chapters 6–11 may indicate something different from later parts of the corpus, the *Epistle* represents "an important clarifying and corrective function within 1 Enoch as a whole" (2001a: 477). Stuckenbruck offers perhaps the most insightful explanation for this discrepancy. Rather than considering it a "blatant contradiction," he instead views it as intending to transfer responsibility to those whom the author views as his opponents, namely the rich and wealthy. Thus, the author of the *Epistle* is offering more than a theological correction, but instead is attempting to "write the opponents of his community into the script" (2007a: 346).

While the specific reasoning and mechanism behind the change of opinion is a matter of some disagreement among scholars, they all agree more basically that there is a marked change at this point in the Enochic corpus. More broadly, however, this text still evinces interest

---

54   The Chester Beatty papyrus of this text clearly portrays a longer reading, but one that is fragmentary. The first half of the verse contains the contested textual history, while it is the content of the second half that is important for present purposes. In both Greek and Ethiopic, it seems clear that the verse is intent on implicating humanity in the origin of evil. For a discussion of the textual issues here, see Milik and Black (1976: 48).

55   This is based on the Chester Beatty Papyrus (Nickelsburg 2001a: 495–6). See also Black and Denis (1970: 40).

in the minutiae of the origin of evil and humanity's role in its genesis on the earth.

d. *Creation in the* Epistle of Enoch

At one level, creation is treated similarly in the *Epistle* when compared to the *Book of Watchers* and the *Astronomical Book*. In chapter 101 the *Epistle* draws a parallel between sailors who fear the sea and sinners who need to fear God. This appears quite similar to the arguments made in chapters 2–5, in which sinners are told to contemplate the obedience of the cosmos as a contrast to their disobedience. The *Epistle* asks: are not sailors, who see ships tossed by the wind and the sea, anxious? If they are anxious, sinners should be all the more. The *Epistle* also shows continuity with previous Enochic material by presuming Enoch's visits to the outer reaches of the cosmos. In 93.11–14 a long list of rhetorical questions asks who is able to contemplate all the activities of heaven. The presumed response is that only Enoch is able. Enoch's repeated oath formulae (e.g., 99.6; 103.1; 104.1) indicate that Enoch has an epistemological basis—his previous revelation—on which to make his pronouncements of woe and blessing. Enoch is most explicit about his previous revelation in 103.1–2, in which he swears the accuracy of his words because of what he previously saw and understood: "I know this mystery, for I have come to know the tablets of heaven and I saw the writing of what is necessary. I know the things written in them and inscribed concerning you."[56] Thus, Enoch's otherworldly journey and his revelation in the *Book of Watchers* and the *Astronomical Book* provide a backdrop for and give authority to his words in the *Epistle*.

From these initial similarities, however, the *Epistle* diverges from earlier portions of the corpus. The *Epistle* presumes and uses Enoch's otherworldly journeys, but it shows no further interest in the cosmic or scientific intricacies explored in those journeys. Similarly, though the *Epistle* uses creation as an analogy in a way reminiscent of chapters 2–5, it pushes the boundary of the analogy by making a metaphorical situation a potentially real one. Earlier portions of the corpus indicated that by "inspired guidance into the mysteries of the cosmos one can arrive at theological truth" (VanderKam 1984: 141) but in the *Epistle* there is less heavenly speculation and a more concrete role for the created order.

The author's extended use of the sea as an analogy (101.1–9) indicates a change in interest in how creation functions. The author of the *Epistle* pushes the sea from analogy to reality; the sea itself becomes a vehicle of judgment.

---

56   This translation is from Chester Beatty Papyrus. See Black and Denis (1970: 42). A lacuna covers the first three lines of chapter 103. The Greek ends here with a second-person object, the Ethiopic with third person. My translation here, "the writing of what is necessary" (τὴν γραφὴν τὴν ἀναγκαίαν), is translated by Stuckenbruck (2007a: 521) as "the urgent writing," although he suggests this is a corruption of what would originally have been closer to the phrase "holy books," which is what the Ethiopic has.

A closer look at 100.10–13 bears out this conclusion. Clouds, rain, and dew—beneficial and necessary aspects of creation—are listed as witnesses against the sinners and they will be withheld in the process of judgment (100.11). With God in control of creation, the author here describes elements of creation as the very implements of judgment. In v. 13 the same judgment is envisaged, this time from frost, snow, and cold, scourges over which the sinners have no control. Furthermore, the maritime scenario expressed in 101.1–9 is more than just an analogy.[57] Sailors do fear the sea as the sinners should fear God, but the sinners should also fear the actual sea, because it just might be the means by which God decides to swallow them up:

> Look at the captains who sail the sea! Their ships are shaken by wave and storm. Being beaten by the storm, they all fear, and all their goods and possessions they throw out into the sea. And in their heart they are apprehensive that the sea will swallow them up, and they will perish in it. Are not all the sea and all its waters and all its movement the work of the Most High? . . . At his rebuke they fear and dry up, and the fish die and all that is in it; but you sinners upon the earth do not fear him.[58]

Nickelsburg nicely states the "theological" thrust of the analogy: "the actions of the captains stem from the wisdom that perceives God's power and judgment in nature" (2001a: 507). Thus, the viewpoint propounded here is an extension of that found in chapters 2–5. Creation is no longer just a "foil" to the action of sinners and a "ground" for judging them. In this new scenario, creation responds "obediently when the creator calls on it to exact judgment from the sinners" (Nickelsburg 2001a: 507).[59]

Thus, we see a parallel development in the view of humanity and creation in the *Epistle* when compared with those in the *Book of Watchers* and the *Astronomical Book*. The two-ways instruction and human culpability in the origin of evil fit nicely with a situation where creation is called upon to execute the judgment on those who choose the wrong path. In the *Book of Watchers*, creation was upheld as the example of order, and evil was explained in terms of a rebellion therefrom. In the *Epistle*, humans have the ability to choose their own path and creation leaves the realm of an exemplar and becomes an "ominous extension" of what, in the *Book of Watchers*, was only an analogy (Nickelsburg 2001a: 507). The human origin of sin, as stated in the *Epistle*, fits with this new role for creation. It is possible that the author of the *Epistle* knew of the theory of the watchers'

---

57   The maritime scenario has been used primarily by scholars to indicate a potential provenance for the *Epistle* (e.g., Milik and Black 1976: 50). Stuckenbruck (2007a: 472–3) adds support to this conclusion.

58   Translation taken from Nickelsburg (2001a: 503).

59   So also Stone, who claims that, in the Second Temple period, there is a "clear attribution of personality and even of will to natural phenomena" (1987: 307).

rebellion and wanted intentionally to contradict its message.[60] By stating unequivocally that humans are responsible for sin, the author gives creation a strong role as a direct extension of God's arm of judgment (cf. 102.1–2) in order to contradict the view that it had been corrupted by the rebellion of the watchers.

V. Conclusion

The collection of apocalyptic materials known as *1 Enoch* shows a great deal of interest in retribution, expressed primarily within arguments about the problem of evil, its origin, and the role of humanity therein. In the *Book of Watchers* clearly, and the *Astronomical Book* implicitly, an effort is made to show the non-human origin of evil. Evil comes instead from a rebellion in heaven that descends, invades, and corrupts humanity and the earth. There is a judgment coming, however, when God will remove the scourge once and for all. In the *Epistle*, the same judgment is coming, but it will be meted out by the created order itself as an extension of God's judgment. This judgment, in contrast to earlier portions of the corpus, is based upon human actions; following the correct path is the way to avoid the judgment. There are several further observations significant for this current project.

As noted above, these texts in *1 Enoch* exhibit an interest in working out the specific details regarding the origin of evil and humanity's complicity in that origin. A similar interest was observed in the thought of Ben Sira. Simply put, these authors, in the period between 300 and 150 BCE, were thinking about such things, offering different viewpoints, and working out the problem in various ways. Some exonerate humanity (or, at least, a certain righteous segment of it) from bearing the guilt of the origin of sin and evil. Others, such as Ben Sira and the author of the *Epistle of Enoch*, are comfortable leaving the onus of righteousness with the choice of the individual, who will receive a reward commensurate with his or her action (even though the timing of this reward may be different).

Within this broad observation about an interest in the problem of evil, we can see even more similarities in how this thinking culminates, even if the point of arrival differs somewhat among the varying perspectives. The major commonality among all these perspectives is the importance of creation.[61] The expression of good and evil and its origin in the world seems irrevocably to be expressed in terms of nature, natural phenomena, or the created order.

---

60   This is the position held by Sacchi, who claims that the author of the *Epistle* "knew the myth of the angelic sin, but consciously opposed this doctrine" (1990: 146).

61   Stone (1987) has pointed up the way in which authors in the Second Temple period presented nature as personified, even to the point of having its own will. He is not so specific as I am here, however, in tying that personification to the working out of the problem of evil.

In some cases, the created order is simply an exemplar for condemning evil derivations from what God intended. At other times, evil itself is explained as a rebellion from the order God created, especially as expressed as stars that deviate from their tasks. Evil also is shown to be a cause that corrupts and invades creation, consuming plants, animals, and even humans. And, as was the case in the *Epistle of Enoch*, and, to some extent, in Sirach, at times the created order rises up as the actual actor in God's judgment.

There is variety within these perspectives, but they all seem to share a central mode of expressing their understanding of retribution by way of created order and/or phenomena. Time and again, natural phenomena are the players in the drama of good and evil. It may be helpful to recall the words of Nickelsburg, who claims that these authors do not "separate science from theology or history from creation" (2001a: 293).[62] As we move forward to chapter 8, these observations provide justification for examining how the created order is treated in the book of Tobit. We have already established that Tobit is interested in many of these issues that relate to retribution—especially the problem of misfortune and human complicity in its origin—that are central in Sirach and parts of 1 Enoch. Our goal as we move forward will not be to map Tobit's expression specifically onto one of the paradigms above. No attempt will be made to claim that Tobit's viewpoint coheres perfectly with the opinions latent in Sirach, the *Book of Watchers*, the *Astronomical Book* or the *Epistle of Enoch*. Rather, noting the interest in the problem of evil and its expression *vis-à-vis* the created order provides justification and points of comparison for understanding how creation, human action, and divine retribution are expressed in the book of Tobit. When this comparison is made, one can better see the complexity of the view of retribution in Tobit. It presents a created order that is unruly and problematic for God's righteous actors. The following chapter will show how this serves to make the book's view of retribution much more complex than a simple correlation between act and consequence.

---

62   Nickelsburg makes his comments specifically with regard to the *Book of Watchers*, but they hold true generally for other parts of 1 Enoch and for Sirach as well.

Chapter 8

RETRIBUTION IN THE BOOK OF TOBIT: FINDING ITS COMPLEXITY

Previous chapters of this study argued that the book of Tobit offers a theological perspective of retribution that is more complex than a simple correlation between act and consequence. Analysis of Sirach and *1 Enoch* concluded that Jewish thinkers in the second and third centuries BCE were struggling with the classical formulation of straightforward retribution and were expressing their views with analogies from the regularity of creation or deviations therefrom. One should not be surprised to find the book of Tobit, written at roughly the same time period, struggling with similar questions and also expressing its answers in terms of the created order. Tobit's fairy tale/novella genre, however, has excluded it from among that pantheon of serious theological thinkers in this time period.[1] This need not be the case.

This penultimate chapter will examine Tobit closely in order to describe more precisely its complex view of retribution. As was the case in chapters 3–5 of this study—in which Sirach provided a body of roughly contemporaneous materials—the work in chapter 7 on *1 Enoch* will provide us with a similar body of material for the current task. The goal here is not to claim shared tradition between Tobit and parts of *1 Enoch*,[2] nor is it to argue that one influenced the other. Rather, the way *1 Enoch* expressed the problem of evil—specifically, by casting it within an expression of the created order—justifies mining the created order in Tobit to look for keys to its understanding of retribution, especially as manifest in the problem of evil.

This penultimate chapter will proceed in four major parts. First will be a comparison between Daniel 9 and Tobit 3, which will provide precedent for the type of complex theological argument Tobit makes. The final three parts will then be organized in the same manner as the explorations of Sirach and *1 Enoch*—according to the heuristic categories of God, humanity, and creation.

---

1   For example, J. Collins (2005) claims that Tobit "is presumably a sample of popular Judaism" (39), and that it is a "popular story and not an ideological one" (40).
2   Recall the arguments of Nickelsburg (1988b; 1996).

I. Daniel 9.3–19 and Tobit 3.1–6: Straightforward Retribution in an Unfriendly Context

Earlier parts of this study (especially chapter 5) argued that Tobit the character works from a strict correlation between act and consequence and that the surrounding narrative events may not support his conclusions. Daniel 9.3–19 offers a very similar scenario. Chronological indeterminacies preclude calling this a "precedent," but it does show similar thinking—and, more importantly, a similar literary strategy—in the same general time period. The prose poem in Daniel 9 provides an example of another author who engages in literary and theological techniques similar to those present in Tobit (Towner 1971; Miller 1994).

Sibley Towner isolates Dan. 9.3–19 along with Ezra 9.6–15, Neh. 1.5–11, and Neh. 9.6–37 as penitential prose poems. Tobit 3.1–6 has previously not been grouped with these prayers in Ezra, Nehemiah, and Daniel, perhaps partly because the book lies outside of the traditional Hebrew canon and because its form is more poetic than the others.[3] These prayers in Ezra, Nehemiah, and Daniel are grouped together partially because of their unique usage of ידה in the hithpael form, meaning to "confess." While Tobit's prayer does not use this specific word, his prayer nevertheless could be classified as penitential and shares many similarities with these other prayers. Tobit's prayer in 3.1–6 declares God to be righteous and just (3.2). Similar language is used in the prayers in Ezra 9.15, Neh. 1.5, and Dan. 9.7. Tobit's penitential disposition (3.3) is similar to that expressed in Ezra 9.6, Neh. 1.6, and Dan. 9.9–10.[4] Such similarities lead Moore (1996: 136–41) and Fitzmyer (2003: 142) to mention the prayers in Ezra, Nehemiah, and Daniel as being similar to that of Tobit.

These prayers in Daniel, Nehemiah, and Ezra also have a strong Diaspora orientation and describe Israel's having been scattered or driven away, a sentiment clearly reflected in Tobit's prayer (3.4). In general, all of these prayers grapple with the very questions one might expect of an exilic or Diaspora community: Why did this happen? (answer: we sinned). And: How do we change our situation? (answer: beg for God's mercy). In this explanation of the national calamity, scholars tend to refer to these prose prayers as being "Deuteronomistic in character" (Miller 1994: 256). Their collective perspective is certainly in line with what previous parts of this study termed a "straightforward doctrine of retribution." Here, also, Tobit concurs. His prayer in chapter three has been described as having a "Deuteronomic theme of retribution in punishment for sin" (Fitzmyer 2003: 143). Moore's commentary is even more adamant in its ascription: "the

---

3   Neither Miller (1994) nor Towner (1971) discusses Tobit's prayer, even though Miller mentions the "apocryphal" Baruch 1.15–3.8 (255).

4   Fitzmyer (2003) notes that Tobit's prayer "echoes" those prayers in Neh. 9.33, Ezra 9.15, and Dan. 9.14 (142).

prayer's basic theology, especially in vv. 2–5, is Deuteronomistic, i.e., 'Do good and prosper; do evil and be punished'" (1996: 142). Although Tobit could be considered among these "late prose prayers," our current goal is not to provide proof of such generic compatibility. Within this group of prayers, Tobit's shows special affinity with that of Daniel in several significant ways.

Daniel's prayer in 9.3–19 has a similar tenor and tone to Tobit's prayer in Tob. 3.1–6. Daniel 9.3 specifically names what follows as a petition and depicts Daniel in sackcloth and ashes. Tobit's prayer is not introduced as a petition, but anguish, weeping, and groaning mark his disposition. In both prayers, God's judgments are righteous (Tob. 3.2; Dan. 9.7), the basis on which the guilt rests. In the admission and recounting of guilt, both prayers oscillate between the first person plural and the third person plural. With reference to his ancestors, Tobit claims, "They sinned against you" (3.3), but he also includes himself and his present community in the guilt: "for we have not kept your commandments" (3.5). Daniel similarly refers to "their unfaithful act that they did against you" (במעלם אשר מעלו־בך), but spends most of the prayer including himself in the guilt, as in 9.9: "We have rebelled against him" (מרדנו). Beyond this, there are several more detailed similarities.

a. Scattering (διασκορπίζω) amongst the Nations

Both prayers share the language of Israel's having been driven, scattered, or dispersed. Daniel 9.7 discusses the fate of the people in Judah and Jerusalem, who now reside in "all the lands to which you have driven them." Daniel here uses the verb נדח (בכל־הארצות אשר הדחתם), which is used frequently in Jeremiah (18 times) and Deuteronomy (10 times), and in most cases is translated into the LXX as διασκορπίζω. Tobit uses διασκορπίζω, although his prayer has the northern deportation to Assyria as its hypothetical historical referent, claiming that he and his people have become a reproach among all the nations in which God has scattered them (ἐν πᾶσιν τοῖς ἔθνεσιν ἐν οἷς ἡμᾶς διεσκόρπισας).[5] The use of this word and concept shows that both of these prayers (and texts) are struggling with the challenge of Israel existing under foreign rule.

b. Angelic Response

The prayers in Dan. 9.3–19 and Tob. 3.1–6 also both elicit an angelic response. At the end of Daniel's prayer, Gabriel comes swiftly to

---

5   There is no surviving Qumran fragment to determine a Semitic original for the word "scattering" in Tobit. A medieval Hebrew text of Tobit does, however, use נדד here: (בכל גויי הארץ אשר הדחתנו). See Weeks, Gathercole, and Stuckenbruck (2004: 111). Nehemiah 1.8 also has the language of the people having been driven or scattered, using the word פוץ, not נדד, although this also is translated as διασκορπίζω in the LXX of Neh. 1.8.

give Daniel wisdom and understanding (9.22). This angelic response is not necessarily an answer to Daniel's prayer, at least in the sense that the prayer itself would have anticipated. Daniel learns what has been decreed, but the shape of the restoration does not work from the assumptions in Daniel's prayer. As R. H. Charles says in his commentary on Daniel: "the conclusion of the chapter takes no account of the subject of the prayer, which supplicates for forgiveness and deliverance. Here a prayer for illumination and not a liturgical confession is required by the context" (1929: 226). This disjunction between Daniel's prayer and the angelic response has led to theories that the prayer is an interpolation into the narrative in Daniel (these will be discussed below).

Tobit's prayer in chapter 3 is also followed by an angelic response. After the intervening narrative of Sarah and her demonic affliction, the prayers of both characters were heard in heaven and Raphael was dispatched to heal both of them (3.17). It is not until the end of the story, however, that Tobit learns of this reality. Raphael finally discloses his identity in 12.11–22. The content of Raphael's self-revelation is similar to that in Daniel. Raphael declares that he will now tell the "whole truth" and conceal nothing. Raphael's revelation is similar to Gabriel's, namely that God's role in the drama of Israel's history is different than the perspective in Tobit's original prayer. Raphael, as God's agent, was actually behind the action of the story all along, despite Tobit's assertions that his own guilt and that of his forebears had produced his situation. The angel does not show up and relieve Tobit's guilt, as Tobit's original formulation of the problem would have required. Instead, Raphael reveals that much of what happened was a test (12.14) and that even Tobit and Tobias' own sight had been manipulated (12.19). Thus, in both Tobit and Daniel, an angel responds to the penitential prayer, but obliquely. The response reveals a divinely ordained reality structured differently than that assumed in the prayer itself.

c. Disjunction between the Prayers and their Contexts

The angelic responses lead to the most striking and important aspect of these prayers in Tobit and Daniel: that the theological perspective in the prayer is dissonant from the context in which it is placed. This has long been recognized as a problem with regard to Daniel 9. Gerald Wilson's comment summarizes the common opinion well: "it is clear that the prayer [in Daniel 9] exhibits a Deuteronomistic view of history that is drastically at variance with the deterministic view characteristic of Daniel outside the prayer" (1990: 91). Or, as J. Collins observes, "the content of the prayer does not represent the theology of the angel or of the author of the book" (1993: 360). The prayer in Daniel 9 is a response to a question about the fulfillment of the prophecy in Jer. 25.11–12 and 29.10. Jeremiah claimed that there would be 70 years until the end of the exile. As this did not come true, authors grappled with the true meaning of Jeremiah's prophecy. The revelation in Daniel

answers that Jeremiah meant 70 weeks of years. Daniel's prayer of petition, marked by a strict connection between act and consequence, elicits
an angelic response. A "word went out" at the beginning of Daniel's
prayer, and an angel came to deliver it. Daniel's prayer is generally
impotent: the end does not come about because Daniel asked that it
might be so, but rather because it was "decreed" (9.24).

Many, including Charles, show the discontinuity[6] between the prayer and
its context, which leads to the conclusion that it was added later or had an
independent existence before its usage in Daniel (1929: 226). Bruce Jones
(1968), however, makes a strong case for its originality. He notes linguistic
and conceptual parallels between the prayer and its larger context. Jones
ultimately claims that the "Deuteronomistic" theology and understanding
of history, at this point in the history of Israel, had become "insufficient"
(1968: 492). He summarizes: "Deuteronomistic retribution was insufficient
to give insight to Israel, but Gabriel's *apokalypsis* could" (1968: 492). For
Jones, the lack of attention to the prayer in the surrounding narrative does
not mean that the prayer was a later interpolation into the narrative, but that
its ostracism is exactly the point: "the calamity was decreed and it will end at
the appointed time, quite apart from prayers and quite apart from previous
ideas of retribution" (1968: 493).

Although scholars have proposed a spate of redactional theories regarding
many parts of Tobit, the prayer in chapter 3 is considered core to the book's
theology. Instead, the opposite is often assumed: that the later chapters, which
have more deterministic and eschatological orientation, are the interpolation.
Because the book of Tobit has a purportedly Deuteronomic viewpoint, the
dissonance between Tobit's prayer and the angelic revelation—discussed
fervently in studies of Daniel 9—is often missed. As previous chapters of this
study have argued, assuming that the whole of Tobit is "Deuteronomistic"
or has a straightforward sense of retribution may not do justice to Tobit's
theological complexity. As this chapter will prove, Tobit's prayer is representative of a theological perspective the author can no longer accept
wholesale. Noticing the prayer in Daniel 9—straightforward retribution in a
more deterministic, revelatory context—helps provide warrant for a similar
occurrence in Tobit. Both texts have a similar, theologically driven narrative
method. Specifically, the current goal is to prove that the strategy in Daniel
9 is also operative in the book of Tobit: that the theology of Tobit's prayer
in 3.1–6 is intentionally at odds with other perspectives in the narrative.

---

6   This discontinuity is based on theology and on the comparably smooth Hebrew
in the prayer as compared to that which surrounds it.

II. God, Humanity, and Creation in the Book of Tobit

a. God in the Book of Tobit

One immediately notices upon reading the book of Tobit that God does not play a role in the narrative in any direct, personal way. God does not appear on earth or speak directly to human actors. God is not anthropomorphized. God is an entity to be blessed, beseeched, and one who sets the course of history.

1. Implications of the throne vision in Tobit

The closest glimpse of God provided by the author is in 3.16 and 12.11–15. In 3.16 we learn that the prayers of Tobit and Sarah are heard (εἰσηκούσθη) simultaneously "before the glory of God" (ἐνώπιον τῆς δόξης τοῦ θεου). In 12.15 Raphael established his identity as one of the seven angels who goes in before the glory of the Lord (ἐνώπιον τῆς δόξης κυρίου). These pericopae hint at a picture of God as one enthroned, surrounded by glory so great that only a select few are granted access. Such glimpses of the heavenly realm in Tobit have profitably been compared to those in *1 Enoch*. The argument of Nickelsburg, discussed in chapter 6 above, claims that "the author of Tobit presumes and employs some important elements" that are evident in *1 Enoch* (1988b: 58). Among these are the named angels, of which Raphael is one (cf., *1 Enoch* 6–11) and the language used to describe approaching the heavenly throne (ἐνώπιον τῆς δόξης is used in *1 En.* 104.1 and Tob. 3.16 and 12.15). In the midst of these similarities, Nickelsburg also points out differences, the most significant of which, in his opinion, is the fact that "Tobit's chief explanation for his own suffering is that God chastises even the righteous because of their sin . . . God is smiting his people, so that they may repent and find mercy" (1988b: 58). Nickelsburg assumes that the theology of Tobit's prayer in 3.1–6 is in concert with the narrative as a whole. As a result, despite the shared language, Nickelsburg thinks the two texts diverge along theological lines, and he does not consider a deeper conceptual similarity a possibility.

Similar language describing God's throne in *1 Enoch* and Tobit does not warrant importing a sectarian understanding of the origin of evil—one that views evil as an incursion into the world and undeservedly onerous for the righteous ones—from *1 Enoch* into Tobit. Such similarities, however, should give us pause. One could draw a conclusion opposite of Nickelsburg's and claim instead that the common language suggests a shared theological perspective. In such a case, the otherworldliness of God necessitates an angelic broker who reveals the true order of justice in the world.[7] In *1 Enoch*, the vision of the throne represents something bigger than just a lofty vision of God. It is a glimpse of an alternative reality and provides confirmation,

---

7   For the role of Raphael in the narrative of Tobit, see Nowell (2007: 227–38).

by way of a vision, that the revelation given to the human recipient is trustworthy. In other words, the vision confirms that there are circles of justice that lie outside of human purview.

A similar conceptual move may be seen in Tobit. Raphael has a unique ability to approach God's throne as one of the seven angels who stand ready (οἱ παρεστήκασιν) to do God's bidding. Such special access legitimizes Raphael as one who is capable of revealing the "whole truth" (πᾶσαν τὴν ἀλήθειαν). The truth revealed, as we saw in chapter 5 above, is that Tobit had not been properly perceiving the story of his own life. There were many ways in which God's role was drastically different than he had assumed.

2. The roles of God and Raphael

The similarities in the throne visions in Tobit and *1 Enoch* lead to a second observation about God in Tobit: that the arc of Tobit the character depends upon God's role being different from how Tobit himself perceived it. This dynamic opens a rift in the narrative and creates irony through situations in which the characters say things more true than they know. Irony in the book of Tobit is not missed by any commentators.[8] Should noting the irony, however, exhaust the implications of this epistemological gap? Did the author create the irony for irony's sake, or is there a more subtle theological intention? As was noted in an earlier portion of this study in chapter 5, Tobit is the only character who works from a straightforward sense of retribution in order to explain the predicaments in the story. The sole exception to Tobit's rhetoric claiming a close connection between act and consequence comes in Raphael's revelation in 12.6–10. In this speech, he claims that those who give alms will have a full life, and those who do sin and unrighteousness are warlike against their own soul (πολέμιοί εἰσιν τῆς ἑαυτῶν ψυχῆς). This would seem initially to cohere with Tobit's own theological explanations of his plight. Raphael continues, however, to say that he will now reveal the "whole truth [πᾶσαν τὴν ἀλήθειαν]" (12.11), which indicates that God's role in the arc of Tobit and the other characters was different from that which Tobit thought.[9]

Raphael's revelation reveals the fact that God has been behind the action of the story the whole time. Raphael presented[10] Tobit and Sarah's memorial of prayer (τὸ μνημόσυνον τῆς προσευχῆς) before God, which resulted in his mission to heal them. In 3.16–17, in the midst of a vision of the heavenly realm, Raphael is dispatched to heal Tobit and Sarah (ἰάσασθαι τοὺς δύο). Raphael is sent on a similar mission in the *Book of Watchers* in

---

8   For example, see Nowell (1983) and McCracken (1995).

9   For some recent studies of the role of Raphael in the story of Tobit, see Barker (2006), Nowell (2007), Ego (2007), and Reiterer (2007).

10   NRSV here reads "brought and read," following the Old Latin (*et legi*), but Sinaiticus has only ἐγὼ προσήγαγον.

1 Enoch, where he is instructed: ἴασαι τὴν γῆν (*1 En.* 10.7).[11] Raphael's healing activity is indicative of the role he actually plays in the story. He encourages Tobias to grab hold of the fish that provides medicinal agents that chase away the demon and remove Tobit's blindness. Raphael also binds Asmodeus in upper Egypt (8.3), which fits his role as a healer and sounds similar to the instructions given to him in *1 En.* 10.4–7.

As Nickelsburg suggests, "This important role played by revelation, even in the received form of the book of Tobit, raises the question of the place of angelic revelation in the sources and traditions behind Tobit" (1988b: 67). Nickelsburg, in other words, notices similarities with *1 Enoch* and decides to surmise similar origins or sources for both texts. Source-critical conclusions, however, are not the only ones that can be drawn. One could also suggest that the angelic revelation and the revelatory disposition are being employed toward similar theological ends in both works. If, as we saw in the *Book of Watchers* and the *Astronomical Book*, the revelatory perspective is a guarantor of justice hidden in the universe, revealing an alternative reality in which God really is in control, then the same could hold true in Tobit.

There are, therefore, still more reasons to think that straightforward retribution may not be the core perspective of the book of Tobit. When compared to parts of *1 Enoch*, we can more fully appreciate the revelatory perspective in Tobit. Raphael comes to reveal a hidden reality to specific human recipients. Furthermore, Raphael orders Tobit to write down all the things that have happened (Tob. 12.20), which situates him as the new convener of Raphael's revelation.[12] The thrust of this new perspective is that the misfortune Tobit had been experiencing was not the type of retribution he thought. It was not punishment for individual and/or collective guilt.

At this point, it will suffice to observe that (1) the revelatory perspective provided by Raphael and his angelophany impinges directly upon the book's view of retribution, and (2) that the role of the angel Raphael is a direct result of a theological understanding of God and the origin and alleviation of misfortune. Tobit is not a full-blown apocalypse, but its revelatory perspective indicates that there is a secret order to things heretofore unavailable to Tobit.[13]

---

11   Syncellus' Greek text and the Ethiopic here have the imperative, ἴασαι. Other manuscripts, including the Panopolitanus Codex, have the future passive, ἰαθήσεται.

12   There is no direct parallel in the *Book of Watchers*, in which Enoch is told specifically to write down what he had observed. He is, however, clearly the scribal guarantor of the revelation. Enoch is called the "scribe of righteousness" in 12.4 because he is entrusted with communicating to the watchers their impending doom.

13   At the point of such an observation, one might be tempted to make speculative diachronic claims or hypotheses. Such concerns, however, are not central to this current project, which distinguishes it from the analysis of Nickelsburg (1988b), who seems interested in diachronic, rather than theological, conclusions. In his comparison of Tobit and *1 Enoch*, he claims that the two texts "reflect an older common stock of ideas, traditions, and terminology . . . which has developed in different directions in the respective texts" (55).

b. Humanity in Tobit: The Role of Blindness and Sight

Human sight and blindness obviously play a significant role in the story of Tobit. This sight, however, may have some interesting resonances with parts of *1 Enoch*. Sight and blindness in the story of Tobit contribute to the argument that the book has an understanding of retribution much more complex than a simple correlation between act and consequence. Blindness is more than the foil and misfortune of the title character. Tobit's blindness is coordinated specifically with his theological perspective, a perspective that changes when his sight returns.

1. Blindness and sight in Tobit and 1 Enoch

Blindness and sight play a subtle but important role in parts of *1 Enoch*. The beginning of the *Book of Watchers* mentions a future judgment and then introduces Enoch as a righteous man whose "eyes were opened by God" (ἐνὼχ ἄνθρωπος δίκαιος ἔστιν ὅρασις ἐκ θεοῦ αὐτῷ ἀνεῳγμένη).[14] Thus, the first thing necessary for Enoch to be an appropriate receptacle for the coming revelation was for his eyes to be opened. Similarly, in the *Animal Apocalypse* (chs. 85–90 of *1 Enoch*), when the author moves into the most recent history, newly acquired sight becomes paramount. The start of the Maccabean revolt begins with the statement: "Then, behold lambs were born from those snow-white sheep; and they began to open their eyes and see . . ." (90.6).[15] This portion of *1 Enoch* obviously dates from a later period than the book of Tobit, but it helps provide some warrant for thinking that there may be some more traditional, revelatory reflection behind the motif of blindness and its alleviation in Tobit.

A more thorough investigation is needed, then, of the role of blindness in the story of Tobit.[16] Is it simply an entertaining part of a fairy tale, or does the author intend it to be more symbolic? If one pays close attention to Tobit the character, a subtle shift in his theological explanations can be viewed. This suggests that Tobit's blindness is coordinated with his theological perspective so as to cast it in a negative light. On the other hand, when his sight returns, he has new theological insight.

2. God's contingent actions

One of the hallmarks of what we have been calling a straightforward theology of retribution is that it purports to explain and predict cir-

---

14   This is from the Greek Panopolitanus text (Nickelsburg 2001a: 137).

15   The general consensus of opinion concludes that the opening of the eyes refers to the start of the Maccabean movement. See, for example, J. Collins (1998: 69), who claims, along with the majority of scholars, that the death of one of these lambs refers to Onias III, and that the horn that grows from one of them assuredly refers to Judas Maccabee.

16   There have been some scholarly treatments of the role of blindness in Tobit. See, for example, Portier-Young (2005) and Just (1997).

cumstances in this current life. The example *par excellence* of such a view is in Sirach. Ben Sira repeatedly asserts that the true character of a person's life will be revealed at his or her death: "at the end of one's life one's actions are revealed. Call no one happy before his death; a person is known by how he ends" (11.27b–28).[17] While there were, at times, adjuncts that helped explain such a strict formulation (Rankin 1936), Ben Sira consistently upholds it, and so does Tobit the character in the initial parts of his story (e.g., 3.3–4; 4.6–10). He is distraught because he, similar to Job, is experiencing misfortune despite his righteousness.

Chapters 13 and 14 of Tobit exhibit such a shift in perspective that they were long considered a later addition to the first 12 chapters. Early in the twentieth century, it was commonly believed among scholars that they were added after 70 CE, responding to the destruction of the temple (e.g., Zimmerman 1958: 25). Such a scenario certainly would fit Tobit's words about a new Jerusalem and a reference to its being destroyed for a time (14.4). Nevertheless, the discovery of fragments of Tobit at Qumran, which include parts of chapters 13 and 14, firmly plants these chapters as part of the story by the first century BCE, if not earlier. Yet, many scholars still consider them extraneous to the core story. According to Lawrence Wills, chapters 13–14 show a "difference in tone," which indicates that "a redactor has added this testamentary ending and done it rather awkwardly" (1995: 86–7). Wills summarizes the impact of the additions by saying: "the spirited novel of chapters 2–12 has become heavily laden with theological pretension" (1995: 91). Thus, even a brief review of past and current scholarly opinions indicates that a shift takes place in the final two chapters; the perspective changes. One does not need to posit different *Erweiterungen* (expansions),[18] however, in order to make sense of the final form of the text.

Ronald Herms has helpfully summarized a modest but focused debate about the shift at the end of Tobit with regard to universalism and the inclusion of the gentiles. He claims that the ending evinces a "dramatic shift" from a "boundary-focused" worldview to one of "eschatological optimism" (2006: 69). Herms contends that such a shift does not mean the chapters were added later, but that the shift is exactly the point— once Tobit experiences and understands God's mercy, he is then able to "make the shift outside of nationalistic boundaries to embrace the Gentile nations into the New Jerusalem" (2006: 74). Herms, in conversation with McCracken (1995) and Cousland (2003), sees the author of Tobit making a complex narrative/theological argument about ethnicity and universalism. The argument to be presented here proceeds along similar lines, but with a focus on the retributional theology latent in the narrative development of the book. The two may actually go hand in

---

17 From Hebrew manuscript A (Beentjes 1997: 38).

18 As is done by Deselaers (1982).

hand; re-evaluating ethnic boundaries may also entail abandoning traditional theological formulae.[19]

When we examine Tobit's words and actions after his sight has returned, one first notices an added contingency that previously did not exist in Tobit's rhetoric. Chapter 13 consists of Tobit's hymn, sung after Raphael has revealed his true identity and God's hidden role throughout the story. The prayer begins with a second-person address, with Tobit telling an anonymous "you" how God acts and how God's people should appropriately respond. It contrasts Tobit's hymns and prayers in 3.1–6 and 11.14–15, which are much more personal and introspective. The content at the beginning of chapter 13 is similar to Tobit's statements earlier in the story, claiming that God afflicts and shows mercy, leads down to Hades and brings up from the abyss (13.2). Tobit's words in chapter 13, however, shift in the second half of verse 6 back to his own personal reflection.[20] The last stanza of v. 6 says: "turn back, you sinners, and do what is right before him; *perhaps* he may look with favor upon you and show you mercy" (NRSV). The Greek (AB) of what the NRSV translates as "perhaps" is: τίς γινώσκει ἢ θελήσει ὑμᾶς καὶ ποιήσει ἐλεημοσύνην ὑμῖν. A better translation would be: "Who knows whether [God] will take pleasure in you[21] and show mercy to you?"[22] Such a phrase casts doubt on Tobit's previous formulations of a direct connection between act and consequence. In light of this lack of predictability, the opening words of chapter 13 offer a more inscrutable God as well, one that recalls Hosea 6.1: "It is God who has torn, and he will heal us; he has struck down, and he will bind us up" (NRSV). In Tobit 13, the formulation of God's actions is framed by a larger sense of unease, marked by a God whose character is no longer as predictable as Tobit once thought and a world that he now realizes does not function with a tightly ordered connection between deed and

---

19   Herms' analysis is helpful for its close attention to context, theology, and narrative concerns. His overall project, however, is concerned with the book of Revelation from the NT. While ethnicity and universalism are aspects of the book of Tobit, it seems its perspective on retribution is a more central concern, and, as will be outlined below, the newly introduced universalism and eschatological perspective are the result of a changed perspective of retribution, and may not result from a reflection on universalism, per se.

20   The second major lacuna in the text of Tobit makes the use of AB necessary here.

21   The Greek construction, θελήσει ὑμᾶς, here is a little awkward. It might seem more natural to take the dative case. Translations vary: "may look with favor upon you" (NRSV and NAB); Fitzmyer (2003: 310) translates as "welcome you."

22   Qumran seems to confirm this question. The Aramaic in 4Q196 frag. 17, in line 5, has קדמוה[י], which corresponds to ἐνώπιον αὐτοῦ in AB (used here because of a lacuna in S). Following, then, is what appears to be ידע, which Fitzmyer (2003: 309–10) supposes would have been preceded by מן. Thus, the Aramaic likely preserves the question "who knows . . .?" This question also parallels the rhetorical question preserved in the Hebrew of 4Q200 in 13.2: ומה אשר יפצה מידו ("and what is there that can snatch from his hand?"). Fitzmyer also translates as "who knows?" (2003: 302).

consequence. Tobit's question, "who knows?" is reminiscent of Joel 2.14: "who knows (מִי יוֹדֵעַ) if he will turn and comfort and cause a blessing to remain behind him."[23] In Joel, the question seems truly contingent; it is not immediately clear whether the prophet believes there is a basis for repentance or not. The words of Tobit seem just as contingent. Although Tobit has again offered words of seemingly straightforward retribution, they are framed by statements that seem closer to an uneasy shrug of the shoulders than a strong assertion of being able to predict God's action. Tobit has come to his senses, both literally and theologically; the revelation of Raphael and God's role in the story has tempered his previously belligerent expression of a close connection between act and consequence.

3. Eschatological shift

Verse seven in chapter 13 continues to display a shift in Tobit's perspective. The second-person address has been removed, and Tobit begins to speak from his own, now amended, perspective. Verse seven begins with a contrasting "I."[24] Thus, the NRSV and NAB translation, "As for me . . ." supplies an appropriate disjunction from the previous statements. More importantly, after this shift to what is Tobit's own perspective, the prayer takes a dramatic eschatological turn toward the future of Jerusalem. Much of what Tobit says is not necessarily remarkable or unique; his statements about all nations coming to Jerusalem are reminiscent of many prophetic texts. Whatever its precursors, Tobit now speaks about a remnant and a rebuilt Jerusalem, which contradicts Tobit's yearly pilgrimage to Jerusalem described at the beginning of the story. This change of focus is what has led scholars to claims, similar to those of J. Collins, that these chapters have been added to the story to provide a "theological and historical frame, from a Judean, Jerusalemite perspective" (2005: 25). One need not posit redactional layers, however. Tobit's change here could simply be the result of new theological insight. He no longer looks for rewards in the present, but instead is forced to hope that God will do something new and better in the future: in this case, a new Jerusalem, built with precious stones. Tobit hopes that a remnant of his people will endure to see such a thing.

Thus, in chapter 13 a correlation between act and consequence has not been completely omitted, but there has been a shift of emphasis. Whereas Tobit previously had traveled to Jerusalem, made his tithes, was charitable and upright, and expected commensurate treatment from God, there is now

---

23   One could also note the same question from the great epistemological contrarian, Qoheleth: "Who knows whether the human spirit goes upward and the spirit of animals goes downward to the earth?" (3.21).

24   The disjunction here is represented consistently across the different manuscript traditions: Greek (AB) has "I and my soul" (ὑψῶ καὶ ἡ ψυχή μου); the Old Latin is similar: (ego, et anima mea); and, the Aramaic, although obviously fragmentary, seems to support the same idea in Fitzmyer's reconstruction: (אנה ונפשי מרומם).

less certainty. The current iteration of Jerusalem—the one to which Tobit had previously traveled—is no longer sufficient.

In chapter 14, the same tension is felt between Tobit's previous theological explanations of his plight and his new "insight" into how God acts. Chapter 14 consists of Tobit's second testament to his son, Tobias. While the testament here repeats some of the core doctrines of his first, like the theology of chapter 13, they are framed in such a way that they no longer hold the same persuasive power. Tobit's words in chapter 14 begin with a directive to flee because all of the Lord's prophecies are going to come true, especially those of Nahum, who predicted destruction for Assyria.[25] As part of this turmoil, the temple will be desolate for a while. But the temple will then be rebuilt, echoing the eschatological sentiment of the hymn in chapter 13. The testament continues as it describes the essential nature of almsgiving and the outcomes it potentially procures (14.8–9), as did chapter 4. But here the directive for immediate flight follows the sapiential formulations. On the day Tobias buries his mother, he is not to stay one more night. Thus, chapter 14 does not completely ignore Tobit's previous theological explanations; some of the sapiential instruction and its assumptions about retribution remain. The calls for flight, however, frame the sapiential statements differently. Just as chapter 13 expressed previous theological formulations with a greater sense of contingency, in chapter 14, almsgiving is required, but it is surrounded by frantic calls for imminent departure. Such a context does two things. First, it questions what almsgiving can accomplish. This is a microcosm of the issue that spawns the book in the first place—why is this bad stuff happening even though Tobit is doing the right thing? Second, the need to flee distracts from the call for almsgiving. A context of imminent danger suggests that flight constitutes a more pressing need. The previously "tight causal weave" (Fretheim 2005: 165) espoused by Tobit is cast in a new light, one where the way God is acting in the world is less predictable and, at the same time, cast far into the future. The book of Tobit ends with Tobias and his family in no better position than when they started; they are still exiles in a foreign land. Yes, Nineveh is destroyed, but Tobias returns to Ecbatana, where he and his family will still be subject to foreign rulers.

Commentators often notice the generally unfinished character of the ending of the book of Tobit. For instance, Nickelsburg summarizes the ending by saying, "whereas the healing of Tobit (and Sarah) brings closure to that plot, the story of Israel's suffering remains unfinished" (1988b: 60). Tobit's healing is often seen as a down-payment for what will eventually be the restoration of Israel. As Moore states in his commentary: the "Deuteronomic principle was still intact" because the help that comes to Tobit and Sarah represents "divine assurance of other more wonderful things to come" (1996: 298). These final two chapters could function differently, however. Rather than representing a protraction of the expected reward

---

25   For a discussion of prophecy in Tobit, see Reiterer (2005: 155–76).

according to a straightforward sense of retribution, they instead question the entire enterprise of expecting a correlation between act and consequence. The need for imminent flight, the eschatological depiction of Jerusalem, and the fact that Tobit's offspring remain under foreign rule, indicate that the author has reached a new stage of reflection. No longer can one expect things to work according to old formulae. Facts on the ground have forced the author to mold the story of Tobit into one that suggests that God is more capricious than was originally, or traditionally, thought. At the same time, hope remains. The hope, however, is not that God will treat individuals according to their actions, as Tobit assumes at the beginning of the story, but rather, that God will do something new. A new Jerusalem is needed (13.16–17; 14.5–6). War is needed in which the oppressors are vanquished (14.15). While this type of thinking need not be labeled apocalyptic, it does have affinities with what we have seen in portions of *1 Enoch*. The *Book of Watchers* offers a scenario that exonerated a segment of humanity from guilt as a catalyst for the evil being experienced. The *Astronomical Book* was also careful to suggest that the wickedness seen on the earth was not the fault of a certain segment of humanity. The way Tobit's insight changes after his sight returns suggests that the author of this text may have come to similar conclusions, although ones not quite as well developed as those in parts of *1 Enoch*. When Tobit's sight returns, he realizes that God does not work according to a strict formula. Righteousness may not be a guarantor of wellbeing after all. Instead, God acts in a way inscrutable to humans unless God decides to reveal the hidden divine workings; the resolution of individual and collective calamity is left entirely in God's hands.

Francis Macatangay sees the ending as a strategy intended specifically for the reader. He notes that the ending does remain "incomplete" and portrays a "tension and foreboding" (2011: 128). This, he claims, appeals to the "hidden and mysterious ways of a providential God" by "alluding to the eschatological day of salvation" (129). He admits there is "yet to be an agreeable resolution" to the characters' tense condition of exile at the end (129). Macatangay's solution to the problem of exile at the end of the book is to posit that the author has left the ending to the imagination of the readers, "placing upon them certain responsibilities" (129). Those reading the story are supposed to go out and emulate Tobit in order to "experience the deliverance Tobit and his family has experienced" (129). One wonders, however, whether the story of Tobit really engenders the kind of confidence Macatangay seems to assume it would. Would a reader of the book of Tobit really want to emulate its title character? Much of the narrative seems to undermine the confident expectations about what righteousness can accomplish that Tobit had at the beginning (and that Macatangay assumes the reader would have at the end).

Some try to make the ending a protracted reward, but one that allows the connection between act and consequence to remain intact. Such logic suggests that the righteous are "eventually rewarded even if they have first to undergo probationary suffering" (Corley and Skemp 2005: xiii). This, however, does not represent the timing in chapters 13 and 14. We have already shown how God's response to human action is no longer as predictable. More pointedly, God's prophecies, particularly those leveled against Assyria by the prophet Nahum, are now what need to be fulfilled in order for resolution to occur. These prophecies will not come true until the "appointed times" (καὶ πάντα συμβήσεται τοῖς καιροῖς αὐτῶν).[26] The scenario in Tobit does not fit the idea of a protracted reward as an adjunct[27] that helped one maintain the *Tun-Ergehen Zusammenhang.*

How one interprets the story of Tobit depends upon how one reads the ending. If the ending is intended to have the restoration of Tobit's sight be a precursor to what is then the assured resolution of Israel's plight, then there is a sense in which the straightforward retributive formula can hold. Such an explanation is not the most likely. Instead, the author breaks from earlier, more traditional views of retribution, especially those that suggest human action as a guarantor of God's blessing. Tobit's sight is restored, but, as shown above, it comes about through no merit of his own. (And, at the same time, it was not initially caused by the personal and corporate reasons he enumerated.) Instead, the fates of individuals and the nation are left in the hands of God, who will be required to establish a new reality on earth, one that is commensurate with the justice that works in the heavens.

c. Creation

One of the major observations made in earlier parts of this study is that texts contemporaneous with Tobit, in this case, Sirach and *1 Enoch*, express their views of retribution and the origin of misfortune in terms of creation theology. Sirach invoked creation as a regulatory force analogous to the predictability of God judging humans in accordance with their actions. On the other hand, the *Book of Watchers* and the *Astronomical Book* used the created realm to show how upheavals in earthly justice originated as departures from the created order. The imbalance of justice is mirrored in created phenomena: stars no longer keep their courses, giants now drink human blood, etc. In the book of Tobit, the created order and its reflection of human predicaments is less celestial. It does not envision a rebellion in heaven, the devouring of creation, or mis-ordered stars. It does, however, present a view of the created order. At several crucial points in the story, the created order

---

26   4Q198 1.5 has כלא יתעבד לזמן]ניהון[. Reconstruction is by Fitzmyer (2003: 326).

27   This is the language of Rankin (1936). He discusses the doctrine of rewards and punishments as one that had "appendices" that helped make it "elastic and durable" as a concept (81). One of the appendices Rankin discusses is the fact that God could "delay action" in bringing about the proper end (82). The explanation of reality that posits straightforward retribution, with its "adjuncts," became "an extremely serviceable and adaptable instrument" (83).

itself rises up and causes problems for the human actors; it does not function according to the ways intended. This indicates a situation similar to that in parts of *1 Enoch*, in which the created order is corrupted. As a result, corrupted creation—here represented especially by birds and fish—causes human misfortune in the story.

Two texts in Israel's scriptures provide an introduction into the type of biblical, theological thinking that may be reflected in Tobit. First, in the story of the plagues in Exodus, creation itself is caught up in the struggle for liberation experienced by the Israelites. Fretheim has shown how the plagues that God levels at Pharaoh and the Egyptians are non-human elements that are "out of kilter with their created way of being" (2005: 119). None of them are represented as the way God intended them to exist; they are "hypernatural" (120). Fretheim carefully points out how it is more than just humans who are impacted. The entire created order faces the brunt of the plagues. Hail destroys all the plant life; boils are apparent not just on humans, but on all the beasts; and the locusts eat every last green plant (Exod. 10.15). For Fretheim, this indicates that these plagues cannot be explained simply as a serendipitous conglomeration of natural occurrences, because the created order itself is severely crippled by them. Instead, the plagues represent a scenario where "the elements of the natural order are not what they were created to be and do"; they have gone "berserk" (120). In this story, the human reality of the bondage of the Israelites is expressed in terms of creation itself: "The collective image presented is that the entire created order is caught up in this struggle, either as a cause or victim. Pharaoh's antilife measures against God's creation have unleashed chaotic effects that threaten the very creation that God intended" (119).

Hosea chapter two also depicts the ongoing drama of human calamity and its explanations with specific references to the created order. Hosea 2.1–13 recounts Israel's infidelity and punishment. Cultivated groves of figs and olives will return to wildness, and wild animals will devour them. A shift occurs in 2.14–23 in its depiction of future reconciliation. In Hos. 2.18, God explains a future covenant: "I will make for them a covenant on that day with the wild animals, with the birds of the air, and with the creeping things of the earth." This covenant is not between humans and the wild animals, but instead is a covenant between God and the wild animals, on behalf of the humans; it is "for them" (לְהֶם). The covenant removes the threat posed by the wild animals in 2.13. (A similar sentiment is expressed in Ezek. 34.25–27.) The core thinking that seems to lie behind such texts is the idea that in the drama of retribution there is a correlation between the human situation and the disposition of creation. In Hosea, the suggestion is that, having run afoul of God through their infidelity, the Israelites face the danger of aspects of creation wielding its ability to devour and destroy. On the other hand, when the relationship with God is restored, it will be accompanied by God's action of subduing creation. While later apocalyptic thinking will express the details differently—namely, that part of the explanation for evil is that this creation has rebelled and lies temporarily outside of God's control—there exists a more basic shared assumption: that the created order is an important factor in the equations of good and evil. Like parts of *1 Enoch*, the created order in Tobit is one that has gone awry, where the elements of creation no longer play the role for which they were intended.

1. Birds

The first example in Tobit of the created order factoring in equations of good and evil is the birds that instigate Tobit's blindness.[28] Tobit may share a core conviction with Exodus and Hosea: that the human situation is expressed in terms of "chaotic effects" within creation. As a way of articulating the calamity of the people's dispersion, the book of Tobit depicts the environment as out of control, crossing boundaries, and troublesome for God's righteous actors.

Before discussing the specific role the birds play in the narrative of Tobit, let us recall the general way that the created order is treated in Ben Sira and *1 Enoch*. For Ben Sira, the created order has been determined by God; its elements do not deviate from their tasks (16.26–30). For vengeance God has created "the fangs of wild animals and scorpions and vipers, and the sword that punishes the ungodly with destruction" (39.30 NRSV). Ben Sira goes on to personify these natural forces; they "rejoice" in doing God's bidding (39.31a). In the *Book of Watchers* in *1 Enoch*, on the other hand, humans are exhorted to examine natural phenomena and observe how they do not alter their courses (e.g., *1 En.* 2.1). Later in this text, evil is described as a rebellion in heaven, which has dramatic consequences for creation. The insatiable giants consumed all human produce and then turned their attention to other aspects of creation: "they began to sin against birds, wild beasts, reptiles, and fish" (*1 En.* 7.5).[29] Finally, the *Epistle of Enoch* suggests a scenario similar to that in Ben Sira: that the created order, when called upon, can rise up and exact God's judgment. Sailors fear the sea, which suggests that sinners should fear God, the one who marked the sea's boundaries and can direct it according to the divine will (*1 En.* 101.5–7). In general, these texts all agree that the created order will do God's will and that its elements function with regularity. The *Book of Watchers*, however, suggests a scenario in which the origin of evil is attributed to a fissure in this regularity. The reality of evil is put forward as a rebellion in heaven that leads to a series of events disrupting the way things are supposed to work.

---

28   Note that it is only after his visit to the doctors and pharmacological treatments that Tobit's iatrogenic blindness is complete (2.10). This puts Tobit in line with other segments of Israel's scriptures that share the same pharmacological skepticism, such as Job 13.4; Jer. 8.22 and 46.11; 2 Chron. 16.12 and *1 En.* 7.1–4. For a contrasting opinion, see Ben Sira, who believes that the physician should be given his place (Sir. 38.9–15).

29   4QEn[a] has a slightly longer reading here that seems to evoke the language of Genesis 1 even more intentionally than the Ethiopic. See Nickelsburg (2001a: 183).

One text in Jeremiah provides an example of similar thinking with regard to creation, and it specifically mentions birds. Jeremiah 8 discusses the obstinacy of the people and their perpetual backsliding. A series of analogies, such as the image of a horse that rushes headlong into battle, are meant to illustrate rash, disobedient behavior. The prophet is upset because, usually, when people fall they get up again. In 8.7, the imagery turns avian: "even the stork in the heavens knows its times; and the turtledove, swallow, and crane observe the time of their coming." The birds provide an example of creatures that know what they are supposed to do. The created order, in this instance, provides a contrast to the perversity of the nation. This shows that birds can function as a small example of what was a more grandiose use of the created order in Ben Sira and *1 Enoch*, both of which use creation and its regularity as a way of defining and condemning deviations therefrom.

If Jeremiah provides birds as an example of regularity and stability, Tobit's birds[30] are the exact opposite. Tobit behaves appropriately, but the birds deviate. The question often asked of Tobit's encounter with the sparrows is whether the situation is comic or tragic (McCracken 1995; Cousland 2003). While answering such a question can help move one toward an interpretation of the story, it may not be the most helpful question to ask. It is slightly different to ask: Do these birds indicate in any way the origin of Tobit's misfortune? As we have seen, authors contemporaneous with Tobit used aspects of creation to make arguments about the origin and causes of evil. Here, the author of Tobit may be doing the same.

Tobit's outdoor slumber would have been unencumbered had the sparrows not intervened. Many commentators point to a story in the Babylonian Talmud (*b. Pesah* 111a) that warns against the indiscretion of sleeping outside because whoever does so will have to bear the consequences.[31] This one Talmudic reference, fraught with temporal problems in its potential relevance in Tobit, should not inoculate the interpreter from having to ask further questions about what, specifically, the birds may be intended to communicate. Is Tobit's misfortune here really just the result of a "simple indiscretion?" (J. Collins 2005: 28).

Tobit's righteous act necessitates his outdoor slumber, even if his actions cannot be correlated with a specific Jewish law.[32] What might the author

---

30   In Tobit 2.10, the birds are called στρουθίον, a word that likely means sparrow or another similar small bird. It is a more specific name for a bird than the general ὄρνεον (e.g., Gen. 6.20) or πετεινόν (e.g., Mark 4.4, 32). There does not, however, seem to be great significance behind the specific type of bird.

31   The saying, as quoted by Zimmerman (1958: 57): "He who sleeps in the shadow of a single palm tree in a courtyard, and who sleeps in the shadow of the moon, has his own blood on his head." This saying is also noted by Moore (1996: 130) and Collins (2005: 28).

32   The necessity of Tobit's ritual washing lies in Num. 19.11 and following, but the necessity of Tobit's outdoor slumber is harder to pinpoint, beyond the obvious irony or misfortune in the fact that Tobit's righteous deed leads to the purification rites, his outdoor slumber, and, eventually, his blindness. See Moore's discussion (1996: 130–1).

be intending to communicate by way of the mechanism of Tobit's ordeal? We have provided ample examples of how the regularity of creation is a guarantor of God's ability to exact punishment with a straightforward correlation between act and consequence. In Tobit, however, the sparrows have proved a nuisance. While one could simply suggest that they interfere with Tobit as a result of Tobit's own indiscretion, the fact that contemporaneous authors were expressing their views of evil and its origin in specific terms of creation indicates that the author of Tobit may have a more subtle intention. The contention in what follows is that the birds provide a mundane example of the type of corrupted and unruly creation seen in the apocalyptic literature in the *Book of Watchers* and the *Astronomical Book* in *1 Enoch*.

There is some evidence of a correlation between birds and demonic activity within Second Temple Judaism. *Jubilees* chapter 11 describes a scenario where birds make human survival difficult: "And Prince Mastema sent crows and birds so that they might eat the seed which was being sown in the earth in order to spoil the earth so that they might rob mankind of their labors . . . and the years began being barren because of the birds" (*Jub.* 11.10–13; *OTP* 2:78). In the next section, Abram is able to chase the birds away, having to turn them back 70 times in one day (11.18–22).[33] The scenario in *Jubilees* is such that it is not just that birds are an annoyance to humans and causing problems. They are instead indicative of a larger, cosmic battle that is taking place.[34] They are the direct agents of the original adversary, Mastema.

Here we might compare a slightly different treatment of birds. Philo, while passing through Ascalon on his way to the temple, notes (*De providentia* 2.64) the large number of pigeons whose lack of wariness was the result of local injunctions against harming them. The birds in *Jubilees* are not a passing, random nuisance, but are indicative of a larger sectarian struggle, which forms part of the exploration of the experience of evil in *Jubilees*.[35] The parable Jesus tells in Mark 4 also suggests a correlation between birds and demonic activity: "And it happened in his sowing that some fell along the road, and birds came and gobbled it up" (Mark 4.4). Jesus interprets this bird as "Satan," who comes and takes away that which had been sown

33   Nickelsburg points out some similarities between Tobit and *Jubilees* (2001b: 41–55).

34   For a discussion of how *Jubilees* constructs its scenario of "disembodied spirits" as an explanation for segments of human reality, see Stuckenbruck (2009: 302). His essay on the origin of evil and interpretation of Gen. 6.1–4 is also relevant to this discussion (2004: 111–15).

35   See, for example, the introduction of Mastema into Genesis 22, which transforms the impetus for Abraham's test into a Job-like conversation between God and an adversary (*Jub.* 17.15–16; 18.9–13). Stuckenbruck (2009: 303) shows how *Jubilees* is actually quite varied in its explorations of the origin of evil. First, he shows that the text's most pressing aim is to explain experienced realities in the author's and reader's world (305), and that the text, in its appropriation of the *Book of Watchers*, "attempts to steer a fine line between human responsibility, on the one hand, and demonic cause, on the other" (303).

(Mark 4.15). Some of this dualistic reflection on the role of birds has led Nickelsburg to suggest: "Perhaps the birds [in Tobit] are agents of a demon like Asmodeus" (1988a: 794).[36] A connection in understanding may be even more likely when one notes that 4Q225 (a text from Qumran called *Pseudo-Jubilees*) seems to envision the binding of Mastema, which is the same fate suffered by Asmodeus (in Tob. 8.3) and Asael (in *1 En.* 10.4) at the hands of Raphael.[37]

It is, of course, a long trip from a few meddlesome sparrows to the cosmological and speculative scenarios in parts of *1 Enoch*. It seems possible, however, that there are some previously unexplored connotations these birds may communicate for the author of Tobit. In light of two facts previously established in this study—that Tobit's own explanations of his situation may not be adequate and that contemporaneous texts use creation as a canvas for expressing their views of retribution and misfortune—we might better be able to perceive the role of the birds in the book of Tobit. The birds suggest a scenario where all is not as it should be. Michael Stone has analyzed the role of what he calls the "natural order" in the Second Temple period (1987: 298–308). He notes that, in this period, there arises a "clear attribution of personality and even of will to natural phenomena" (307). This is a distinct innovation compared to earlier resistance in the Hebrew Bible to such views. There is thus a recognizable motif in the time period of Tobit in which natural phenomena can function as "independent personalities" (Stone 1987: 303). As we have seen, these independent personalities can often be indicative of a more apocalyptic, sectarian understanding of the origin of evil, one in which evil is imposed on humanity, through no guilt of those who are righteous. The birds that oppose Tobit, a paradigmatically righteous character, hint at a more sectarian understanding of the origin of Tobit's misfortune. In a way akin to the scenarios in the *Book of Watchers* and the *Astronomical Book*, Tobit's sparrows are indicative of the extent to which evil has corrupted the world. The frustration of existing under Gentile rule is conveyed as a created order that no longer functions as intended, manifest in some of its smallest and seemingly innocuous constituents.

2. Fish

When working to understand the meaning inherent in the fish in Tobit, *Jubilees* may again provide a helpful comparison. Tzvi Novick (2007: 763) argues that the book of Tobit's narrative strategy was to present a biblicized narrative that resembles Genesis 22. Part of his argument includes the possibility that, at the time Tobit was written, Mastema was assumed to be operative in the story of the sacrifice of Isaac.

---

36   Owens (2007) claims that Tobit and Sarah's situations are different. Tobit's is accidental, while Sarah's is "malicious." Other parallels between them, however, especially their prayers' reception simultaneously in heaven, may indicate that they should be closely regarded, and that they both may be malicious.

37   The line in 4Q225 2.ii.13 reads: ושר המשטמה [blank] אסור.

According to Novick, the "elliptical nature" of the role of Mastema in the Genesis 22 episode is evidence that such a tradition had become "well known" (760). Novick suggests that the demonic figure that opposes Tobias may function similarly to the demonic work that threatens Isaac. If this is indeed the case, then it opens the question of the origin of all of the opposition Tobias faces. Novick, in his analysis of the similarities between Genesis 22 and the journey of Tobias and Raphael, focuses on the similarities in Tobit 6. Use of the word for "lad" (Greek: παιδίον/παιδάριον; Aramaic: עול ימא‎) and the language of the two of them "going on together" (Tob. 6.2) suggest intentional resonances between the two stories (Novick 2007: 758–9). Although the specter of Asmodeus looms over the conversation between Tobias and Raphael in chapter 6, there is a more immediate threat that Novick passes over. The large fish that leaps from the river and tries to attack Tobias' "foot" or "leg" may function as a more immediate example of the sectarian opposition already experienced in the birds and soon to find more obvious expression in the challenge from Asmodeus.[38]

The book of Tobit helps explain the threat to Tobias by evoking the biblical theme of God's destruction of a monster in the primordial waters of creation. Tobit uses the material in a subtle way. A great fish jumps from the Tigris River and attacks Tobias, an episode that becomes intelligible in light of Jewish creation mythology. Israel's scriptures contain different ideas of creation, one of which is the conception of a battle in which God enters the chaotic primordial waters and slays a mythical beast.[39] In this myth, subduing the opposition constitutes creation; God defeats the chaotic primordial water and keeps it off the land, thereby creating space for life. While most of the creation accounts in the beginning of Genesis have been scrubbed clean of this imagery,[40] the motif crops up in many strata of Israel's scriptures.

The creation battle myth exists in early literature such as the song of praise after the Exodus: "The Lord is a Warrior!" (Exod. 15.3) and remains prominent in late post-exilic apocalyptic texts like Daniel: "the four winds of heaven stirred up the great sea, from which emerged four immense beasts" (Dan. 7.2–3). The mythical beast appears under three different names in the Hebrew Bible. The most common, Leviathan

---

38   See also Nickelsburg (2001b: 50), who claims that the type of history in Tobit is closer to that in *Jubilees* than in Genesis. His actual claim is made with specific reference to the use of Genesis in both Tobit and *Jubilees*: "Our comparison with *Jubilees* indicates that the story of Tobit is closer to the *Jubilees* account of the story of Jacob than it is to the Genesis version" (50).

39   Much work has been done to show the syncretistic way in which these conceptions of creation within Israel were appropriated from other Ancient Near East sources. Especially helpful in finding influences have been the Ugaritic texts and the Canaanite Marduke–Tiamat battle.

40   The Priestly creation account actually contradicts the creation-battle motif by claiming that it was God who created the sea monsters (Gen. 1.21).

(לִוְיָתָן), is usually a many-headed sea creature that God destroyed:

> You stirred up the sea in your might
> You smashed the heads of the dragons on the waters
> You crushed the heads of Leviathan
> Tossed him for food to the sharks.
>
> (Ps. 74.13–14, NAB)

Another name for this mythical creature is Rahab (רַהַב):

> He marked out a circle on the face of the waters,
> at the boundary of light and darkness.
> The pillars of heaven shook,
> and were astounded at his roar.
> By his power he stilled the sea,
> and by his understanding he smote Rahab.
> By his wind the heavens were made fair,
> his hand pierced the twisting serpent.
>
> (Job 26.10–13)

Leviathan and Rahab are distinctly different names that play the same role—creatures opposed to God whom God destroyed at creation. A third name for this creation monster is *Tannin* (תַּנִּין). While Leviathan and Rahab never appear together in the same context (indicating that they were proper names distinguished from one another), Tannin appears parallel with both (Wakeman 1973: 72).[41] Tannin is never used as a proper noun, and probably refers to a general concept of "sea-monster" (Wakeman 1973: 73). Tannin receives the same treatment and suffers the same fate as Rahab and Leviathan; Tannin is crushed, pierced, slain, and so forth. Mary Wakeman concludes that Tannin was "a mythological term (rather than the name of some real animal), referring to the monster who was struck down . . . by Yahweh when he established his dominion" (1973: 73). Wakeman's conclusion is important because a general concept of the beast can flexibly be applied and appropriated into different contexts throughout Israel's history. John Day (1985) calls this process "historicization"[42] while Jon Levenson terms it a "dialectical counterstatement" (1994: 23). Both would agree that their terminology describes a situation where "the old myth is applied to historical events" (Levenson 1994: 23).

The most common example of historicization occurs in appropriating the creation battle mythology into the story of the Exodus. Pharaoh is an apt

41   With Rahab (Isa. 51.9) and with Leviathan (Ps. 74.13).
42   Day has an entire chapter titled, "The Historicization of the Divine Conflict with the Dragon and the Sea and the Origin of the 'Conflict with the Nations' Motif" (pp. 88–139).

evil force who meets his demise in the stormy sea (as did Rahab/Leviathan in creation). Thus Isaiah, discussing the futility of an alliance with Egypt, can say:

> Egypt's help is worthless and empty,
> Therefore I have called her
> "the silenced Rahab."

(Isa. 30.7)[43]

In second Isaiah, the exilic situation produces a further application of the imagery:

> Awake, awake, put on strength, O arm of the Lord!
> Awake as in the days of old, in ages long ago!
> Was it not you who crushed Rahab, you who pierced the dragon?
> Was it not you who dried up the sea, the waters of the great deep,
> Who made the depths of the sea into a way for the redeemed to pass over?
> Those whom the Lord has ransomed will return
> And enter Zion singing, crowned with everlasting joy;
> They will meet with joy and gladness, sorrow and mourning will flee.

(Isa. 51.9–11, NAB)

Here, the text from Deutero-Isaiah appropriates the Rahab myth in order to describe the battle at creation, to understand the liberation of the Exodus, and to hope for liberation from the exile in the future.[44] The dragon is associated with Egypt in many places, such as Ps. 77.17–21, Ezek. 29.3–5, 32.2–8, and with Babylon in Jer. 51.34. The chaotic sea, generally a part of the dragon imagery, is applied to Assyria (Isa. 17.12–14), Babylon (Hab. 3.8–10, 15), and to the nations in general (Ps. 46.3–4). In all of these examples, we find that "the powers of chaos, though subdued at the creation, were still liable to manifest themselves in the present on the historical plane" (Day 1985: 88).

Yahweh's battle at creation is a noticeable motif at various points in Israel's scriptures, often reappropriated by the community in light of a changing situation. The above examples share a method: a past event becomes necessary or useful in explaining the present. Does noticing this methodology help explain the phenomena of opposition and suffering in the book of Tobit? We have already explored the possibility that Tobit's birds represent a supra-human struggle that underlies the origin of Tobit's blindness. Tobias' visit to the banks of the Tigris River in 6.3 is a further extension of this struggle that evokes the *Chaoskampf* embedded in Israel's

---

43   Here I have followed Day's translation (1985: 89).
44   So Day, "Rahab is both the monster defeated at creation and Egypt at the time of the Exodus and also, by implication, it may be argued, the thought is extended to Babylon at the time of the prophet himself" (1985: 9).

cultural memory and textual history. While Tobias is going down to wash, a large fish (ἰχθὺς μέγας) jumps out of the water and prepares to eat his foot. This is not a little guppy that comes for a nibble of Tobias' toe. The fish is ready to consume (ἀναπηδήσας[45] ἰχθὺς μέγας ἐκ τοῦ ὕδατος ἐβούλετο καταπεῖν τὸν πόδα τοῦ παιδαρίου) and causes Tobias to cry out (ἔκραξεν).[46] The reference to Tobias' foot may also be meant as a euphemism for the male genitalia.[47] Fitzmyer rejects such innuendo outright: "it is sheer eisegesis to interpret 'foot' as a euphemism for private parts" (2003: 206). Fitzmyer's rejection of this possibility may be hasty, however. An attack on Tobias' genitalia fits the tenor of his story in general. Tobias fears for his own life in part because he is an only child (6.15). When Raphael tells him of Sarah, Tobias already knows the tale and the threat from Asmodeus (6.14–15). Tobias fears that his death will leave his parents childless; his survival and promulgation are key plot elements. More pointedly, the threat to his virility is the very one provided by the demon Asmodeus to all who attempted to approach consummation of a marriage to Sarah. Since Asmodeus threatens his ability to consummate the marriage, a parallel threat from the great fish is actually appropriate to the context and is not eisegesis. The ichthyic attack on Tobias' reproductive ability further explicates his exclamation, and also qualifies the type of opposition the fish embodies as being similar to that faced from Asmodeus.

A "great fish" coming out of the water and preparing to devour Tobias could be intelligible in light of the creation battle motif. The words Levenson used to describe the chaotic seas in Israel's intermittent dalliances with ancient creation mythology appropriately describe Tobias' encounter at the Tigris: this great fish is a "sinister force" that could possibly "forestall the ordered reality we call creation" (1994: 15). Any attempt to pinpoint what type of aquatic creature the author envisions is to miss the point entirely. As Moore notes, "*what* [the great fish] symbolizes in the tale is the important thing" (1996: 199). The journey on which Tobias has set out begins the defeat of the opposition and also provides the material for renewal and creation. The heart and liver, when burned, become the odor of deliverance, causing Asmodeus to flee. The gall will restore Tobit's sight. For Israel, the "heart of [their] deliverance took place at sea" (Day 1985: 89) (in both the destruction of Leviathan and the parting of the waters), leading to the genesis

---

45   Jacobs (2005: 135) makes an interesting observation that the language of the fish jumping from the water here echoes that of Tobit leaping from his meal in 2.4 to bury his dead kinsman.

46   AB shortens the episode considerably. No adjective modifies the fish, and its goal is simply "to eat the child." 4Q197 4.i.6–7 contains fragments of this episode, and it seems to confirm what is contained in S: [א]מי[ל למב]לע רגל עלימן חד רב מן [נו]ן ושור. Thus, the Aramaic supports the phrase, "great fish" ([נו]ן חד רב), and its desire to eat Tobias' foot ([א]למב]לע רגל עלימן). See Fitzmyer (2003: 205).

47   This is a fairly common Semitic euphemism. See, for example, Exod. 4.25; Ruth 3.4–7.

of their religion (i.e., the covenant at Sinai and entrance into the land). For the book of Tobit, the heart of deliverance is literally a heart, one that has been wrested from the innards of an aggressive fish.

Tobias not only thwarts the opposition—he eats it. In some later apocalyptic literature, Leviathan, after his defeat, is served as eschatological food for the community: "And the angel of peace who was with me said to me, 'These two monsters [i.e., Leviathan and Behemoth] are prepared for the great day of the Lord when they shall turn into food'" (*1 En.* 60.24; *OTP* 1:41–42). *2 Baruch* offers a similar tradition: "And Behemoth will reveal itself from its place, and Leviathan will come from the sea, the two great monsters which I created on the fifth day of creation and which I shall have kept until that time. And they will be nourishment for all who are left" (29.4; *OTP* 1:630). These traditions in *1 Enoch* and *2 Baruch* could help explain Raphael's statement in Tob. 12.19 in which he claims that he did not eat or drink anything. Here, in Tob. 6.6, only Tobias eats the fish. Many proposals have been offered to explain why Raphael could not eat, most of them suggesting that angelic corporeality (or lack thereof) would not require or allow such a human activity.[48] The fact that only Tobias eats the fish, however, could simply be because it was food meant only for him. As *2 Baruch* states, the food from the primordial adversary is intended for those who are left. It is proper food for the "remnant," a word specifically used later in the narrative's eschatological section (13.16). The food from the thwarted fish is meant for Tobias and is not appropriate for God's angelic agent.

The most likely historical context for the book of Tobit corresponds in kind with those investigated above in the appropriation of the creation battle. Tobit was most likely written at some point during the Hellenistic period and its central struggle is with what Cousland calls "the subjection of a scattered Israel to the rule of powerful Gentiles" (2003: 551). Such a situation spurs the author of Tobit to suggest that, in some sense, the primordial foe endures, which revives "all the anxiety that goes with this horrific thought . . . The experience of this world sorely tries the affirmation of [an] ever vigilant, ever faithful God" (Levenson 1994: 18). It was in these types of situations that the *Chaoskampf* proved particularly generative, especially for those trying to explain why the world is "inherently unsafe" (Levenson 1994: 17). When discussing the application of the creation battle motif to powers such as Egypt and Babylon, Day concludes:

> It is clear that it was the experience of exile itself which led to the fondness for the imagery, for Israel was now totally subject to a foreign power in a way which had not been the case in pre-exilic times. Thus it was that the

---

48   See, for example, Moore (1996: 272), who suggests that "in the thinking of the day, angels neither ate nor drank." He does admit, however, that Lot's angels in Gen. 19.3 provide evidence to the contrary. The Vulgate here suggests that he did eat and drink, but that he used invisible food (*cibo et potu inuisibili*).

dragon and sea were apt terms to be applied to Babylon, for it appeared that the powers of chaos defeated at creation and in the Exodus had reasserted themselves. (187–8)

The book of Tobit portrays a world where all is not well because "the order that is supposed to prevail in the cosmos has been profoundly subverted and inverted" (Cousland 2003: 548). In the book of Tobit, the creation battle between God and the dragon provides a template through which the current situation of suffering can be understood. The usage is subtle, an evocation that takes the form of a fish from the Tigris. Irene Nowell agrees with the association of Tobias' fish with the primordial waters:

> The struggle with the fish occurs at night, a traditional time for the dominance of evil . . . The fish symbolizes not only the beginning of this struggle with death, but also the means to life . . . Thus the fish recalls the traditional symbolism of water and water monsters which signify chaos, but once conquered become the means of creation. (1983: 219)

According to the book of Tobit, part of the experience of suffering is the feeling that the primordial battle of creation is still being played out. God's victory over the sea creature is not in doubt, but the battle has reappeared in the narrative of Tobit. There are forces of the world opposed to God and God's people, but God can overcome these powers in a way that liberates (like Sarah from the demon) and restores (like Tobit from blindness) the community.[49]

III. Conclusion

The book of Tobit ultimately does not offer a satisfactory resolution to the problems it addresses. Tobit's sight is restored and Nineveh is destroyed, but the core problem of subjection to foreign rule is never resolved. The text seems to vacillate between the extremes of restoration and continued subjugation. Levenson's words, although not specifically about Tobit, summarize the situation well:

> The present is bereft of the signs of divine triumph. It is a formidable challenge to faith and a devastating refutation of optimism. On the other hand, the dialectic of this vision does not allow for an unqualified acceptance of the pessimism that attributes to innocent suffering the immovability of fate. (1994: 24)

---

49 Moore offers a caveat on this point. When discussing potential resonances with the *Chaoskampf* in Tobit, he suggests: "to what an extent an ancient audience of men, women, and children would have perceived such symbolism is unknown" (1996: 199).

In other words, Tobit shares some significant concerns with contemporaneous apocalyptic thinkers and its later inheritors. Events on the ground suggest that injustice has somehow seeped its way into the structure of the world.[50] This is where the opposition to Tobit and other characters comes from. It is clearly not the result of his own iniquity, despite his own estimations to the contrary. We have sufficiently proven that his words do not hold up to scrutiny of the events in the narrative. The birds, the fish, and the demon are all elements of a larger creation that has been penetrated and corrupted, representing a more dualistic understanding of the origin of evil. There are sufficient points of contact between Tobit and apocalyptic texts to sustain such an understanding. Tobit, however, is not fully an apocalypticist, nor should his text be categorized as an apocalypse. In Tobit there is not an "unqualified acceptance of the pessimism" that attributes suffering to inexorable fate (Levenson 1994: 24). The text of Tobit is too infused with suggestions to the contrary, most notably those statements of the title character who proposes a close connection between act and consequence. To push Tobit to one of these poles or the other would not adequately describe the complexity of its perspective of retribution. What the story of Tobit ultimately does is, to coin a word, complexify. The book's theology is complex and unresolved because its view of reality is equally so. A close connection between act and consequence is shown to be problematic. So, too, however, is a complete turn to skepticism and determinism.[51]

The very argument about the origin of evil that scholars have delimited between Ben Sira and the tradents of *1 Enoch* is one in which Tobit wants to engage.[52] Because Tobit has the appearance of being a simple folk tale and has been so construed by its interpreters, it is all the more remarkable that such a great degree of astute theological thinking is embedded in so simple a genre. The book's genre may actually augment its impact. A folk tale, both then and now, has a quotidian appeal. Such a seemingly mundane vehicle lends its message greater clout. The author's contribution is to tell an entertaining folk tale which refuses to be limited to one theological supposition. The book of Tobit offers a scenario that respects the ambiguity and inconsistency experienced in everyday life.[53]

---

50   Gustavo Gutierrez's (1973) language of a "hamartiosphere" comes to mind here.

51   One could again note here the complexity of the representation of evil in *Jubilees* for which Stuckenbruck argues when he notes that "the writer of Jubilees thus attempts to steer a fine line between human responsibility, on the one hand, and demonic cause on the other" (2009: 303). At the same time, his overall argument concludes that *Jubilees* has reshaped the watchers tradition so as "to reinforce the responsibility humans ultimately have before God" (307).

52   A debate well delineated by Argall (1995).

53   This is a conclusion similar to what Stuckenbruck says about *Jubilees*, that its primary concern is "not actually deliberating about the origin of evil per se," but that "it functions to explain 'why things are the way they are experienced and perceived' in the author's and his reader's world" (2009: 305).

Chapter 9

Conclusion

I. Retrospect: "Who knows if he will look with favor upon you?" (Tob. 13.6)

The argument presented in this study has shown that scholars' alacrity to claim that the book of Tobit hews closely to the lines of a straight-forward sense of retribution does not adequately explain the book's complexity. While the book of Tobit does make statements that work from an assumption that there is a close connection between act and consequence, such statements are limited to the title character himself. Raphael, God's agent, avers that only a newly revealed "whole truth" can adequately allow Tobit to understand his situation. God's role in this story is different than Tobit the character assumed; in a strik-ingly similar way, many scholars who study the book have inadequately assessed the complexity of Deuteronomic theology, its influence on Tobit, and the subtle influence of apocalyptic theology in Tobit.

a. Summary
Before offering several conclusions from the work of the present study, a robust summary will prove salutary.

Chapter one
Chapter one introduced the idea that there are two significant prob-lems with how scholars have attached the "Deuteronomistic" label to the book of Tobit. On one hand, the word "Deuteronomistic" is most often used to refer to Tobit's perspective on retribution, which does not do justice to the complexity of either the book of Tobit or the book of Deuteronomy itself. Second, studies of Tobit have not paid close enough attention to the parsing of retribution in the entire story of Tobit. There is certainly so-called "Deuteronomistic" retributive theology in Tobit, but this neither exhausts nor exemplifies the overall perspective of the book.

Chapter two
Chapter two argued for the integrity of the text of Tobit, most specifi-cally, that the framing chapters (1 and 13–14) were not later editions

but are integral to the overall text. They were written intentionally by
the author in a way roughly similar to how we find them today through
our variegated textual traditions. The assessment of Tobit's provenance
and likely time of composition also provided warrant for comparing it
with Sirach and *1 Enoch*.

Chapter three
Chapter three traced the history of how scholars have come to discuss
"Deuteronomism" broadly within the study of the Hebrew Bible and
more specifically within the book of Tobit. While there certainly is
evidence of an ideological thread in the biblical materials that could be
called "Deuteronomistic," its influence and pervasiveness can often be
oversimplified and overstated. The same holds true for its existence in
Tobit. Alexander Di Lella's original argument (1979) about the influence
of Deuteronomy on Tobit launched a scholarly trajectory in assessing
the book's overall theological perspective that has lost its tether to the
full details of the story the book of Tobit tells. This chapter ended with
two significant observations. First, most scholarly treatments of Tobit
as "Deuteronomistic" do not pay sufficient attention to variant forms
of retributive theology in the Second Temple period. Influence directly
from Deuteronomy to Tobit is certainly possible, but some contextualization of so-called "Deuteronomistic" theology is often not a mainstay
in treatments of Tobit. Second, scholarly assessment of the book of
Tobit's purported "Deuteronomistic" perspective do not attend to the
whole story. Statements by Tobit the character himself, which at points
certainly do posit a close connection between act and consequence, are
taken to be in concert with the point of the view of the author. This need
not be the case. The two chapters that follow (four and five) discuss in
sequence the two conclusions from chapter three.

Chapter four
Chapter four took up the challenge of a close parsing of the retributive
perspective in the book of Sirach. Ben Sira offers a roughly contemporaneous offering and a wisdom text that obviously has been influenced
by Deuteronomy and is often labeled "Deuteronomistic." Ben Sira offers
an erudite, well-formulated view of retribution, incorporating his own
experience and how it intersects with Israel's past and its scriptures. His
view of retribution was generally expressed in the language of creation
theology and evinced significant reflection and nuance in its manifestation in the sapiential forms of his writing. At the same time, the chapter
concluded that the terms "Deuteronomic" or "Deuteronomistic" are
simply not adequate. They tend to oversimplify and do not do justice to
the complexity of Deuteronomy itself nor to those texts that purportedly
are "Deuteronomistic." I opted instead to refer to a "straightforward"
sense of retribution, one that portrays a "close connection" between

act and consequence. This language describes a distinct retributive perspective without attaching to it an unhelpful and potentially misleading macro-label.

Chapter five
Chapter five addressed the second significant observation from chapter three, which was the need for a close parsing of the view of retribution in the whole story in the book of Tobit. While there certainly is language that works from an idea of a close connection between act and consequence (e.g., Tob. 3.1–6), this ideology is limited to Tobit the main character himself. None of the other characters in the story seem to make the same assumptions about the connection between act and consequence that the title character himself does. If one looks beyond Tobit the character, an assumed connection between act and consequence fades from the story. In fact, by the end of the story, the reader (and Tobit) discover that the events of the story have a very different role for God than that which Tobit had been assuming throughout. The role of Raphael in the narrative creates an epistemological gap between Tobit the character and the reader. This gap allows the narrator to critique Tobit's theological formulations with use of narrative events and statements that offer conclusions contrary to Tobit's.

Chapter six
Chapter six explored an alternate ideology in the ancient world conceptually gathered around a very different focal point: apocalypticism. One finds little consensus on a host of issues when discussing apocalypticism in ancient Judaism, especially in determining its original catalyst and historical development. George W. E. Nickelsburg (1988b; 1996) is one of very few scholars who have explored connections between Tobit and some motifs in insipient apocalypticism. His conclusions, however, are very modest, and although he finds conceptual parallels between Tobit and the traditions that are behind parts of *1 Enoch*, he does not allow these parallels to influence a theological assessment of the book of Tobit in any way at all. The argument presented here concluded differently. If the book of Tobit can be shown to have some traditions and narrative techniques shared with some apocalyptic texts, then this could call for a reassessment of the book of Tobit's theological perspective.

Chapter seven
Chapter seven, in a way similar to chapter four, which focused on Sirach, closely examined portions of the apocalyptic collection known as *1 Enoch*. Both the *Book of Watchers* and the *Astronomical Book* showed the extensive reflection and theological thinking being done in the third century BCE about retribution and the problem of evil. The answer given in these texts is essentially sectarian: that evil was not

wrought by human action but is imposed upon a certain righteous segment of humanity by unruly outside forces. *1 Enoch* is not univocal on
this topic, and a later part of the corpus, *The Epistle of Enoch*, offers a
revised role for humanity, but this only highlights the way humanity is
exonerated in the *Book of Watchers* and the *Astronomical Book*. Similar
to Ben Sira, many parts of *1 Enoch* express their views of retribution in
terms of creation theology, and are preoccupied with the complicity (or
lack thereof) of humanity in retribution and equations of good and evil.

Chapter eight
Chapter eight returns specifically to the book of Tobit to build upon
the observations of chapter seven. The interest in the problem of evil,
retribution, and the role of humanity therein in both Ben Sira and
1 Enoch more than justifies a close examination of the book of Tobit
along similar lines. The close parsing of the understanding of the origin
of evil in parts of *1 Enoch* is not just folderol, but reveals a helpful
conclusion: that authors contemporaneous with the book of Tobit
were explaining their views of retribution in terms of creation theology. Creation in Tobit rises up in direct rebellion against what God
intends. One finds in Tobit a created order that is unruly, that has
gone "berserk" (Fretheim 2005: 120).[1] Birds and fish, both of which
share some traditional associations with unruly creation in apocalyptic
texts, arise in opposition to the righteous characters in Tobit. Thus,
Tobit's guilt (or that of his forebears) is not the sole reason for his misfortune. He is not experiencing direct retribution. Instead, humans are
caught up in the drama of evil, even if they are not directly responsible
for its origin or its alleviation. When Tobit's sight returns at the end of
the book, his theological point of view changes. The newly amended
perspective no longer contains the same tight connection between act
and consequence, and an entirely new conception of how God interacts
with humanity and creation becomes necessary for Tobit to make sense
of his life. This role for God is specifically revealed by the angel Raphael.
The book of Tobit is not an apocalypse, but its story does reveal theological affinities with some of Israel's earliest apocalyptic literature that
need to be taken into account in order fully to comprehend the complex
view of reality and retribution that the book offers.

1   Fretheim does not make this comment specifically with regard to the book of
Tobit, but the application of this terminology seems appropriate nonetheless.

b. Conclusions

The work of this present study leads to the following succinct conclusions:

1. *The pervasive references to the "Deuteronomistic theology" of the book of Tobit are inadequate.* As noted repeatedly in the pages above, Tobit does contain some straightforward retributive language, but the book's ultimate perspective is much more complex. At the same time, as the work of John Gammie has shown (1970: 1–12), the actual theology of Deuteronomy and its view of retribution is much more complex than is often assumed (Olson 2003: 209). Tobit may be Deuteronomic, but only in an ironic sense: it shares with Deuteronomy a penchant for complexity and a refusal to offer trite explanations for human predicaments.

2. *Tobit's affinities with some aspects of Jewish apocalypticism recommend rethinking its view of retribution.* The book of Tobit has a revelatory perspective that impinges directly upon the book's view of retribution. God's role is different than that assumed by the title character. What is often interpreted as straightforward retribution (by both Tobit and interpreters of the book) is instead the result of a cosmic clash between good and evil, the resolution of which is dependent solely upon God doing something new in the future. Thus, the book of Tobit has a more dualistic and sectarian view of the origin of evil than has generally been noticed in previous assessments of the book's view of retribution.

3. *The book of Tobit deserves a place at the table as a serious theological offering in the Second Temple period.* Scholars have delimited debates about the origin of evil in many texts of this period. These debates are passionate, interesting, complex, learned, mytho-poetic, and multifarious. The book of Tobit, generally, has not been a serious conversation partner in the reconstructions and assessment of these debates. The text's own internal struggles with issues of retribution and the problem of evil and its erudition in the traditions of Israel (and the wider culture), in addition to the complex answer it gives, recommend it be given a louder voice.

4. *The complex theological point of view the book offers may provide clues about its place of composition.* Scholars who study Tobit face a conundrum: the book's Diaspora setting and interest in how to live in such a situation do not seem to make sense in light of more recent studies that are tending to find its location closer and closer to Jerusalem.[2] My main interest in this monograph has been a proper reading of the book of Tobit's theological perspective, not to pinpoint its place of composition, but its theology may hint at its provenance. If the book of Tobit is seen as a narrative in service of a theological statement, then its Diaspora/exilic setting need not pose a problem of a likely

---

2   For example, two recent monographs place the book of Tobit in drastically different locales. Macatangay (2011) goes so far as to call the author of Tobit a Jerusalem-based sage (303). Miller (2011) seems to view the book as a Diaspora composition (e.g., 132–3).

Sitz im Leben for the author. These elements are simply part of the story, intended to contribute to the overall theological intentions of the author. Dimant (2009a) has gone so far as to suggest that Tobit may have origins or affinities with the Qumran community, and the theology of the book, as presented in this study, would certainly be at home in such a setting. This observation would fit with the conclusions of Fröhlich that Tobit may have been a "popular work in the [Qumran] community" (2005: 69).[3]

II. Prospect: "If I give my soul, will he stop my hands from shaking?"[4]

The idea of straightforward retribution, of a close connection between action and consequence, is still pervasive today. So-called "Deuteronomistic theology" is not an antiquated, vestigial explanation of human predicaments. The theological dictum that God always rewards righteousness and punishes wickedness endures. We began this study with Puccini's *Tosca*, which provides an example of very similar theological thinking:

> Always with a sincere faith,
> I placed flowers on the altar.
> In the hour of ache,
> Why, why, O Lord
> Why have you repaid me like this?

The successful book and DVD series, *The Secret*, by Rhonda Byrne (2006) has become immensely popular and has the same conceptual underpinning. Byrne's book spent over 80 weeks on the *New York Times'* bestseller list. It peddles a scenario in which the power of positive thinking can procure specific, concrete results in a person's life:

> A perfect example to demonstrate The Secret and the law of attraction in action is this: You may know of people who acquired massive wealth, lost it all, and within a short time acquired massive wealth again. What happened in these cases, whether they know it or not, is that their dominant thoughts were on wealth; that is how they acquired it in the first instance. Then they allowed fearful thoughts of losing the wealth to enter their minds, until those

---

3   Fröhlich makes the further observation that the Diaspora setting of the book may have functioned metaphorically for those sharing the sectarian worldview of the Qumran community, since they may have "felt themselves living in a kind of exile" (2005: 70).

4   From "If I Give my Soul" by Bill Joe Shaver, recently reinterpreted by Johnny Cash on his album, *Unearthed I: Who's Gonna Cry?*

fearful thoughts of loss became their dominant thoughts. (Byrne 2006: 6)

The Secret is built upon the "law of attraction." Do you have cancer? Think positively enough about your health and the disease will leave. Want more money? Tap into the law of attraction by thinking the right, disciplined thoughts and you will get what you want. This is nothing other than a straightforward sense of retribution in sheep's clothing. God has been removed from the equation, but this perspective still assumes that the world works as a tightly ordered machine and that humans can expect consequences that are commensurate with specific actions.

Many forms of religious expression today are also redolent with this point of view. Those who propound the prosperity gospel focus on obedience as the key to God's blessing (usually manifest as this-worldly financial success). For example, in a recent book, the very popular preacher and author Joel Osteen says that: "God's plan for each of our lives is that we continually rise to new levels. But how high we go in life, and how much of God's favor and blessings we experience, will be directly related to how well we follow His directions" (2007: 301). This, again, suggests that the world runs like a machine and that God can be leveraged toward blessing with human obedience. Such views of how humans secure their own destiny have repeatedly suffered devastating critiques. The human experience has been trumping such mechanistic views of retribution for a long time—one only need mention Qoheleth.

It is precisely because of the continuance of such straightforward views of retribution that the theological proposition in the book of Tobit seems so timely. The book of Tobit refuses to accept The Secret. It contains enough traditional formulations of straightforward retribution that they are not all there simply to be undercut; the book of Tobit's game is not simply to be subversive. The book does, however, allow experience to influence the party line. Real life is messy. Things do not always work out according to a strict formula. The book of Tobit, at its core, suggests that humans do not have the ability to secure their future by way of their righteousness; God cannot be leveraged toward blessing. This is not because of an inability to be righteous, but because God has created a different world, one that does not run like a machine. In crafting this scenario, the book of Tobit wrests an incredible amount of control from humans. It offers, ultimately, an uncomfortable portrait of human contingency and our dependence on God's willingness to reveal to us the "whole truth."

BIBLIOGRAPHY

Aberle, David (1962), "A Note on Relative Deprivation Theory as Applied to Millenarian and Other Cult Movements," in Sylvia Thrupp (ed.), *Millennial Dreams in Action: Essays in Comparative Study* (The Hague: Mouton): 209–14.

Abrahams, I. (1893), "Tobit and Genesis," *JQR* 5: 348–50.

Alexander, Philip (1997), "'Wrestling against Wickedness in High Places': Magic in the Worldview of the Qumran Community," in S. Porter and C. Evans (eds.), *The Scrolls and the Scriptures: Qumran Fifty Years After* (Sheffield: Sheffield Academic Press): 318–37.

Anderson, Bernhard (1987), *Creation Versus Chaos: The Reinterpretation of Mythical Symbolism in the Bible* (Philadelphia: Fortress Press).

Anderson, Gary A. (2008), "The Book of Tobit and the Canonical Ordering of the Book of the Twelve," in J. Ross Wagner, C. Kavin Rowe, and A. Katherine Grieb (eds.), *The Word Leaps the Gap: Essays on Scripture and Theology in Honor of Richard B. Hays* (Grand Rapids: Eerdmans): 67–75.

Argall, Randal (1995), *1 Enoch and Sirach: A Comparative Literary and Conceptual Analysis of the Themes of Revelation, Creation, and Judgment* (SBL Early Judaism and its Literature, 8; Atlanta: Scholars Press).

Auwers, Jean-Marie (2005), "La Tradition Vielle Latine Du Livre De Tobi: Un Etat de la Question," in Géza Xeravits and József Zsengellér (eds.), *The Book of Tobit: Text, Tradition, Theology* (JSJSup, 98; Leiden: Brill): 1–22.

—— (2006), "Traduire le livre de Tobie pour la liturgie," *Revue Théologique du Louvain* 37: 179–99.

Bakan, David (1968), *Disease, Pain and Sacrifice: Toward a Psychology of Suffering* (Chicago: University of Chicago Press).

Baltzer, Klaus (1971), *The Covenant Formulary: In Old Testament, Jewish, and Early Christian Writings* (Philadelphia: Fortress Press).

Barclay, John (1996), *Jews in the Mediterranean Diaspora: From Alexander to Trajan* (Edinburgh: T&T Clark).

Barker, Margaret (2006), "The Archangel Raphael in the Book of Tobit," in Mark Bredin (ed.), *Studies in the Book of Tobit: A*

Multidisciplinary Approach (LSTS, 55; London: T&T Clark): 118–28.

Bauckham, Richard (2006), "Tobit as a Parable for the Exiles of Northern Israel," in Mark Bredin (ed.), *Studies in the Book of Tobit: A Multidisciplinary Approach* (LSTS, 55; London: T&T Clark): 140–64.

Beckwith, Roger (2005), *Calendar, Chronology and Worship* (Ancient Judaism and Early Christianity, 61; Leiden: Brill).

Bede (1983), *In Tobiam; In Proverbia; In Cantica Canticorum* (Corpus Christianorum Series Latina, 119b; Turnholt: Brepols).

Beentjes, Pancratius Cornelis (1997), *The Book of Ben Sira in Hebrew* (VTSup, 68; Leiden: Brill).

——— (2003), "Theodicy in the Wisdom of Ben Sira," in A. Laato and J. C. de Moor (eds.), *Theodicy in the World of the Bible* (Leiden: Brill): 509–24.

——— (2011), "The Book of Ben Sira and Deuteronomistic Heritage: A Critical Approach," in Hanne Von Weissenberg, Juha Pakkala, and Marko Marttila (eds.), *Changes in Scripture: Rewriting and Interpreting Authoritative Traditions in the Second Temple Period* (BZAW, 419; Berlin: Walter de Gruyter): 275–96.

Betz, Hans Deiter (1969), "On the Problem of the Religio-Historical Understanding of Apocalypticism," in Robert W. Funk (ed.), *Apocalypticism* (JTC, 6; New York: Herder & Herder): 134–56.

Beyer, Klaus (1984), *Die Aramäischen Texte vom Toten Meer* (Göttingen: Vandenhoeck & Ruprecht).

Beyerle, Stefan (2005a), *Die Gottesvorstellungen in der antik-jüdischen Apokalyptic* (JSJSup, 103; Leiden: Brill).

——— (2005b), "'Release Me to Go to My Everlasting Home . . .' (Tob 3:6): A Belief in an Afterlife in Late Wisdom Literature?" in Géza Xeravits and József Zsengellér (eds.), *The Book of Tobit: Text, Tradition, Theology* (JSJSup, 98; Leiden: Brill): 71–88.

Bhayro, Siam (2005), *The Shemihazah and Asael Narrative of 1 Enoch 6–11: Introduction, Text, Translation and Commentary with Reference to Ancient Near Eastern and Biblical Antecedents* (AOAT, 322; Münster: Ugarit-Verlag).

Black, Matthew and Albert Marie Denis (1970), *Apocalypsis Henochi Graece* (PVTG, 3; Leiden: Brill).

Black, Matthew, James C. Vanderkam, and Otto Neugebauer (1985), *The Book of Enoch or 1 Enoch: A New English Edition with Commentary and Textual Notes* (SVTP, 7; Leiden: Brill).

Blenkinsopp, Joseph (2002), *Isaiah 40–55: A New Translation with Introduction and Commentary* (AB, 19b; New York: Doubleday).

Boccaccini, Gabriele (ed.) (2005), *Enoch and Qumran Origins: New Light on a Forgotten Connection* (Grand Rapids: Eerdmans).

Boccaccini, Gabriele and John J. Collins (eds.) (2007), *The Early Enoch Literature* (JSJSup, 121; Leiden: Brill).

Bow, Beverly and George W. E. Nickelsburg (1991), "Patriarchy with a Twist: Men and Women in Tobit," in Amy-Jill Levine (ed.), *Women Like This: New Perspectives on Jewish Women in the Greco-Roman World* (Atlanta: Scholars Press): 127–43.

Boyce, Mary (1975), *A History of Zoroastrianism I: The Early Period* (Handbuch der Orientalistik, I.8.1; Leiden: Brill).

—— (1984), "On the Antiquity of Zoroastrian Apocalyptic," *BSO(A)S* 47: 57–75.

Braulik, Georg (1994), "The Development of the Doctrine of Justification in the Redactional Strata of the Book of Deuteronomy," in *The Theology of Deuteronomy: Collected Essays of Georg Braulik, O.S.B.* (Richland Hills, TX: BIBAL Press): 151–64.

Burridge, Kenelm (2005), *New Heaven, New Earth: A Study of Millenarian Activities* (Oxford: Oxford University Press).

Byrne, Rhonda (2006), *The Secret* (New York: Atria Books/Beyond Words Publishing).

Carr, David (2005), *Writing on the Tablet of the Heart: Origins of Scripture and Literature* (Oxford: Oxford University Press).

Carroll, Robert P. (1979), "Twilight of Prophecy or Dawn of Apocalyptic?" *JSOT* 14: 3–35.

—— (1998), "Exile! What Exile? Deportation and the Discourses of Diaspora," in Lester L. Grabbe (ed.), *Leading Captivity Captive: "The Exile" as History and Ideology* (JSOTSup, 278; Sheffield: Sheffield Academic Press): 63–79.

Charles, R. H. (1929), *A Critical and Exegetical Commentary on the Book of Daniel* (ICC; Oxford: Clarendon Press).

Charles, R. H. (ed.) (1913), *Apocrypha and Pseudepigrapha of the Old Testament in English* (2 vols.; Oxford: Clarendon Press).

Charlesworth, James H. (1969), "A Critical Comparison of the Dualism in 1 QS 3:13–4:26 and the 'Dualism' Contained in the Gospel of John," *NTS* 15: 389–418.

—— (1993), "In the Crucible: The Pseudepigrapha as Biblical Interpretation," in James H. Charlesworth and Craig A. Evans (eds.), *The Pseudepigrapha and Early Biblical Interpretation* (JSPSup, 14; Sheffield: JSOT Press): 20–43.

—— (2003), "Theodicy in Early Jewish Writings," in A. Laato and J. C. de Moor (eds.), *Theodicy in the World of the Bible* (Leiden: Brill): 470–508.

—— (2005), "Summary and Conclusions: The Books of Enoch or 1 Enoch Matters: New Paradigms for Understanding Pre-70 Judaism," in Gabriele Bocaccini (ed.), *Enoch and Qumran Origins: New Light on a Forgotten Connection* (Grand Rapids: Eerdmans): 436–54.

—— (2006), "Where Does the Concept of Resurrection Appear and How Do We Know That?" in James H. Charlesworth (ed.), *Resurrection: The Origin and Future of a Biblical Doctrine* (New York: T&T Clark): 1–21.

—— (ed.) (1983), *The Old Testament Pseudepigrapha* (2 vols.; New York: Doubleday).

Charlesworth, James H. and Michael A. Daise (eds.) (2003), *Light in a Spotless Mirror: Reflections on Wisdom Traditions in Judaism and Early Christianity* (Harrisburg: Trinity Press International).

Chatman, Seymour (1978), *Story and Discourse: Narrative Structure in Fiction and Film* (Ithaca: Cornell University Press).

Clifford, Richard (1998), "The Roots of Apocalypticism in Near Eastern Myth," in John J. Collins (ed.), *The Encyclopedia of Apocalypticism – Volume One: The Origins of Apocalypticism in Judaism and Christianity* (New York: Continuum): 3–38.

Coggins, Richard (1999), "What does 'Deuteronomistic' Mean?" in Linda Schearing (ed.), *Those Elusive Deuteronomists: The Phenomenon of Pan-Deuteronomism* (JSOTSup, 268; Sheffield: JSOT Press): 22–35.

Collins, Adela Yarbro (1996), *Cosmology and Eschatology in Jewish and Christian Apocalypticism* (JSJSup, 50; Leiden: Brill).

Collins, John J. (1975), "The Court-Tales in Daniel and the Development of Apocalyptic," *JBL* 94: 21–34.

—— (ed.) (1979), *Apocalypse: The Morphology of a Genre* (Semeia, 14; Missoula: Scholars Press).

—— (1982), "The Apocalyptic Technique: Setting and Function in the Book of the Watchers," *CBQ* 44: 91–111.

—— (1991), "Genre, Ideology and Social Movements in Jewish Apocalypticism," in John J. Collins and James H. Charlesworth (eds.), *Mysteries and Revelations: Apocalyptic Studies since the Uppsala Colloquium* (JSPSup, 9; Sheffield: JSOT Press): 11–32.

—— (1993), *Daniel: A Commentary on the Book of Daniel* (Hermeneia; Minneapolis: Fortress Press).

—— (1997a), *Apocalypticism in the Dead Sea Scrolls* (London: Routledge).

—— (1997b), *Jewish Wisdom in the Hellenistic Age* (OTL; Louisville: Westminster/John Knox Press).

—— (1998), *The Apocalyptic Imagination: An Introduction to Jewish Apocalyptic Literature* (2nd edn.; Biblical Resource Series; Grand Rapids: Eerdmans).

—— (2000), *Between Athens and Jerusalem: Jewish Identity in the Hellenistic Diaspora* (2nd edn.; Biblical Resource Series; Grand Rapids: Eerdmans).

—— (2002), "Temporality and Politics in Jewish Apocalyptic Literature," in C. Rowland and J. Barton (eds.), *Apocalyptic in History and Tradition* (JSPSup, 43; Sheffield: Sheffield Academic Press): 26–43.

———— (2003a), "An Enochic Testament? Comments on George Nickelsburg's Hermeneia Commentary," in *George W. E. Nickelsburg in Perspective: An Ongoing Dialogue of Learning* (2 vols.; JSJSup, 80; Leiden: Brill): 2: 373–8.

———— (2003b), "The Mysteries of God: Creation and Eschatology in 4QInstruction and the Wisdom of Solomon," in F. García-Martínez (ed), *Wisdom and Apocalypticism in the Dead Sea Scrolls and in the Biblical Tradition* (Leuven: Peeters-Leuven University Press): 287–306.

———— (2003c), "Prophecy, Apocalypse and Eschatology: Reflections on the Proposals of Lester Grabbe," in Lester L. Grabbe and Robert D. Haak (eds.), *Knowing the End from the Beginning: The Prophetic, the Apocalyptic and their Relationships* (JSPSup, 46; London: T&T Clark): 44–52.

———— (2005), "The Judaism of the Book of Tobit," in Géza Xeravits and József Zsengellér (eds.), *The Book of Tobit: Text, Tradition, Theology* (JSJSup, 98; Leiden: Brill): 23–40.

———— (2011), "Changing Scripture," in Hanne Von Weissenberg, Juha Pakkala, and Marko Marttila (eds.), *Changes in Scripture: Rewriting and Interpreting Authoritative Traditions in the Second Temple Period* (BZAW, 419; Berlin: Walter de Gruyter): 23–45.

Connolly, Sean (1997), *Bede on Tobit and on the Canticle of Habakkuk* (Dublin: Four Courts Press).

Cook, Edward M. (1996), "Our Translated Tobit," in K. Cathcart and M. Maher (eds.), *Targumic and Cognate Studies: Essays in Honour of Martin Mcnamara* (JSOTSup, 230; Sheffield: Sheffield Academic Press): 153–62.

Cook, Stephen (1995), *Prophecy and Apocalypticism: The Postexilic Setting* (Minneapolis: Fortress Press).

Corley, Jeremy (1999), "Rediscovering Tobit," *Scritpure Bulletin* 29: 22–31.

Corley, Jeremy and Vincent Skemp (eds.) (2005), *Intertextual Studies in Ben Sira and Tobit: Essays in Honor of Alexander A. Di Lella, O.F.M.* (CBQMS, 38; Washington, D.C.: Catholic Biblical Association of America).

Corley, Jeremy and Vincent Skemp (2005), "Introduction," in Jeremy Corley and Vincent Skemp (eds.), *Intertextual Studies in Ben Sira and Tobit: Essays in Honor of Alexander A. Di Lella, O.F.M.* (CBQMS, 38; Washington, D.C.: Catholic Biblical Association of America): xiii–xiv.

Cousland, J. R. C. (2003), "Tobit: A Comedy in Error?" *CBQ* 65: 535–53.

Craghan, John (1982), *Esther, Judith, Tobit, Jonah, Ruth* (Wilmington: Michael Glazier).

Crenshaw, James H. (1969), "Method in Determining Wisdom Influence upon 'Historical' Literature," *JBL* 88: 129–42.

—— (1975), "The Problem of Theodicy in Sirach: On Human Bondage," *JBL* 94: 47–64 (reprinted in James H. Crenshaw (ed.), *Theodicy in the Old Testament* [Issues in Religion and Theology, 4; London: SPCK Press, 1983]: 119–40).

—— (1978), "The Shadow of Death in Qoheleth," in John Gammie (ed.), *Israelite Wisdom: Theological and Literary Essays in Honor of Samuel Terrien* (Missoula: Scholars Press): 205–16.

—— (1980), "The Birth of Skepticism in Ancient Israel," in James Crenshaw and Samuel Sandmel (eds.), *The Divine Helmsman: Studies on God's Control of Human Events* (New York: Ktav): 1–19.

—— (ed.) (1983), *Theodicy in the Old Testament* (Issues in Religion and Theology, 4; Philadelphia: Fortress Press).

—— (1998), *Old Testament Wisdom: An Introduction* (Louisville: Westminster/John Knox Press).

—— (2005), *Defending God: Biblical Responses to the Problem of Evil* (Oxford: Oxford University Press).

Cross, Frank Moore (1973), *Canaanite Myth and Hebrew Epic: Essays in the History of the Religion of Israel* (Cambridge, MA: Harvard University Press).

Dahmen, Ulrich (2003), "Das Deuteronomium in Qumran als Umgeschriebene Bibel," in G. Braulik (ed.), *Das Deuteronomium* (Frankfurt am Main: Peter Lang): 269–309.

Davies, Philip R. (1989), "The Social World of Apocalyptic Writings," in R. E. Clements (ed.), *The World of Ancient Israel: Sociological, Anthropological and Political Perspectives, Essays by Members of the Society for Old Testament Study* (Cambridge, UK: Cambridge University Press): 251–71.

Day, John (1985), *God's Conflict with the Dragon and the Sea: Echoes of a Canaanite Myth in the Old Testament* (University of Cambridge Oriental Publications, 35; Cambridge, UK: Cambridge University Press).

Deselaers, Paul (1982), *Das Buch Tobit: Studien zu seiner Entstehung, Komposition und Theologie* (OBO, 43; Freiburg: Universitätsverlag).

Di Lella, Alexander A. (1966), "Conservative and Progressive Theology: Sirach and Wisdom," *CBQ* 28: 139–54.

—— (1979), "The Deuteronomic Background of the Farewell Discourse in Tob 14:3–11," *CBQ* 41: 380–9.

—— (1999), "Health and Healing in Tobit," *TBT* 37: 69–73.

—— (2000), "The Book of Tobit and the Book of Judges: An Intertextual Analysis," *Henoch* 22: 197–205.

—— (2004), "Two Major Prayers in the Book of Tobit," in Renate Egger-Wenzel and Jeremy Corley (eds.), *Prayer from Tobit to Qumran: Inaugural Conference of the ISDCL at Salzburg, Austria, 5–9 July 2003* (Deuterocanonical and Cognate Literature Yearbook 2004; Berlin: Walter de Gruyter): 95–115.

—— (2009a), "A Study of Tobit 14:10 and its Intertextual Parallels," *CBQ* 71: 497–506.

—— (2009b), "Tobit 4,19 and Romans 9,18: An Intertextual Study," *Bib* 90: 260–3.

Dimant, Devorah (1974), "The Fallen Angels in the Dead Sea Scrolls and in the Apocryphal and Pseudepigraphic Books Related to Them" (Ph.D. Diss., Hebrew University) [Hebrew].

—— (2008), "The Family of Tobit," in Károly D. Dobos and Miklós Köszeghy (eds.), *With Wisdom as a Robe: Qumran and other Jewish Studies in Honor of Ida Fröhlich* (Hebrew Bible Monographs, 21; Sheffield: Sheffield Phoenix Press): 23–58.

—— (2009a), "The Book of Tobit and the Qumran Halakhah," in Devorah Dimant and Reinhard G. Kratz (eds.), *The Dynamics of Language and Exegesis at Qumran* (Forschungen zum Alten Testament, 2. Reihe, 35; Tübingen: Mohr Siebeck): 121–43.

—— (2009b), "Tobit in Galilee," in Gershon Galil, Mark Geller, and Alan Millard (eds.), *Homeland and Exile: Biblical and Ancient Near Eastern Studies in Honour of Bustenay Oded* (Leiden: Brill): 347–59.

Duyndam, Joachim (2004), "Hermeneutics of Imitation: A Philosophical Approach to Sainthood and Exemplariness," in M. Poorhuis and J. Schwartz (eds.), *Saints and Role Models in Judaism and Christianity* (Jewish and Christian Perspectives Series, 7; Leiden: Brill): 7–24.

Ego, Beate (1999), *Buch Tobit* (JSHRZ, 6; Gütersloh: Gütersloher Verlagshaus).

—— (2005), "The Book of Tobit and the Diaspora," in Géza Xeravits and József Zsengellér (eds.), *The Book of Tobit: Text, Tradition, Theology* (JSJSup, 98; Leiden: Brill): 41–54.

—— (2006), "Textual Variants as a Result of Enculturation: The Banishment of the Demon in Tobit," in Wolfgang Kraus and R. Glenn Wooden (eds.), *Septuagint Research: Issues and Challenges in the Study of the Greek Jewish Scriptures* (SBLSCS, 53; Atlanta: Society of Biblical Literature): 371–8.

—— (2007), "The Figure of the Angel Raphael According to His Farewell Address in Tob 12:6–20," in Friedrich Reiterer, Tobias Nicklas, and Karin Schöpflin (eds.), *Angels: The Concept of Celestial Beings – Origins, Development and Reception*

(Deuterocanonical and Cognate Literature; Berlin: Walter de Gruyter): 239–54.

Fassbeck, Gabriele (2005), "Tobit's Religious Universe between Kinship Loyalty and the Law of Moses," *JSJ* 36: 173–96.

Festinger, Leon (1956), *When Prophecy Fails* (Minneapolis: University of Minnesota Press).

Fitzmyer, Joseph A. (1979), *A Wandering Aramean: Collected Aramaic Essays* (Missoula: Scholars Press).

——— (1995), *Qumran Cave 4: Parabiblical Texts, Part 2* (DJD, 19; Oxford: Clarendon Press).

——— (2000), "The Significance of the Hebrew and Aramaic Texts of Tobit from Qumran for the Study of Tobit," in Lawrence H. Schiffman, et al. (eds.), *The Dead Sea Scrolls: Fifty Years after their Discovery – Proceedings of the Jerusalem Congress, July 20–25, 1997* (Jerusalem: Israel Exploration Society): 418–25.

——— (2003), *Tobit* (Commentaries on Early Jewish Literature; Berlin: Walter de Gruyter).

Fraser, P. M. (1972), *Ptolemaic Alexandria* (3 vols.; Oxford: Clarendon Press).

Fretheim, Terence (2005), *God and World in the Old Testament: A Relational Theology of Creation* (Nashville: Abingdon Press).

Fries, Carl (1910), "Das Buch Tobit und Die Telemachie," *ZWT* 53: 54–87.

Fritzsche, Otto and Carl Ludwig Grimm (1953), *Kurzgefasstes Exegetisches Handbuch zu den Apokryphen des Alten Testamentes* (2nd vol.; Leipzig: S. Hirzel).

Fröhlich, Ida (2005), "Tobit against the Background of the Dead Sea Scrolls," in Géza Xeravits and József Zsengellér (eds.), *The Book of Tobit: Text, Tradition, Theology* (JSJSup, 98; Leiden: Brill): 55–70.

Frost, Stanley Brice (1952), *Old Testament Apocalyptic: Its Origins and Growth* (London: Epworth Press).

Frye, R. N. (1962), "Reitzenstein and Qumran Revisited by an Iranian," *HTR* 55: 261–8.

Gager, John G. (1975), *Kingdom and Community: The Social World of Early Christianity* (Englewood Cliffs, N.J.: Prentice-Hall).

Gamberoni, Johann (1977), "Das 'Gesetz des Mose' im Buch Tobias," in G. Braulik (ed.), *Studien zum Pentateuch* (Wien: Herder): 227–42.

Gammie, John (1970), "The Theology of Retribution in the Book of Deuteronomy," *CBQ* 32: 1–12.

——— (1990), "The Sage in Sirach," in John Gammie and Leo Perdue (eds.), *The Sage in Israel and the Ancient Near East* (Winona Lake: Eisenbrauns): 355–72.

García-Martínez, Florentino (1992), *Qumran and Apocalyptic: Studies on the Aramaic Texts from Qumran* (STDJ, 9; Leiden: Brill).

—— (ed.) (2003), *Wisdom and Apocalypticism in the Dead Sea Scrolls and in the Biblical Tradition* (Leuven: Leuven University Press).

Gathercole, Simon (2006), "Tobit in Spain: Some Preliminary Comments on the Relations between the Old Latin Witnesses," in Mark Bredin (ed.), *Studies in the Book of Tobit: A Multidisciplinary Approach* (LSTS, 55; London: T&T Clark): 5–11.

Gerould, Gordon Hall (1908), *The Grateful Dead: The History of a Folk Story* (Publications of the Folk Lore Society, 60; London: D. Nutt).

Gilbert, Maurice, Núria Calduch-Benages, and J. Vermeylen (eds.) (1999), *Treasures of Wisdom: Studies in Ben Sira and the Book of Wisdom* (BETL, 143; Leuven: Leuven University Press).

Grabbe, Lester L. (1987), "The Scapegoat Ritual: A Study in Early Jewish Interpretation," *JSJ* 18: 152–67.

—— (1989), "The Social Setting of Early Jewish Apocalypticism," *JSP* 4: 27–47.

—— (1995), *Priests, Prophets, Diviners, Sages: A Socio-historical Study of Religious Specialists in Ancient Israel* (Valley Forge: Trinity Press International).

—— (2000), *Judaic Religion in the Second Temple Period: Belief and Practice from the Exile to Yavneh* (New York: Routledge).

—— (2003a), "Introduction and Overview," in Lester L. Grabbe and Robert D. Haak (eds.), *Knowing the End from the Beginning: The Prophetic, the Apocalyptic and Their Relationships* (JSPSup, 46; London: T&T Clark): 2–43.

—— (2003b), "Prophetic and Apocalyptic: Time for New Definitions—and New Thinking," in Lester L. Grabbe and Robert D. Haak (eds.), *Knowing the End from the Beginning: The Prophetic, the Apocalyptic and Their Relationships* (JSPSup, 46; London: T&T Clark): 107–33.

Grabbe, Lester L. and Robert D. Haak (eds.) (2003), *Knowing the End from the Beginning: The Prophetic, the Apocalyptic and Their Relationships* (JSPSup, 46; London: T&T Clark).

Grabbe, Lester L. and Obed Lipschits (eds.) (2011), *Judah between East and West: The Transition from Persian to Greek Rule (ca. 400–200 BC)* (LSTS, 75; London: T&T Clark).

Greenfield, Jonas (1981), "Ahiqar in the Book of Tobit," in M. Carrez, J. Dore, and P. Grelot (eds.), *De la Tôrah au Messie: Etudes d'Exégèse et D'herméneutique Bibliques Offertes à Henri Cazelles pur ses 25 Annees d'Enseignement a l'Iinstitut Catholique de Paris* (Paris: Desclée): 329–36.

Griffen, Patrick J. (1984), "The Theology and Function of Prayer in the Book of Tobit" (Ph.D. diss.; The Catholic University of America).

Gruen, Erich (2002), *Diaspora: Jews amidst Greeks and Romans* (Cambridge, MA: Harvard University Press).

Gunkel, Hermann (1895), *Schöpfung und Chaos in Urziet und Endzeit: Eine Religionsgeschichtliche Untersuchung über Gen 1 und Ap Joh 12* (Göttingen: Vandenhoeck und Ruprecht).

Gutiérrez, Gustavo (1973), *A Theology of Liberation: History, Politics, and Salvation* (Maryknoll: Orbis Books).

Hanhart, Robert (1984), *Text und Textgeschichte des Buches Tobit* (Philologisch-Historische Klass, 3; Göttingen: Vandenhoeck und Ruprecht).

Hanson, Paul D. (1971), "Jewish Apocalyptic against its Near Eastern Environment," *RB* 78: 31–58.

—— (1975), *The Dawn of Apocalyptic: The Historical and Sociological Roots of Jewish Apocalyptic Eschatology* (Philadelphia: Fortress Press).

—— (1976a), "Apocalypticism," in *IDBSup*, 27–34.

—— (1976b), "Prolegomena to Study of Jewish Apocalyptic," in Frank Moore Cross, Werner E. Lemke, and Patrick D. Miller (eds.), *Magnalia Dei: The Mighty Acts of God – Essays on the Bible and Archaeology in Memory of G. Ernest Wright* (New York: Doubleday): 389–413.

—— (1977), "Rebellion in Heaven, Azazel, and Euhemeristic Heroes in 1 Enoch 6–11," *JBL* 96: 195–233.

—— (1992), "Apocalypses and Apocalypticism," *ABD*: 1: 279–82.

Harrington, Daniel J. (1996), *Wisdom Texts from Qumran* (London: Routledge).

—— (1999), "Prayers in Tobit," *TBT* 37: 86–90.

Hartman, Lars (1979), *Asking for a Meaning: A Study of 1 Enoch 1–5* (ConBNT, 12; Lund: Liber Laromedel/Gleerup).

Hays, Richard B. (1989), *Echoes of Scripture in the Letters of Paul* (New Haven: Yale University Press).

Hellholm, David (ed.) (1983), *Apocalypticism in the Mediterranean World and the Near East: Proceedings of the International Colloquium on Apocalypticism* (Tübingen: J. C. B. Mohr).

Hempel, Charlotte, Armin Lange, and Hermann Lichtenberger (eds.) (2002), *The Wisdom Texts from Qumran and the Development of Sapiential Thought* (BETL, 159; Leuven: Peeters).

Herms, Ronald (2006), *An Apocalypse for the Church and for the World: The Narrative Function of Universal Language in the Book of Revelation* (BZNW, 143; Berlin: Walter de Gruyter).

Hilgenfeld, Adolf (1857), *Die Jüdische Apokalyptik in ihrer Geschichtlichen Entwickelung ein Beitrag zur Vorgeschichte des Christenthums* (Jena: Friedrich Mauke).

Hinnells, John (1973), "The Zoroastrian Doctrine of Salvation in the Roman World: A Study of the Oracle of Hystaspes," in E. Sharpe and J. Hinnells (eds.), *Man and his Salvation: Studies in Memory of S. G. F. Brandon* (Manchester, N.J.: Manchester University Press): 125–48.

Hofmann, Norbert Johannes (2003), "Die Rezeption des Dtn im Buch Tobit, in der Assumptio Mosis und im 4. Esrabuch," in G. Braulik (ed.), *Das Deuteronomium* (Frankfurt am Main: Peter Lang): 311–42.

Huizenga, Leroy Andrew (2002), "The Battle for Isaac: Exploring the Composition and Function of the Aqedah in the Book of Jubilees," *JSP* 13: 33–59.

Hultgard, Anders (1983), "Forms and Origins of Iranian Apocalypticism," in David Hellholm (ed.), *Apocalypticism in the Mediterranean World and the Near East* (Tübingen: Mohr Siebeck): 387–411.

—— (1991), "Bahman Yasht: A Persian Apocalypse," in John J. Collins and James H. Charlesworth (eds.), *Mysteries and Revelations: Apocalyptic Studies since the Uppsala Colloquium* (Sheffield: JSOT Press): 114–34.

—— (1998), "Persian Apocalypticism," in John J. Collins (ed.), *The Encyclopedia of Apocalypticism – Volume One: The Origins of Apocalypticism in Judaism and Christianity* (New York: Continuum): 39–83.

Humback, Helmut and Pallan R. Ichaporia (1994), *The Heritage of Zarathushtra: A New Translation of his Gathas* (Heidelberg: Universitätsverlag C. Winter).

Ilgen, Karl David (1800), *Die Geschichte Tobi's Nach Drey Verschiedenen Originalen dem Griechischen, dem Lateinischen des Hieronymus und einem Syrischen Uebersetzt und mit Anmerkungen Exegetischen und Kritischen Inhalts* (Jena: J. C. Goepferdt).

Jackson, David (2004), *Enochic Judaism: Three Defining Paradigm Exemplars* (LSTS, 49; London: T&T Clark).

Jacobs, Naomi (2005), "'You Did Not Hesitate to Get Up and Leave the Dinner': Food and Eating in the Narrative of Tobit with some Attention to Tobit's Shavuot Meal," in Géza Xeravits and József Zsengellér (eds.), *The Book of Tobit: Text, Tradition, Theology* (JSJSup, 98; Leiden: Brill): 121–38.

Jones, Bruce William (1968), "The Prayer in Daniel IX," *VT* 18: 488–93.

Juel, Donald H. (2002), *A Master of Surprise: Mark Interpreted* (Mifflintown, PA: Sigler Press).

Just, Felix (1997), "From Tobit to Bartimaeus, from Qumran to Siloam: The Social Role of Blind People and Attitudes toward the Blind in New Testament Times" (Ph.D. diss.; Yale University).

Keck, Leander E. (1988), *Paul and His Letters* (2nd edn.; Philadelphia: Fortress Press).

Kiel, Micah D. (2008), "Tobit and Moses Redux," *JSP* 17: 83–98.

—— (2010), Review of Robert J. Littman, *Tobit: The Book of Tobit in Codex Sinaiticus, Journal of Hebrew Scriptures* 10.

—— (2011), "Tobit's Theological Blindness," *CBQ* 73: 281–98.

Knibb, Michael (1978), *The Ethiopic Book of Enoch: A New Edition in the Light of the Aramaic Dead Sea Fragments* (2 vols.; Oxford: Clarendon Press).

—— (2003), "The Book of Enoch in the Light of the Qumran Wisdom Literature," in F. García-Martínez (ed.), *Wisdom and Apocalypticism in the Dead Sea Scrolls and in the Biblical Tradition* (BETL, 168; Leuven: Peeters-Leuven University Press): 193–210.

—— (2007), "The Book of Enoch or Books of Enoch? The Textual Evidence for 1 Enoch," in Gabriele Boccaccini and John J. Collins (eds.), *The Early Enoch Literature* (JSJSup, 121; Leiden: Brill): 21–40.

Koch, Klaus (1955), "Gibt es ein Vergeltungs-Dogma im Alten Testament?" *ZTK* 52: 1–42; ET (1983): "Is there a Doctrine of Retribution in the Old Testament?" in James Crenshaw (ed.), *Theodicy in the Old Testasment* (Issues in Religion and Theology, 4; Philadelphia: Fortress Press): 57–87.

—— (1970), *Ratlos vor der Apokalyptik* (Gütersloh: Mohn).

—— (1972), *The Rediscovery of Apocalyptic: A Polemical Work on a Neglected Area of Biblical Studies and its Damaging Effects on Theology and Philosophy* (Biblical Theology, 22; London: S.C.M. Press).

—— (2007), "The Astral Laws as the Basis of Time, Universal History, and the Eschatological Turn in the Astronomical Book and the Animal Apocalypse of 1 Enoch," in Gabriele Boccaccini and John J. Collins (eds.), *The Early Enoch Literature* (JSJSup, 121; Leiden: Brill): 119–37.

Kolenkow, Anitra Bingham (1975), "The Genre Testament and Forecasts of the Future in the Hellenistic Jewish Milieu," *JSJ* 6: 57–71.

Kottsieper, Ingo (2009), "'Look, son, what Nadab did to Ahikaros . . .': The Aramaic Ahiqar-Tradition and its Relationship to the Book of Tobit," in Devorah Dimant and Reinhard G. Kratz (eds.), *The Dynamics of Language and Exegesis at Qumran* (Forschungen zum Alten Testament, 2. Reihe, 35; Tübingen: Mohr Siebeck).

Kraft, Robert A. (2007), "Para-mania: Beside, Before and Beyond Bible Studies," *JBL* 126: 5–27.

—— (2009), *Exploring the Scripturesque: Jewish Texts and their Christian Contexts* (JSJSup, 137; Leiden: Brill).

Laato, Antti (2003), "Theodicy in the Deuteronomistic History," in A. Laato and J. C. de Moor (eds.), *Theodicy in the World of the Bible* (Leiden: Brill): 183–235.

Lacocque, Andre (1976), "The Liturgical Prayer in Daniel 9," *Hebrew Union College Annual* 41: 119–42.

Leppäkari, Maria (2006), *Apocalyptic Representations of Jerusalem* (Numen Book Series, 111; Leiden: Brill).

Levenson, Jon D. (1994), *Creation and the Persistence of Evil: The Jewish Drama of Divine Omnipotence* (Princeton: Princeton University Press).

Levine, Amy-Jill (1992a), "Diaspora as Metaphor: Bodies and Boundaries in the Book of Tobit," in A. Overman and R. Maclennan (eds.), *Diaspora Jews and Judaism: Essays in Honor of, and in Dialogue with, A. Thomas Kraabel* (Atlanta: Scholars Press): 105–19.

——— (1992b), "Tobit: Teaching the Jews How to Live in the Diaspora," *BR* 8: 42–51.

Liesen, Jan (1999), "Strategical Self-References in Ben Sira," in N. Calduch-Benages and J. Mermeylen (eds.), *Treasures of Wisdom: Studies in Ben Sira and the Book of Wisdom* (Leuven: Leuven University Press): 63–74.

——— (2000), *Full of Praise: An Exegetical Study of Sir 39:12–35* (JSJSup, 64; Leiden: Brill).

Littman, Robert J. (2008), *Tobit: The Book of Tobit in Codex Sinaiticus* (Septuagint Commentary Series; Leiden: Brill).

Lohfink, Norbert (1999), "Was There a Deuteronomistic Movement?" in Linda Schearing and Steven McKenzie (eds), *Those Elusive Deuteronomists: The Phenomenon of Pan-Deuteronomism* (JSOTSup, 268; Sheffield: JSOT Press): 36–66.

Lücke, Friedrich (1848), *Versuch einer Vollständigen Einleitung in die Offenbarung des Johannes, oder, Allgemeine Untersuchungen über die Apokalyptische Litteratur überhaupt und die Apokalypse des Johannes Insbesondere* (Bonn: E. Weber).

Macatangay, Francis M. (2011), *The Wisdom Instructions in the Book of Tobit* (Deuterocanonical and Cognate Literature Studies, 12; Berlin: Walter de Gruyter).

MacDonald, Dennis R. (2001), "Tobit and the Odyssey," in Dennis R. MacDonald (ed.), *Mimesis and Intertextuality in Antiquity and Christianity* (Harrisburg: Trinity Press International): 11–40.

Mannheim, Karl (1936), *Ideology and Utopia: An Introduction to the Sociology of Knowledge* (trans. L. Wirth and E. Shils; New York: Harcourt Brace Jovanovich).

McCracken, David (1995), "Narration and Comedy in the Book of Tobit," *JBL* 114: 401–18.

McKenzie, Stephen, "Deuteronomistic History," *ABD* 2: 162.

Meeks, Wayne A. (1983), *The First Urban Christians: The Social World of the Apostle Paul* (New Haven: Yale University Press).

Milik, J. T. (1966), "La Patre de Tobie," *RB* 73: 522–30.

Milik, J. T. and Matthew Black (1976), *The Books of Enoch: Aramaic Fragments of Qumran Cave 4* (Oxford: Clarendon Press).

Miller, James E. (1991), "The Redaction of Tobit and the Genesis Apocryphon," *JSP* 8: 53–61.

Miller, Geoffrey David (2008), "Attitudes toward Dogs in Ancient Israel: A Reassessment," *JSOT* 32: 487–500.

—— (2011), *Marriage in the Book of Tobit* (Deuterocanonical and Cognate Literature Studies, 10; Berlin: Walter de Gruyter).

Miller, Patrick D. (1994), *They Cried to the Lord: The Form and Theology of Biblical Prayer* (Minneapolis: Fortress Press).

—— (2000), "God's Other Stories: On the Margins of Deuteronomic Theology," in *Israelite Religion and Biblical Theology* (JSOTSup, 267; Sheffield: Sheffield Academic Press): 593–601.

Molenberg, Corrie (1984), "A Study of the Roles of Shemihaza and Asael in 1 Enoch 6–11," *JJS* 35: 136–46.

Montgomery, James A. (1927), *A Critical and Exegetical Commentary on the Book of Daniel* (New York: Scribner).

Moore, Carey A. (1971), *Esther: Introduction, Translation and Notes* (AB, 7b; New York: Doubleday).

—— (1989), "Scholarly Issues in the Book of Tobit before Qumran and After: An Assessment," *JSP* 5: 65–81.

—— (1996), *Tobit: A New Translation with Introduction and Commentary* (AB, 40a; New York: Doubleday).

Moore, George Foot (1927), *Judaism in the First Centuries of the Christian Era: The Age of the Tannaim* (3 vols.; Cambridge, MA: Harvard University Press).

Moulton, James (1900), "The Iranian Background of Tobit," *ExpTim* 11: 257–60.

Mowinckel, Sigmund (1951), *Han som kommer* (Copenhagen: Gad); ET: *He that Cometh* (trans. G. W. Anderson; Oxford: Blackwell, 1956).

—— (2005), *He that Cometh: The Messiah Concept in the Old Testament and Later Judaism* (Grand Rapids: Eerdmans).

Nelson, Milward Douglas (1988), *The Syriac Version of the Wisdom of Ben Sira Compared to the Greek and Hebrew Materials* (SBLDS, 107; Atlanta: Scholars Press).

Nelson, Richard D. (1981), *The Double Redaction of the Deuteronomistic History* (JSOTSup, 18; Sheffield: JSOT Press).

Neugebauer, Otto (1985), "Appendix: The 'Astronomical' Chapters of the Ethiopic Book of Enoch (72–82)," in M. Black (ed.), *The Book of Enoch or 1 Enoch: A New English Translation* (Leiden: Brill): 386–418.

Neusner, Jacob and Alan Avery-Peck (2003), *George W. E. Nickelsburg in Perspective: An Ongoing Dialogue of Learning* (2 vols.; JSJSup, 80; Leiden: Brill).

Newsom, Carol A. (1980), "The Development of *1 Enoch* 6–19: Cosmology and Judgment," *CBQ* 42: 310–29.

—— (2003), *The Book of Job: A Contest of Moral Imaginations* (Oxford: Oxford University Press).

Nickelsburg, George W. E. (1977a), "Apocalyptic and Myth in 1 Enoch 6–11," *JBL* 96: 383–405.

—— (1977b), "The Apocalyptic Message of 1 Enoch 92–105," *CBQ* 39: 309–28.

—— (1981), *Jewish Literature between the Bible and the Mishnah: A Historical and Literary Introduction* (Philadelphia: Fortress Press).

—— (1983), "Social Aspects of Palestinian Jewish Apocalypticism," in David Hellholm (ed.), *Apocalypticism in the Mediterranean World and the Near East* (Tübingen: Mohr Siebeck): 641–54.

—— (1988a), "Tobit," in James Mays (ed.), *Harper's Bible Commentary* (San Francisco: Harper and Row): 791–803.

—— (1988b), "Tobit and Enoch: Distant Cousins with a Recognizable Resemblance," in David J. Lull (ed.), *Society of Biblical Literature 1988 Seminar Papers* (SBLSP, 27; Atlanta: Scholars Press): 54–68.

—— (1993), "Response to Robert Doran," in Jacob Neusner and Alan J. Avery-Peck (eds.), *George W. E. Nickelsburg in Perspective: An Ongoing Dialogue of Learning* (2 vols.; JSJSup, 80; Leiden: Brill): 1:263–6.

—— (1996), "The Search for Tobit's Mixed Ancestry: A Historical and Hermeneutical Odyssey," *RevQ* 8: 339–49.

—— (1997), Review of Merten Rabenau, *Studien zum Buch Tobit*, *JBL* 116: 348–50.

—— (2001a), *1 Enoch: A Commentary on the Book of 1 Enoch* (Hermeneia; Minneapolis: Fortress Press).

—— (2001b), "Tobit, Genesis, and the Odyssey: A Complex Web of Intertextuality," in Dennis R. MacDonald (ed.), *Mimesis and Intertextuality in Antiquity and Christianity* (Harrisburg: Trinity Press International): 41–55.

—— (2007), "Enochic Wisdom and its Relationship to the Mosaic Torah," in Gabriele Boccaccini and John J. Collins (eds.), *The Early Enoch Literature* (JSJSup, 121; Leiden: Brill): 81–94.

Nickelsburg, George W. E. and James C. VanderKam (2004), *1 Enoch: A New Translation Based on the Hermeneia Commentary* (Minneapolis: Fortress Press).

Nicklas, Tobias and Christian J. Wagner (2003), "Thesen zur textlichen Vielfalt im Tobitbuch," *JSJ* 34: 141–53.

Nogalski, James (1993), *Literary Precursors to the Book of The Twelve* (Berlin: Walter de Gruyter).

Noll, Kurt L. (2007), "Deuteronomistic History or Deuteronomic Debate? (A Thought Experiment)," *JSOT* 31: 311–45.

Noth, Martin (1948), *Überlieferungsgeschichte Des Pentateuch* (Stuttgart: W. Kohlhammer).

—— (1957), *Überlieferungsgeschictliche Studien: Die Sammelnden und Bearbeitenden Geschichtswerke im Alten Testament* (Tübingen: M. Niemeyer).

—— (1981), *The Deuteronomistic History* (JSOTSup, 15; Sheffield: JSOT Press).

Novick, Tzvi (2007), "Biblicized Narrative: On Tobit and Genesis 22," *JBL* 126: 755–64.

Nowell, Irene (1983), "The Book of Tobit: Narrative Technique and Theology" (Ph.D. diss., Catholic University of America).

—— (1988), "The Narrator in the Book of Tobit," in David J. Lull (ed.), *Society of Biblical Literature 1988 Seminar Papers* (SBLSP, 27; Atlanta: Scholars Press): 27–38.

—— (1995), "Irony in the Book of Tobit," *TBT* 33: 79–83.

—— (2005), "The Book of Tobit: An Ancestral Story," in Jeremy Corley and Vincent Skemp (eds.), *Intertextual Studies in Ben Sira and Tobit: Essays in Honor of Alexander A. Di Lella O.F.M.* (CBQMS, 38; Washington D.C.: Catholic Biblical Association of America): 3–13.

—— (2007), "The 'Work' of Archangel Raphael," in Friedrich Reiterer, Tobias Nicklas, and Karin Schöpflin (eds.), *Angels: The Concept of Celestial Beings—Origins, Development and Reception* (Deuterocanonical and Cognate Literature; Berlin: Walter de Gruyter): 227–38.

O'Leary, Stephen (1994), *Arguing the Apocalypse: A Theory of Millennial Rhetoric* (New York: Oxford University Press).

O'Leary, Stephen and Glen S. McGhee (eds.) (2005), *War in Heaven/Heaven on Earth: Theories of the Apocalyptic* (Millennialism and Society, 2; London: Equinox).

Olson, Daniel C. (2004), *Enoch: A New Translation – The Ethiopic Book of Enoch, or 1 Enoch* (Richland Hills, TX: BIBAL Press).

Olson, Dennis T. (2003), "How does Deuteronomy do Theology? Literary Juxtaposition and Paradox in the New Moab Covenant in Deuteronomy 29–32," in Brent A. Strawn and Nancy Bowen (eds.), *A God So Near: Essays on Old Testament Theology in Honor of Patrick D. Miller* (Winona Lake: Eisenbrauns): 201–13.

—— (2005), "Between Disappointment and Hope at the Boundary: Moses' Death at the End of Deuteronomy," in Beverly Roberts Gaventa and Patrick D. Miller (eds.), *The Ending of Mark and the Ends of God: Essays in Memory of Donald Harrisville Juel* (Louisville: Westminster/John Knox Press): 127–38.

Osteen, Joel (2007), *Become a Better You: 7 Keys to Improving your Life Every Day* (New York: Free Press).

Otzen, Benedikt (2002), *Tobit and Judith* (London: Sheffield Academic Press).

Owen, Paul (2004), "The Relationship of Eschatology to Esoteric Wisdom in the Jewish Pseudepigraphal Apocalypses," in Craig A. Evans (ed.), *Of Scribes and Sages: Early Jewish Interpretation and Transmission of Scripture* (2 vols.; LSTS, 50; London: T&T Clark): 122–33.

Owens, J. Edward (2007), "Asmodeus: A Less than Minor Character in the Book of Tobit – A Narrative-Critical Study," in Friedrich Reiterer, Tobias Nicklas, and Karin Schöpflin (eds.), *Angels: The Concept of Celestial Beings – Origins, Development and Reception* (Deuterocanonical and Cognate Literature; Berlin: Walter de Gruyter): 277–92.

Perdue, Leo G. (1991), *Wisdom in Revolt: Metaphorical Theology in the Book of Job* (JSOTSup, 112; Sheffield: Almond Press).

––––––– (1994), *Wisdom and Creation: The Theology of Wisdom Literature* (Nashville: Abingdon Press).

Person, Raymond F. (1993), *Second Zechariah and the Deuteronomic School* (JSOTSup, 167; Sheffield: JSOT Press).

Plöger, Otto (1959), *Theokratie und Eschatologie* (WMANT, 2; Neukirchen: Neukirchener Verlag).

––––––– (1968), *Theocracy and Eschatology* (Oxford: Blackwell).

Pope, Marvin (1965), *Job* (AB, 15; New York: Doubleday).

Portier-Young, Anathea (2001), "Alleviation of Suffering in the Book of Tobit: Comedy, Community, and Happy Endings," *CBQ* 63: 35–54.

––––––– (2005), "'Eyes to the Blind': A Dialogue between Tobit and Job," in Jeremy Corley and Vincent Skemp (eds.), *Intertextual Studies in Ben Sira and Tobit: Essays in Honor of Alexander A. Di Lella, O.F.M.* (CBQMS, 38; Washington, D.C.: Catholic Biblical Association of America): 14–27.

Pritchard, James Bennett (1969), *Ancient Near Eastern Texts Relating to the Old Testament* (3rd edn.; Princeton: Princeton University Press).

Propp, Vladimir (1968), *Morphology of the Folktale* (trans. Laurence Scott; Austin: University of Texas Press).

Pyper, Hugh (2006), "'Sarah is the Hero': Kierkegaard's Reading of Tobit in *Fear and Trembling*," in Mark Bredin (ed.), *Studies in The Book of Tobit: A Multidisciplinary Approach* (LSTS, 55; London: T&T Clark): 59–71.

Pyysiäinen, Ilkka (2001), *How Religion Works: Toward a New Cognitive Science of Religion* (Cognition and Culture Book Series, 1; Leiden: Brill).

Rabenau, Merten (1994), *Studien zum Buch Tobit* (BZAW, 220; Berlin: Walter de Gruyter).

Rankin, Oliver Shaw (1936), *Israel's Wisdom Literature: Its Bearing on Theology and the History of Religion* (Edinburgh: T&T Clark).

Reardon, Patrick Henry (1999), "Under the Gaze of God and Angels: The Meaning of Tobit for the Christian Reader," *Touchstone* 12: 41–45.

Redditt, Paul L. (2000), "Daniel 9: Its Structure and Meaning," *CBQ* 62: 236–49.

Reiterer, Friedrich (2005), "Prophet und Prophetie in Tobit und Ben Sira: Berührungspunkt und Differenzen," in Géza Xeravits and József Zsengellér (eds.), *The Book of Tobit: Text, Tradition, Theology* (JSJSup, 98; Leiden: Brill): 155–76.

——— (2007), "An Archangel's Theology: Raphael's Speaking about God and the Concept of God in the Book of Tobit," in Friedrich Reiterer, Tobias Nicklas, and Karin Schöpflin (eds.), *Angels: The Concept of Celestial Beings – Origins, Development and Reception* (Deuterocanonical and Cognate Literature; Berlin: Walter de Gruyter): 255–76.

Rendtorff, Rolf (1990), *The Problem of the Process of Transmission in the Pentateuch* (JSOTSup, 89; Sheffield: JSOT Press).

Ricoeur, Paul (1969), *The Symbolism of Evil* (trans. Emerson Buchanan; Boston: Beacon Press).

Rist, Martin (1962), "Apocalypticism," *IDB* I: 157–61.

Roberts, J. J. M. (1976), "Myth versus History: Relaying the Comparative Foundations," *CBQ* 38: 1–13.

Römer, Thomas (ed.) (2000), *The Future of the Deuteronomistic History* (BETL, 147; Leuven: Leuven University Press).

Rost, Leonard (1976), *Judaism Outside the Hebrew Canon: An Introduction to the Documents* (Nashville: Abingdon).

Rowland, Christopher and John Barton (eds.) (2002), *Apocalyptic in History and Tradition* (JSPSup, 43; London: Sheffield Academic Press).

Rowley, H. H. (1944), *The Relevance of Apocalyptic: A Study of Jewish and Christian Apocalypses from Daniel to Revelation* (London: Lutterworth Press).

——— (1970), *Job* (The Century Bible; London: Nelson).

Russell, D. S. (1964), *The Method and Message of Jewish Apocalyptic 200 BC – AD 100* (OTL; Philadelphia: Westminster Press).

Sacchi, Paolo (1990), *Jewish Apocalyptic and its History* (trans. W. Short; JSPSup, 20; Sheffield: JSOT Press).

—— (2000), *The History of the Second Temple Period* (JSOTSup, 285; Sheffield: Sheffield Academic Press).

Sanders, James (1965), *The Psalms Scroll of Qumran Cave 11* (DJD, 4; Oxford: Clarendon Press).

Schearing, Linda S. and Steven McKenzie (eds.) (1999), *Those Elusive Deuteronomists: The Phenomenon of Pan-Deuteronomism* (JSOTSup, 268; Sheffield: Sheffield Academic Press).

Schmid, H. H. (1984), "Creation, Righteousness, and Salvation: 'Creation Theology' as the Broad Horizon of Biblical Theology," in B. Anderson (ed.), *Creation in the Old Testament* (Issues in Religion and Theology, 6; Philadelphia: Fortress Press): 102–17.

Schmithals, Walter (1975), *The Apocalyptic Movement: Introduction and Interpretation* (Nashville: Abingdon Press).

Schnabel, Eckhard (1985), *Law and Wisdom from Ben Sira to Paul: A Tradition Historical Enquiry into the Relation of Law, Wisdom, and Ethics* (WUNT, 16; Tübingen: Mohr Siebeck).

Seow, C. L. (1997), *Ecclesiastes: A New Translation with Introduction and Commentary* (AB, 18C; New York: Doubleday).

Simpson, David (1913), "The Book of Tobit: Introduction," in R. H. Charles (ed.), *Apocrypha and Pseudepigrapha of the Old Testament* (2 vols.; Oxford: Clarendon Press): 1:174–201.

Skehan, Patrick W. and Alexander Di Lella (1987), *The Wisdom of Ben Sira: A New Translation with Notes* (AB, 39; New York: Doubleday).

Skemp, Vincent (2000), *The Vulgate of Tobit Compared with Other Ancient Witnesses* (SBLDS, 180; Atlanta: Society of Biblical Literature).

Smith, Jonathan Z. (1975), "Wisdom and Apocalyptic," in Berger A. Pearson (ed.), *Religious Syncretism in Antiquity* (Missoula: Scholars Press): 131–56.

Soll, William (1988), "Tobit and Folklore Studies, with Emphasis on Propp's Morphology," in David J. Lull (ed.), *Society of Biblical Literature 1988 Seminar Papers* (SBLSP, 27; Atlanta: Scholars Press): 39–53.

—— (1989), "Misfortune and Exile in Tobit: The Juncture of a Fairy Tale Source and Deuteronomistic Theology," *CBQ* 51: 209–31.

—— (2001), "The Book of Tobit as a Window on the Hellenistic Jewish Family," in L. Luker (ed.), *Passion Vitality, and Foment: The Dynamics of Second Temple Judaism* (Harrisburg: Trinity Press International): 242–74.

Spencer, Richard (1999), "The Book of Tobit in Recent Research," *Currents in Research* 7: 147–80.

Stone, Michael (1976), "Lists of Revealed Things in the Apocalyptic Literature," in Frank Moore Cross, Werner E. Lemke, and Patrick D. Miller (eds.), *Magnalia Dei: The Mighty Acts of God*

– *Essays on the Bible and Archaeology in Memory of G. Ernest Wright* (New York: Doubleday): 414–52.

————— (1978), "The Book of Enoch and Judaism in the Third Century B.C.E.," *CBQ* 40: 479–92.

————— (1987), "The Parabolic Use of Natural Order in Judaism of the Second Temple Period," in S. Shaked, D. Schulman, and G. G. Strousma (eds.), *Gilgul: Essays on Transformation, Revolution and Permanence in the History of Religions* (Leiden: Brill): 298–308.

Stuckenbruck, Loren T. (1995), *Angel Veneration and Christology: A Study in Early Judaism and in the Christology of the Apocalypse of John* (WUNT, 70; Tübingen: Mohr Siebeck).

————— (2002), "The Book of Tobit and the Problem of Magic," in Hermann Lichtenberger and Gerbern S. Oegema (eds.), *Jüdische Schriften in ihrem antik-jüdischen und urchristlichen Kontext* (JSHRZ Studien, 1; Gütersloh: Gütersloh Verlagshaus): 258–69.

————— (2004), "The Origins of Evil in Jewish Apocalyptic Tradition: The Interpretation of Genesis 6:1–4 in the Second and Third Centuries B.C.E.," in Christoph Auffarth and Loren T. Stuckenbruck (eds.), *The Fall of the Angels* (Themes in Biblical Narrative, 6; Leiden: Brill): 87–118.

————— (2007a), *1 Enoch 91–108* (Commentaries on Early Jewish Literature; Berlin: Walter de Gruyter).

————— (2007b), "The Early Traditions Related to 1 Enoch from the Dead Sea Scrolls: An Overview and Assessment," in Gabriele Boccaccini and John J. Collins (eds.), *The Early Enoch Literature* (JSJSup, 121; Leiden: Brill): 41–64.

————— (2009), "The Book of Jubilees and the Origin of Evil," in Gabriele Boccaccini and Giovanni Ibba (eds.), *Enoch and the Mosaic Torah: The Evidence of Jubilees* (Grand Rapids, MI: Eerdmans): 294–308.

————— (2011), "Early Enochic Tradition and the Restoration of Humanity: The Function and Significance of *1 Enoch* 10," in Lester L. Grabbe and Obed Lipschits (eds.), *Judah between East and West: The Transition from Persian to Greek Rule (ca. 400–200 BC)* (LSTS, 75; London: T&T Clark): 225–41.

Thomas, J. D. (1972), "The Greek Text of Tobit," *JBL* 91: 463–71.

Tigchelaar, E. J. C. (1987), "More on Apocalyptic and Apocalypses," *JSJ* 18: 137–44.

Toloni, Giancarlo (2004), *L'originale del Libro di Tobia: Studio Filological-Linguistico* (Madrid: Instituto de Filologia, Departamento de Filologia Biblica y de Oriente Antiguo).

Torrey, Charles (1922), "'Nineveh' in the Book of Tobit," *JBL* 41: 237–45.

Towner, W. Sibley (1968), "'Blessed Be YHWH' and 'Blessed Art Thou,

YHWH': The Modulation of a Biblical Formula," *CBQ* 30: 386–99.

——— (1971), "Retributional Theology in the Apocalyptic Setting," *USQR* 26: 203–14.

Troeltsch, Ernst (1931), *The Social Teaching of the Christian Churches* (trans. O. Wyon; 2 vols.; New York: Macmillan).

Uhlig, Siegbert (1984), *Das Äthiopische Henochbuch* (JSHRZ, 5.6; Gütersloh: Mohn).

Valeta, David (2002), "The Satirical Nature of the Book of Daniel," in Christopher Rowland John Barton (eds.), *Apocalyptic in History and Tradition* (JSPSup, 43; Sheffield: Sheffield Academic Press): 81–93.

Van den Eynde, Sabine (2005), "One Journey and One Journey Makes Three: The Impact of the Readers' Knowledge in the Book of Tobit," *ZAW* 117: 273–80.

Van Deventer, Hans (2000), "The End of the End: Or, What is the Deuteronomist (Still) Doing in Daniel?" in Johannes C. de Moor and Harry F. van Rooy (eds.), *Past, Present, Future: The Deuteronomistic History and the Prophets* (Leiden: Brill): 62–75.

VanderKam, James C. (1984), *Enoch and the Growth of the Apocalyptic Tradition* (CBQMS, 16; Washington, D.C.: Catholic Biblical Association of America).

——— (1995), *Enoch: A Man for All Generations* (Studies on Personalities in the Old Testament; Columbia: University of South Carolina Press).

——— (2003), "Response to George Nickelsburg, '1 Enoch: A Commentary on the Book of 1 Enoch: Chapters 1–36; 81–108,'" in *George W. E. Nickelsburg in Perspective: An Ongoing Dialogue of Learning* (2 vols.; JSJSup, 80; Leiden: Brill): 2:379–86.

Veijola, Timo (2006), "Law and Wisdom: The Deuteronomistic Heritage in Ben Sira's Teaching of the Law," in Jacob Neusner et al. (eds.), *Ancient Israel, Judaism, and Christianity in Contemporary Perspective: Essays in Memory of Kar-Johan Illman* (Lanham: University Press of America): 429–48.

von der Osten-Sacken, Peter (1969), *Die Apokalyptic in Ihrem Verhältnis zu Prophetie und Weisheit* (Theologische Existenz Heute, 157; München: C. Kaiser).

von Rad, Gerhard (1965), *Old Testament Theology* (trans. D. M. G. Stalker; 2 vols.; New York: Harper & Row).

——— (1972), *Wisdom in Israel* (trans. James D. Martin; Nashville: Abingdon Press).

Velcic, Bruna (2005), "The Significance of the Relation of 4QTobit^e Fr. 6 with Greek Texts," *Henoch* 27: 149–62.

Wagner, Christian J. (2003), *Polyglotte Tobit-Synopse: Griechisch, Lateinisch, Syrisch, Hebräisch, Aramäisch: Mit einem Index zu den Tobit-Fragmenten vom Toten Meer* (Philologisch-Historische Klasse, 258; Göttingen: Vandenhoeck & Ruprecht).

Wakeman, Mary K. (1973), *God's Battle with the Monster: A Study in Biblical Imagery* (Leiden: Brill).

Weber, Max (1963), *The Sociology of Religion* (Boston: Beacon Press).

Weeks, Stuart (2006), "Some Neglected Texts of Tobit: The Third Greek Version," in Mark Bredin (ed.), *Studies in the Book of Tobit: A Multidisciplinary Approach* (LSTS, 55; London: T&T Clark): 12–42.

——— (2011), "A Deuteronomic Heritage in Tobit?" in Hanne Von Weissenberg, Juha Pakkala, and Marko Marttila (eds.), *Changes in Scripture: Rewriting and Interpreting Authoritative Traditions in the Second Temple Period* (BZAW, 419; Berlin: Walter de Gruyter): 389–404.

Weeks, Stuart, Simon Gathercole, and Loren T. Stuckenbruck (2004), *The Book of Tobit: Texts from the Principal Ancient and Medieval Traditions – With Synopsis, Concordances, and Annotated Texts in Aramaic, Hebrew, Greek, Latin, and Syriac* (Fontes et Subsidia ad Bibliam Pertinentes, 3; Berlin: Walter de Gruyter).

Weinfeld, Moshe (1972), *Deuteronomy and the Deuteronomic School* (trans. M. Freundlich; Oxford: Clarendon Press).

Weitzman, Steven (1996), "Allusion, Artifice, and Exile in the Hymn of Tobit," *JBL* 115: 49–61.

Wellhausen, Julius (1883), *Prolegomena zur Geschichte Israels* (Berlin: Druck und Verlag von G. Reimer).

——— (1957), *Prolegomena to the History of Ancient Israel* (trans. Allan Menzies and John Sutherland Black; New York: Meridian Books).

West, Edward William (1880), *Pahlavi Texts* (The Sacred Books of the East, 5, 18, 24, 37, 47; Oxford: Clarendon Press).

Wicks, Henry J. (1971), *The Doctrine of God in the Jewish Apocryphal and Apocalyptic Literature* (New York: Ktav).

Wills, Lawrence M. (1990), *The Jew in the Court of the Foreign King: Ancient Jewish Court Legends* (HDR, 26; Minneapolis: Fortress Press).

——— (1995), *The Jewish Novel in the Ancient World* (Myth and Poetics; Ithaca: Cornell University Press).

Wills, Lawrence M. and Benjamin G. Wright (eds.) (2005), *Conflicted Boundaries in Wisdom and Apocalypticism* (SBLSymS, 35; Atlanta: Society of Biblical Literature).

Wilson, Brittany E. (2006), "Pugnacious Precursors and the Bearer of Peace: Jael, Judith and Mary in Luke 1:42," *CBQ* 68: 436–56.

Wilson, Gerald H. (1990), "The Prayer of Daniel 9: Reflection on Jeremiah 29," *JSOT* 48: 91–9.

Winston, David (1965), "The Iranian Component in the Bible, Apocrypha, and Qumran: A Review of the Evidence," *History of Religions* 5: 183–216.

Wright, Archie T. (2005), *The Origin of Evil Spirits: The Reception of Genesis 6.1–4 in Early Jewish Literature* (WUNT, 198; Tübingen: Mohr Siebeck).

Wright, Benjamin G. (1997), "'Fear the Lord and Honor the Priest': Ben Sira as Defender of the Jerusalem Priesthood," in P. C. Beentjes (ed.), *The Book of Ben Sira in Modern Research: Proceedings of the First International Ben Sira Conference* (BZAW, 255; Berlin: Walter de Gruyter): 189–222.

—— (1989), *No Small Difference: Sirach's Relationship to its Hebrew Parent Text* (Septuagint and Cognate Studies, 26; Atlanta: Scholars Press).

—— (2007), "1 Enoch and Ben Sira: Wisdom and Apocalypticism in Relationship," in Gabriele Boccaccini and John J. Collins (eds.), *The Early Enoch Literature* (JSJSup, 121; Leiden: Brill): 159–76.

Wright, Benjamin G. and Claudia Camp (2001), "'Who has been Tested by Gold and Found Perfect?' Ben Sira's Discourse of Riches and Poverty," *Henoch* 23: 153–74.

Xeravits, Géza G. and József Zsengellér (eds.) (2005), *The Book of Tobit: Text, Tradition, Theology* (JSJSup, 98; Leiden: Brill).

Zimmerman, Frank (1958), *The Book of Tobit: An English Translation with Introduction and Commentary* (Jewish Apocryphal Literature; New York: Harper & Brothers).

Zsengellér, József (2005), "Topography as Theology: The Theological Premises of the Geographical References in the Book of Tobit," in Géza Xeravits and József Zsengellér (eds.), *Tobit: Text, Tradition, Theology* (JSJSup, 98; Leiden: Brill): 177–88.